BLOODTHIRSTY

BITCHES

and

PIOUS PIMPS

OF POWER

ALSO BY GERRY SPENCE

BLOODTHIRSTY
BITCHES

and

PIOUS PIMPS
OF POWER

* * * * * * * * * * * * * * * * *

The Rise and Risks of the New

Conservative Hate Culture

* * * * * * * * * * * * * * * * *

GERRY SPENCE

St. Martin's Press ❧ *New York*

www.stmartins.com

Library of Congress Cataloging-in-Publication Data

Spence, Gerry.
    Bloodthirsty bitches and pious pimps of power : the rise and risks of the new conservative hate culture / Gerry Spence.—1st ed.
       p. cm.
    Includes bibliographical references (p. 253).
    ISBN-13: 978-0-312-36153-2
    ISBN-10: 0-312-36153-X
      1. Television   personalities—United   States—Biography. 2. Radio personalities—United States—Biography. 3. Talk shows—United States. 4. Conservatism—United States. 5. Hate—Political aspects—United States. 6. Bullying—Political aspects—United States. 7. Propaganda, American. 8. Mass media—Political aspects—United States. 9. United States—Politics and government—1989– I. Title.

PN1992.4.A2S66 2006
791.4502'8092273—dc22
[B]   2006042972

First Edition: October 2006

10 9 8 7 6 5 4 3 2 1

To George W. Bush (George II)

and Richard Cheney,

and the gang of seven

who have laid the dreadful egg

Contents

Acknowledgments

I am deeply indebted to Peter Lampack, my stalwart, patient friend and agent who saw where certain of my arguments were frayed or missed their mark and who often led me back to more solid premises. I lay no blame at his feet for any failures of the work nor do I cloak him with any responsibility for what may be seen by some as its far-out tincture, but I acknowledge with gratitude his thoughtful and tolerant insights as the work progressed.

I thank George Witte, my editor, whose solid support of the book and whose intelligent edits lent both structure and sense to the work and, in fact, made the book possible, and I do not forget the many faithful folks at St. Martin's Press who have joined in both enthusiasm and help along the way.

My brother-in-law, Mendel Peterson Jr., has always believed that love prevails. His friendship and comments from time to time have kept me aware of that truth, for which I am grateful. Hate without love is hell.

I thank Imaging Spence, my darling, who read the book with

understanding both of its message and of the man who sought to make it. Her encouragement gave a better life to the effort and provided me confidence when I doubted the project was worth it. In the short term, nothing seems to change. On the other hand, the admonition of Edmund Burke, who proclaimed, "All that is necessary for the triumph of evil is that good men do nothing," continues to push me on.

I thank Tom Spence, my brother, who read the manuscript in its early form and lovingly offered his always powerful and honest views.

I remember Rex Parris, Joey Lowe, and John Zelbst, who listened to the beginning chapters of the book and generously shared their time and comments. There are some I will remember as soon as this has gone to print and it becomes too late to acknowledge them. To them I offer my apologies. The failure is attributable not to an ungrateful heart but to the stubborn demons of the mind that fight against an always fitting recall.

A Beginning Thought

Let's understand the language: What do I mean by *bitches?* The word is well defined both by common usage and by *Webster's Third New International Dictionary.* Besides being a female dog, a bitch is defined as "a lewd or immoral woman, trollop, slut" (a definition I do not adopt here), *or* "a malicious, spiteful and domineering woman," a definition I think applies at times. But I intend to embrace the term in its more modern usage—one that among feminists approaches endearment, even pride.

A magazine calls itself *Bitch.* The publishers defend their title: "When it's being used as an insult, 'bitch' is most often hurled at women who speak their minds, who have opinions and don't shy away from expressing them. If being an outspoken woman means being a bitch, we'll take that as a compliment, thanks." As one woman puts it, "Sometimes you have to learn how to open your mouth for more than just giving head." Bette Davis once observed, "When a man gives his opinion, he's a man. When a woman gives her opinion, she's a bitch."

Still, this is not a sex-specific matter. Let me hasten to say, before I am sued, that when I refer to the gentlemen herein as "pimps" I mean it. They pimp for big business, for the irreligious right, for war, for those who hate the poor and the voiceless. They pimp for corporate welfare and for the ultimate vaporization of the middle class. They have, in important ways, spawned the new American hate culture, and I hold them equally culpable—no, *more* culpable than the women, because these men began with more power, more opportunity, and supposedly more credibility than their female counterparts.

These members of *Team Hate* are the new conservative mouthpieces for a power structure that's selling us into a murky, dead world where people can no longer love, where God is money, where the earth is a commodity to be destroyed for profit, where people are just digits in a money machine, where the ideals of a Christian society are mocked so that greed is now its favored value, where the Good Samaritan is a piteous fool, and violence against our fellow creatures is celebrated in the name of Christ.

We have become a culture that is fed hate, that has grown to crave hate, a hate-addicted culture that, like any psychotic entity, can destroy itself absent treatment at the hands of those who still retain their ability to love and to forgive. Time does not change much. We remember Henry David Thoreau, who observed more than a century ago that which is still alarmingly apparent—his compatriots were living "lives of quiet desperation."

Too much of America's goodness has been too long in suspension. Unless we retrieve it, we're destined to the same fate as all great nations that devoted themselves to a conquest fueled by the power of hate and greed. If we are free, we will always be different from one another. But if we are to save ourselves, it is our task to discover the common ground we occupy and to disrupt this legacy of loathing.

As will soon become obvious, this is not meant to be a scholarly treatise but a polemic. What else would one expect from a man who's spent his lifetime arguing? Scholars are no more likely to be right than the howling of babes. Out of the bulging heads of scholars are born every good and every evil ever conceived by man, and despite the heavy intellectual burdens scholars endure, and perhaps because of them, scholars are unable to agree on the simplest ideas, like what is right and what is wrong.

Such evils as genocide, eugenics, racism, sexism, the destruction of the earth for profit, intellectual machinations for a nuclear holocaust, for every war, indeed, for our current war, have been thought up or buoyed up by scholars. And bad laws are often spawned from the brainy wombs of good men and good women.

The argument here is that the new conservative hate culture in America is leading us resolutely and irretrievably to the Fourth Reich. And *Team Hate* provides the mouthpieces that spew its dangerous propaganda.

—GERRY SPENCE
Jackson Hole, Wyoming

BLOODTHIRSTY

BITCHES

and

PIOUS PIMPS

OF POWER

1. Hate Sells

Meet Its Prime-time Peddler, Nancy Grace

I can see them now—endless waves of humanoids, one might suppose from another planet; an angry mob stretching from coast to coast; millions of staring, hating voyeurs melded to their screens, watching some bloodthirsty blonde eviscerate whoever has been tabbed as the day's victim. In times past, say, in Rome at the Colosseum, the crowd was enthralled by blood and gore and human entrails torn from the prey of starved beasts. The lionesses then were as vicious as the ripping blondes on our television screens.

Today's worldwide Colosseum is called television. No metaphor is ever perfect, but the similarities are startling; and but for the damage these women wreak on human dignity and truth, perhaps vaguely amusing. CNN, on the cliff's edge of bankruptcy, needed a lioness. Their ratings were headed over the cliff. Then they found Nancy Grace and released her into the arena. Some say she saved the network.

As you remember, the issue in the Michael Jackson case was simple: Did the state prove its case against Jackson as a child molester *beyond a reasonable doubt?* This is still America. Her lady-ship, Ms. Grace, found Michael Jackson guilty from the first day. Maybe he was. Maybe not. But there was no doubt in her mind, although she was never in the courtroom. She didn't observe the witnesses, didn't see their faces, hear their voices, watch the lawyers, or listen to the judge, as did the jury. She sat in her studio a couple of thousand miles away, and before the case took its first judicial breath she found Michael Jackson guilty. Presumably be-yond a reasonable doubt. The presumption of innocence, a sacred American right—what has happened to it?

After the verdict, the jury foreman, Mr. Rodriguez, foolishly agreed to jump into the arena with the lioness. The poor man, like the rest of us, had no idea whether or not Mr. Jackson was actually guilty of the charges. He, as we, had his own opinion, but ours and his suspicions are not *proof*. We do not guess people into the penitentiary in this country. So watch the snarling Grace take after this man, who had been doing his job as a good citizen.

Grace: Yes, Mr. Rodriguez, I understand the theory of rea-sonable doubt. I was a prosecutor many years. But before I let you go, I've got a question for you. What do you *think* Jackson, a forty-year-old man, was doing with these little boys all those nights in bed alone?

Rodriguez: Well, that's a personal view that I don't want to talk about right now. . . . We all have our thoughts. [He's saying 'I may have my own idea about this, but I'm limited to the proof the state presented'—a position that every lawyer should respect, especially Nancy Grace.]

Grace: You tried him for that. You were on the jury. That's what he was accused of. What do you *think* he was doing? [Again note, the question isn't what did the evidence show. The question is what did the juror *think* Jackson was doing.]

Rodriguez: We had to just rely on the—I'm not going to stick my neck out there on this. We're just—*I'm going to base it again on the testimony that was presented to us.* . . . [my italics]

Grace: What do you mean, stick your neck out?

Rodriguez: Well . . .

Grace: You don't want to say what you *thought* Jackson was doing with those little boys every night?

Rodriguez: Because it's our own personal beliefs and our own thoughts, and that's not what we have to work with. *We had to work with the testimony of the witnesses and the credibility of the witnesses, and that's all we can base it on.* [still my italics]

Here we see a Grace-mauled jury foreman, one who followed the law, come bleeding out of his experience in the television arena, a man who had the integrity to hold to the Constitution. It's not what we *believe.* It's what the state *proved.* After ten years as a prosecutor, Ms. Grace seems unable to grasp that basic idea of American justice. If you can convince a jury that they should convict a person merely on personal belief and the evidence be damned, then, of course, you can win a hundred straight, as is her claimed record.

On the same show, Debra Opri, attorney for Jackson's parents, fared better.

Opri: Well, this is the bitter pill you're going to have to swallow, Nancy. This is the reality, not the reality you have created for the last year. Michael Jackson is not guilty. Let him live his life in peace and stop trying to retry the case, and that's what you're doing.

Grace: [The snarl.] You know what? You're right. So I guess I don't need to hear from the defense, either, and that would be you! What are you doing? Don't you think you're doing a little rehash yourself, Miss Opri?

Opri: No. I just want the world to know that our system works. We had a trial. We had a jury acquit him, and he is innocent. He walked out of that courtroom. To use Mesereau's words, justice was served. . . .

Grace: [The roaring.] Wait a minute! Wait a minute! Wait a minute! We know what happened. Why are you rehashing it?

Opri: Sneddon [the prosecutor] said, I accept the jury's verdict. Why don't you, Nancy?

CNN's gamble on Grace paid off. She hissed and clawed and jumped up CNN's ratings overnight. I tell you, *hate sells*. And why not? You have a choice between good-old-kind-of-blank-staring Wolf Blitzer and Nancy Grace, a choice between a sing-songy sound, a man droning out the facts as a competent, honest journalist leaving you to make up your own mind, and an honest-to-God ripping-feline hatemonger pounding at the cage, one who attacks and convicts and massages her audience's need to kill. There he is, Mr. Henry Smith, bonded to his TV screen. The boss has kicked him around all day and he can't yell back, and he's fought through an hour of traffic gridlock surrounded by stupid, pushy assholes, and he comes home to a house full of yelling kids and a supper of Campbell's Chunky Chicken Noodle Soup, and what does he want to do? He wants to kill!

This is a little oversimplified, but there's a lot of nasty, unreleased aggression lying out there, and Nancy Grace knows how to tap into it. It's not all bad. By sublimation she helps the viewer get rid of some of his hostility. She's angry just like he is. And she's right, of course. Anyone can see that. They should hang 'em high, all those worthless accuseds, whoever they are, and the lawyers who represent them, and the juries who turn them loose, and the judges who let this happen. If that old rag, the Constitution, gets in the way, well, dump it. It just makes it harder for prosecutors to do their jobs—and to keep us safe. The inquisitors of old weren't held back by such arcane ideas as constitutional rights. Torture the witch until she confesses. Then burn her!

And about the persecution of witches? Michael Jackson was clearly a suspect. A magical warlock, perhaps. So consider the *Malleus Maleficarum,* better known as "the Witch's Hammer," the bible of the fifteenth-century inquisitors. That tome laid out in detail the method of trying and torturing those accused of witchcraft, and the *Malleus* "acquired especial weight and dignity" from the famous December 9, 1484, bull of Pope Innocent VIII embracing it. It was said, "The *Malleus* lay on the bench of every judge, on the desk of every magistrate. It was the ultimate, irrefutable, unarguable authority" on the prosecution of witches.

So what can we learn about the trials of such as Jackson from this ancient, learned treatise? It proclaims, "For common justice demands that a witch should not be condemned to death unless she is convicted by her own confession . . . and in this case she is to be exposed to questions and torture to extort a confession of her crimes." Jackson, the warlock, protected by the Constitution, escaped. Can we understand the frustration of Ms. Grace's failed Inquisition?

Here then is what Grace says about the constitutional process: "There are systems of justice on this planet where both sides seek the truth, but that isn't the case in this country."

What does she mean? We revisit a *Larry King Show* in which Ms. Grace was Larry's guest. They were discussing the Elizabeth Smart kidnapping case.

Caller: Hi. Is it possible for the FBI or the law officers involved in the case to use sodium pentothal on Mr. Ricci and find out if he has any involvement with this girl's disappear-ance? Whether or not it can be used against him after? [Ricci was suspected of abducting Elizabeth Smart but later proved innocent. He died in jail but no one, including Nancy Grace, apologized.]

King: Nancy, is that allowed?

Grace: *Oh, how I wish, Larry! Unfortunately, it's not allowed under our Constitution. No sodium pentothal, truth serum, no beating, no torture. We have to wait for Ricci to crack. That's right.* (my emphasis)

She's tracking pretty well with the *Malleus.* The format of her tabloid show seems more like a witch hunt than a panel discussion of legal issues. The prosecutorial gene of the *Malleus* is a stubborn one to eradicate. Ms. Grace said to *The New Republic,* "Think back to the Salem witch trials. Trials have always been a source of con-troversy. . . . Trials will always be a spectator sport." Yes, a specta-tor sport! One may wonder if the witch trials of old are not a part of our genetic memory.

The *Malleus* admonishes that the witch must "be stripped by honest women of good reputation," the reason being that they must search her clothing for instruments of witchcraft sewn therein, "for they often make such instruments, at the instruction of devils, out of the limbs of unbaptized children. . . . And when such instruments have been disposed of, the Judge shall use his own persuasions and those of other honest men zealous for the faith to induce her to confess the truth voluntarily; and if she will not, let him order the officers to bind her with cords, and apply her to some engine of torture: and then let them obey at once but not joyfully, rather appearing to be disturbed by their duty." (Please. Do not show your glee in your torture of the naked witch!)

Nancy Grace is an angel of justice. And yes, to CNN she was

an angel. She boosted ratings in her 8:00 p.m. time slot by 126 percent over the same time slot of a year before through a steady diet of bloody, sensational cases where hate was the principal dessert.

"We're very pleased," Ken Jautz of CNN says. He should be. She saved their corporate fannies. And the way CNN proved their pleasure was for *Headline News* to reschedule its programming by moving the *Nancy Grace* replay (previously airing at 11:00 p.m.) to the 10:00 p.m. slot, providing the lady with *two* full prime-time hours every weeknight. She averaged half a million viewers nightly.

But in the distance we heard a quiet protest (a protest that CNN did not air, of course) from David Allen, a gentle professor of journalism and mass communication at the University of Wisconsin-Milwaukee. He said benignly, "Broadcasters seem to have become far more interested in marketing personalities to consumers than giving citizens information that will help them function in a democracy."

And Jason Zengerle, a senior editor at *The New Republic*, opined: "She [Grace] has become the leading practitioner of the relatively new and increasingly popular cable news format: the legal shout-fest."

I do not blame Nancy Grace. She is who she is. She's honest about it. She says, "I have never, ever pretended to be impartial, never. Frankly, I have no interest in being a robot that reads a prompter." Truth is, her gimmick is wrath, pure clean merchantable loathing.

I haven't forgotten the story that she claims is the foundation of, not only her judicial philosophy, but her life's work as well. She says that when she lost her betrothed, a young man named Keith Griffin, to a murderer it changed her. She told Larry King that had he lived they would have been married, that she would have been a schoolteacher with a family. After his murder she went to law school and became a prosecutor and, in her mind, her duty was to stand up for the victims of crimes. In part, here's what she told Larry King when he interviewed her:

King: How was he [her boyfriend] killed?

Grace: Keith had a summer job with a friend of his father's. They were out in a remote area in a construction site, building in a very rural area. And he left that day, as a favor, to go get everybody their soft drinks. They were so far away from anything to have with their lunches. And when he came back . . .

King: He was how old?

Grace: Keith was 25. [He was twenty-three.] When he came back, he was basically ambushed and mugged, en route back.

King: For profit, you mean?

Grace: Yes. [The murderer, a marginally retarded black youth, killed Griffin because he'd been fired from his job and, in apparent revenge, he shot the first fellow employee he came upon. It turned out to be Nancy's boyfriend. The defendant was cleared of robbery and at the trial the prosecutor based part of his case on the assailant killing a friend.]

Grace: I think he had $35 and a picture of me in his wallet. And that is one of the ways everyone was identified. The wallet was later discovered in the possession of the man that killed him. [No, Griffin's wallet was found several days after the incident in the Bronco where he was shot, by one Eli Ingram. It was not found in the possession of the killer.] He was shot five times, Larry. And he was still alive when he got to the hospital. And to this day, I just pray that he could not feel . . . [He was pronounced dead at the scene.]

King: Was the killer apprehended quickly?

Grace: Yes. He was caught quickly. And that is one of the many disturbing things. There are so many disturbing things about a short life, a young life being cut down that way. But this perpetrator had been in and out of trouble. And I always wonder, if someone had cared about the case, not necessarily throw him behind bars and toss the key. But to rehab the person, or to throw him behind bars, to get him off the street. [The perpetrator was not on parole and had no record of prior convictions.]

King: How old was he?

Grace: He was—the perp [short for "perpetrator," a common term used by cops] was twenty-four. [Tommy McCoy, the "perp," was nineteen, not twenty-four.]

Ms. Grace told Tim Russert in 2005 that Griffin was "I guess you would say, mugged by someone—he didn't even know him—and shot five times. . . ." She said that the man who killed him was a "repeat offender," and that the law "let him slip through their fingers."

The jury was not out three days but a few hours. Probably the jury did not return the death penalty, as requested by the prosecutor, because the boy was retarded, and not, as Ms. Grace suggests, because she asked that his life be spared.

When the verdict was read, McCoy turned to Billy Prior, his lawyer. "He asked me, 'What does it mean?'" Prior said. "I told him it meant he was not going to the electric chair."

She claimed to CNN's Art Harris in 1995 that "I am part of the system, and it failed that time, and I hate to see it ever fail again." Of course, if every person charged with a crime is convicted, guilty or not, the criminal will not escape.

After years of painful memories, that Ms. Grace might forget certain of the details of this case is understandable. But Ms.

Grace has proven to be a powerful storyteller and, as it is said, every good story is entitled to embellishment.

Columnist Matt Zoller Seitz recently wrote that her method was obvious: "If you question me, you spit on my dead fiancé."

"I've seen Grace invoke the murder a dozen times in the past two months. On *Russert's Show,* she used it to explain her advocacy of what she calls 'behavioral evidence,' which translates as 'odd and/or shifty behavior that makes Nancy Grace think a person is guilty, and that should be admissible in court because Nancy Grace says so.

"It's impossible to know how much of Grace's flamboyant anger is organic and how much is shtick. It's possible not even she can tell the difference anymore.

"Either way, it represents a short-circuiting of reason, and a passionate embrace of the lynch mob mentality America has been grappling with for more than 200 years."

Media critics say that Grace thinks all suspects are guilty, that is until *they* prove they are innocent, a reading of the Constitution upside down. According to Libby Copeland of *The Washington Post,* "She's passionate about putting guilty people in jail, and it just so happens she doesn't need juries to tell her who those guilty people are." It makes no difference. She knows who is guilty and who is not. And, as observed in the *Malleus,* "For the deeds of witches in conjunction with devils are done in secret, and the accuser cannot in this case, as in others, have definite evidence by which he can make his statements good."

I remember being with her as a guest on *Court TV.* She was the host. In the course of the evening I said, "Nancy, you've never seen a defendant who wasn't guilty or a man you didn't hate." All hell broke loose. I was making a personal attack on her, and what right did I have to do that? She was right. Later I stopped in the control room to say good-bye and they were laughing. Probably at me.

Steven Brill, the founder of *American Lawyer* magazine who created *Court TV* in 1991, said in his day TV anchors were not permitted to express their views on stories they were covering. "And as *Court TV* has changed," he said, "so has Ms. Grace. I regret what her persona on television has become because I think it just contributes to the overall scream culture that is too often cable television. I feel like I owe a debt to society for putting her on television."

On three separate occasions, appeals courts have made severely critical comments about Ms. Grace's conduct in the criminal cases she has prosecuted, reprimands that would cause scarring embarrassment to most lawyers.

These courts' measured findings include such language as found in *Carr v. State:* "Our review of the record supports Carr's [the accused's] contention that the prosecuting attorney [Grace] engaged in an extensive pattern of inappropriate and, in some cases, *illegal conduct* in the course of the trial. . . . We conclude that the conduct of the prosecuting attorney in this case demonstrated her disregard of the notions of due process and fairness, and was *inexcusable.*" (my italics)

The court went on to establish the boundaries of good conduct for a prosecutor. "The responsibility of a public prosecutor differs from that of the usual advocate; his duty is to seek justice, not merely to convict. . . . It has often been stated that it is the duty of a prosecuting attorney to see that justice is done and nothing more. That duty should not be forgotten in an excess of zeal or the eager quest for victory in his case. The people of the state desire merely to ascertain beyond a reasonable doubt that the accused is guilty of the crime charged, and do not countenance any unfairness upon the part of their representatives in court."

The court overturned this arson-murder verdict, also finding that Ms. Grace withheld the names of the state's witnesses until the eve of trial, but in her book, *Objection,* she decries defense lawyers "hiding evidence from the jury." The *Malleus* disposes of the problem once and for all: "And if the accused again and again insists that she should know the names of the witnesses against her, he [the inquisitor] can answer her as follows: You can guess from the charges which are made against you who are the witnesses." Our sense of fairness hasn't evolved much since the fifteenth century.

In an earlier 1994 case the Georgia high court voted 6–1 to reverse a heroin trafficking conviction won by Grace because she "exceeded the wide latitude of closing argument" by referring to drug-related murders and serial rapes, crimes not at issue or related to the case—in short, her employing prejudice, not fact, to obtain a conviction.

In a third case, the Eleventh Circuit Court of Appeals held in 2005 that she *"played 'fast and loose' with her ethical duties,* and that *her conduct demonstrated her disregard of the notions of due process and fairness and was inexcusable."* (my italics)

The open presentation of the prosecution's case without gamesmanship, that is, for example, without withholding witnesses, has always been a problem for prosecutors. Back in the fifteenth century the same issue was raised, but the *Malleus* provided comfort and guidance for the inquisitor. "For although different Popes have had different opinions on this matter, none of them has ever said that in such a case the Judge is bound to make known to the accused the names of the informers or accusers. . . . On the contrary, some have thought that in no case ought he do so."

Grace's inalterable duty as a prosecutor was to see that the trial of an accused was fairly conducted. It can never be the lawful objective of a prosecutor through any means, fair or foul, to drag people into the penitentiary or to stretch them on the gurney awaiting the executioner's needle. The prosecutor's duty, Grace's duty, was simple: to *fairly* present her case.

These cases calling into question the prosecutorial conduct of Ms. Grace are a matter of public record and should have been known to the executives of CNN. Such repeated inappropriate conduct by an experienced lawyer who must have known better was simply a prelude to her approach on her CNN show. Yet despite this record, CNN hired her in order to retain some segment of the market. They brought her into the CNN fold with full knowledge that she would provide the same turgid streams of loathing to a vast television audience that yearned for a quick fix of their underlying hate.

Now listen to a dialogue between Ms. Grace and Marc Klass, another well-known victim's advocate, the father of a girl who was abducted and murdered:

"I think the common theme of this show tonight, Nancy, is very clear," Klaas said during one of his fourteen appearances with her. "There are people on this earth *who should never be allowed to give birth.*" [my emphasis] This sounds for all the world like *eugenics,* the discredited science of human improvement by better breeding, a favorite idea of the Nazis.

Here is Grace's response: "Marc Klaas, stinging indictment! But you know what? I think a lot of people share your sentiment. But *you have the guts to say it, friend.*" [my emphasis] To hate the unborn?

I've repeatedly said I don't blame Nancy Grace. One can't blame her any more than one might blame the bullet. It's who fires the gun, and against whom is it fired? CNN put the Grace-bullet in its gun, fired it at millions of people, hit its targets, and pocketed the profit. That it has peddled hate for profit seemingly creates little shame for those who manage this corporation.

Peter Hartlaub wrote in the *San Francisco Chronicle,* "Grace's mob-mentality panel discussions aren't illegal, or even especially unique. In picking Grace's show as the prime-time centerpiece for *Headline News,* they're using the same hateful-language-attracts-viewers template that Bill O'Reilly has used to win the time period. But Grace's rants are even more dangerous, because they turn the simplest principles of our judicial system upside down."

Hartlaub went on to observe, ". . . The *Nancy Grace* show is already strangely skewed from the real world. Guests who advocate a wait-and-see attitude toward suspects are used as punching bags. Guests who bring a scary amount of anger are praised, often becoming regulars." He says, "Public stonings used to be popular, and they don't belong on CNN either . . . the program more closely resembles a torch-bearing mob than the 'legal issues' show that CNN promised. Grace has created her own parallel universe in which guests are berated for advocating due process, panelists are invited back frequently if they make *ad hominem* attacks and suspects are seemingly guilty until proven innocent."

I make room for the possibility that her snarls and flared nostrils, her rage and verbal assaults, are a means by which she can more successfully bear the tragedy of her life. She has no family of her own making. She has no advertised mate after having lost hers twenty-six years ago. She seems alone. Sometimes she even seems frightened. Does she cure herself through her diatribes where all who come into focus are guilty? Guilty before the jury has spoken? She says in her book, "In trying to cure the injustices heaped upon other victims of violent crime, I was cured."

Sadly, I don't think so.

The problem, is, of course, that one cannot cure one's pain or ease another's by inflicting more pain. Yet rarely is this woman interviewed without her telling her heartbreaking story.

I think the lady yearns to be understood and to understand herself, as most of us do. Perhaps she is unaware of how she transfers the fruit of her pain on to millions, many of whom are not acquainted with the source of her hate, who cannot evaluate it, and who can only take what she says as competent judgments. Why else, one might wonder, would CNN, a respected network, air her rants? Perhaps she does not understand that her own biting cynicism can call to life the same hate-filled but dormant sentiment of her viewers.

> *She hates,*
> *We hate,*
> *We all hate,*
> *Ain't that great?*

I think of how this phenomenon works, that is, how we are influenced by the attitudes of the people we listen to and are expected to respect. If we listen to the love of Billy Graham, the love in us tends to rise to the surface. If we hear the call for love and justice of Martin Luther King Junior, we respond in kind. But anger is the mother of hate. And it is dangerous. I am not comparing her to Hitler. But in a later chapter we shall see how a similar stirring of the people's latent hate led unalterably to the Third Reich.

Ms. Grace is not a bad woman. She is a hurt woman turned loose on the public. Only the network that profits from it can stop the damage. Not only can her charismatic personality open the valve to that store of preexisting anger that most in a civilized society suppress to varying degrees, but she can create hate where none existed before. Those in the television business know the truth of this. They know their audience. Through the hard lessons of descending ratings and plummeting profits, the TV gurus know there is a mob out there brimming with anger, and that mining this anger is like mining gold.

Here is the journalist Joy Press, of the *Village Voice:* "Watching Nancy Grace I can feel two sides of myself in bitter conflict. There's the irony-soaked Gen X'er in me who treats the show as a spectator sport, delighting in every sleazy line of inquiry. And then there's the more earnest me who understands how many people watch Grace in utter seriousness—the me who agrees with Jon Stewart's contention that this kind of blowhard demagoguery is 'hurting America.' May the better half win."

Yes, may the better half win. But at risk is a vast multitude of Americans, good law-abiding folks trained from childhood to accept as gospel whatever those in authority tell them. It isn't that they're stupid, although the power structure in this country has done its best to stupefy them. It's because when people hear strong, attractive, intelligent, and well-qualified people argue against the very rights that ensure their freedom, hear such pronouncements over and over, people begin to think they must be true, especially because what Nancy Grace says has been broadcast by CNN, the honest network, the objective source of news and information.

The networks, all of them, know that out across the land await the grinding, benignly seething millions. As we shall see there is no broad-based conspiracy among the media sources here. The sale of hate is not limited to CNN. All the networks show us the murders, the rapes, the sodomizing of children, the horror galore in their news shows that could only be matched in the bowels of hell. They compete with each other to see which can garner the greatest ratings by dipping the deepest and the most frequently into the public's cauldron of hate and feeding it back to the people, not warmed over, but heated to still a higher degree. As for Ms. Grace, she understands: "I am proud to say that I get more hate mail than anyone at *Court TV*."

A plentiful diet of hate is doled out every day to America's television audiences because the people crave and demand it. They have become addicted to it. And any network that ignores that fact, and none do, is destined to extinction. But what about America? What is happening to the "the land of the free"? As we shall see, our freedoms are teetering on the brink!

2. The Queen of Hate

Ann Coulter

Ann Coulter, the Queen of Hate, claimed on a CNN segment about the dragging death of James Byrd, an African-American man in Texas, that "there is a constitutional right to hate." I suppose in this she's right. We can hate anyone we wish, even the haters. This *is* still America.

But the lady does not take responsibility for the violence such hate engenders. If hate explodes into killing she would say give them the chair, the needle, the chamber, while we all watch and eat popcorn. And she would say, as she has said, that "normal people, unlike lawyers, didn't care if heinous murderers were insane or Caucasian or ate too many Twinkies." This sort of mocking cynicism undermines the basic protection of our legal system, the presumption of innocence and the right to a fair trial. And it denounces all lawyers whose duty is to ensure fair trials.

Ms. Coulter leans so far to the right that she talks in dizzy, clockwise circles and says things like, "We should invade their countries [the Muslims], kill their leaders and convert them to

Christianity," or, as she told an interviewer for the *New York Observer,* "I'm getting a little fed up with hearing about, oh, *civilian* casualties. I think we ought to nuke North Korea right now just to give the rest of the world a warning . . . it would be fun to nuke them."

Who is this woman anyway? She's a media creature who's learned that an intelligent dialogue doesn't sell. She's become a shameless self-promoter who has discovered that if she shrieks enough contemptible and poisonous stuff she can draw attention to herself, sell a ton of books, and appear on the hate shows of radio and television. She's become a sideshow attraction who sadly fails to provide anything useful toward drawing a divided nation together. Her scorn spares not even her own gender: ". . . Women should be armed but should not [be allowed to] vote."

According to Coulter, liberals promote sex and abortion—they go together, you know—and they hug the gays and want them to marry. They preach peace in the world—probably even love the French—and holler for bigger wages for the lazy bastards who want to put a kink in good American business. They encourage single mothers to have more babies so we can support them on welfare, and, and, and . . . with her trademark hiss, "There are 22 million Americans on food stamps. And 39 million greedy geezers collecting Social Security. The greatest generation rewarded itself with a pretty big meal."

I can hear millions of Americans asking, "How come I worked all my life, paid into Social Security, held an honest job for thirty-five years like good Americans are supposed to; and now I'm an old, greedy geezer when I get my twelve hundred dollars a month?"

Why should we consider what this venal comic has to say; why give it dignity? Alone she's harmless enough, like a single pregnant rat in the granary. But her views, mostly adopted by the conservatives of America, are the evil poison being fed an angry and, in ways, an innocent American people.

Still some media have actually turned away from her. Example: When she left the *National Review* in a huff, claiming they were censoring her, the editor, Jonah Goldberg, wrote, in a lengthy and equally huffy response, "Ann is fearless, in person and in her writing. But fearlessness isn't an excuse for crappy writing or crappier behavior." She was allegedly fired from MSNBC when she told a disabled Vietnam veteran, "People like you caused us to lose that war," and *USA Today* canceled her as a correspondent to cover the Democratic convention.

We have a geyser in Wyoming's Yellowstone National Park known as Old Faithful. Every hour, more or less, it spews out boiling, smelly sulfur water—shoots high in the air and makes quite an impressive display. People gather from across the world to see Mother Nature's show. The geyser has no responsibility for whom it might scald. It just blows off. Reminds me a lot of our lady.

She doesn't care much about the millions of innocent people she may be burning with her disparagements. I mean, people love to be on food stamps, right? High living. Over 35 million people exist below the poverty level in this land of milk and honey. Already by the end of 2003 nearly 13 million children lived in poverty. It's worse today. But Old Faithful just incessantly, mindlessly spews on. And the networks expose her to their audiences without warning. She looks human enough; some think she's pretty. She makes those high-end intellectual noises. She is introduced as someone of importance, and she speaks down to us.

Recently appearing before the student body of the University of Connecticut, she was unable to continue in her speech—brimming with her usual invectives—because of the boos and jeers. She abandoned her speech to a question-and-answer session, saying, "I love to engage in repartee with people who are stupider than I am." Then she said boringly stupid things like, "I think there should be a literacy test and a poll tax for people to vote."

Remember, if you get too close to Old Faithful you *will* get burned. While Nancy Grace labors to make us angry at people charged with crimes and those who defend them and the courts that protect their rights, Coulter says, "Liberals love America like O.J. loved Nicole."

Back at the University of Connecticut: Eric Knudsen, a nineteen-year-old sophomore journalism and social-welfare major who heads the campus group Students Against Hate, said, "We encourage diverse opinion at UConn, but this is blatant hate speech." It wasn't the first time she ran into trouble with her Old Faithful mouth. In October of 2004, two boys ran onstage and threw custard pies as she was giving a speech at the University of Arizona. Harding University in Arkansas dropped her from its lecture series in September, citing her abrasive image.

How is it that we're entertained by someone who says in all solemnity, "[Canadians] better hope the United States doesn't roll over one night and crush them. They are lucky we *allow* them to exist on the same continent." Is this spewing geyser serious, or is she just pimping us for profit?

Following her own logic, Ms. Coulter would deprive herself of the right to vote but run around with a gun on her hip. She's not married. Never has been. She claims the longest-running romance she's had was around eighteen months. The man, if he is still alive, should get a medal. She can't seem to get a date in Washington, D.C., because she can't handle the idea that women can ask for dates these days the same as men. So she says she doesn't answer the phone calls left on her answering machine. She just sends off an e-mail. Doesn't even touch her ear to the phone.

If there's a thing she could say that would engender more anger than she has already authored, one would be hard-pressed to find it. David Brock, the one-time conservative journalist who had a long-term political association with Coulter, wrote in *The Washington Post:* "Ann is an illustration of how a certain kind of virulent right-wing politics is based on emotion, not reason. Almost to a one, I found that the most hateful voices on the right were venting their own deep-seated problems and frustrations."

I've appeared with her on several of those talking-head shows.

She was always there to create her brand of commotion, to start the screaming, to get the people riled up with her sarcasm, her wild intellectual swinging, like a kid with boxing gloves on for the first time. But in my opinion the woman is not delusional. She is playing a very simple American game. It's called, "Chase the Money," because her high nastiness sells like many other forms of violence.

She's made millions on her bestselling books that peddle hate. No one would buy a book on how to kill, skin, and eat puppies, but we buy books, such as hers, that tell us "Democrats . . . want to liberate women to behave like pigs, to have sex without consequences, prance about naked, and abort children." Vintage Coulter. The sad part is that the networks know that a shouting match between Ann Coulter and some sacrificial opponent who will provide her a modicum of dignity by taking her on will boost their ratings. Sort of like verbal mud wrestling.

We continue to fall for the merciless game of this sometimes seemingly unhinged ogress who acts as if she could even eat the flesh off the bones of the widows of 9/11 in order to sell her books. Four of the widows sought answers to the terrorist attack on the World Trade Center that led to the creation of the 9/11 Commission. In her latest book she calls these women the "witches of East Brunswick" and says, "These broads are millionaires, lionized on TV and in articles about them, reveling in their status as celebrities and stalked by griefparrazies. I have never seen people enjoying their husband's death so much."

She knows what we know—that the shortest route to a bestseller and millions more in royalties is to simply punch into America's hate canker and let the feculence ooze out. And NBC, who promoted the book on the *Today* show knows that to keep its ratings it must tune in on the likes of Coulter from time to time. It's not that NBC is peopled with bad folks. They are simply in business, and, as always, they know that hate sells. Any thoughtful listener must also know that this is part of Coulter's rummage sale of hate taken to the extreme—to hold up widows of husbands who were burned alive in the World Trade Center as publicity seekers, to claim that these women have enjoyed the deaths of their husbands.

Please.

The media world has endured an overlong run with this evil-mouthed woman. Ms. Coulter has spewed out her hurtful hate messages for years. Matt Lauer of the *Today* show knew what she was going to say when he quoted the above passage from her book. And the world pretended to be shocked. Hillary Clinton jumped on the "Oh-my-goodness" bandwagon and said the book should have been entitled *Heartless,* and called Coulter's remarks, "A vicious, mean-spirited attack," and Governor Pataki, New York's Republican governor, said he was "stunned" by Coulter's remarks. And I have devoted a couple of paragraphs myself to her book-selling cause by even mentioning her latest deranged attack. I do so only to again make the point: No one should take this woman seriously any more than one stops to argue with the raging, wild-eyed soapboxer on the corner. But we all take part in the sale of hate. Everyone profits: Coulter gets rich, the networks get richer with elevated ratings, and we, the public, get our hate fix for the day, and, indeed, I, too, am given a further opportunity to make my case.

One wonders how such malice found a home in this woman. One imagines her as a child. She must have been cute and precocious. Children often grow up mean when they don't get their needs met. I think of the millions who fill our penitentiaries. Most reside there because they were unjustly punished simply by being born—born innocently into steaming poverty or they were beaten or had role models who provided them with a violent vision of life. But Coulter is quicker than most, and she claims she had a marvelous, loving childhood. Somewhere along the way she must have learned that meanness sells—like a junkyard dog that learns he gets an extra bone from his master if he bites trespassers on their butts.

She obviously loves her father, who must have been a well-meaning parent. One of her books is dedicated to him, and she claims she learned to argue effectively by verbally tussling with him at the dinner table. He's a lawyer who fought labor unions—a man whose energies were laid against the working class. He represented Phelps Dodge Corporation, the mining and manufacturing behemoth, and presided over the largest union decertification ever. You can imagine how her view of ordinary people might have been formed. We hear little of her mother, but she dedicated a book to her as well. After law school she followed in her father's footsteps and worked for a corporate law firm for four years, where most often people are seen as digits on a page.

She claims she worked in the summertime in an open pit mine in Arizona. How long she worked there she hasn't told us or what her duties were as a fragile, blonde Eastern girl-child. But she obviously didn't bond with the workers. She thought it was absurd that the union was striking for more wages. After all, "They get very high wages, they get all their health care taken care of, and it's an open-pit mine, so you're working on the side of a mountain." Sounds like fun.

I doubt she ever visited one of those noisy factories, the air filled with poisonous chemical mist, to see how corporate profits are gleaned through the damaged lungs of the worker—or the hospitals and shanties that house what's left of men injured in unsafe workplaces. Nor, likely, was she ever introduced to the widows of men who died of black lung, who labored in the bowels of the earth for the profit of their corporate masters.

We are who we are. I wish Ms. Coulter had taken on Mother Teresa as her role model or Rosa Parks—those hated liberals—or at least the single mother who put her five kids through college and who lived out her old age in a three-story walk-up and subsisted on Social Security—one of Ann Coulter's "greedy geezers." Instead Ms. Coulter has had a postmortem love affair with Joseph McCarthy, the notorious commie-baiter, who, she claims, was an American hero.

Her attack on liberals is relentless and equally mindless. She says, "These liberals are fanatics about privacy when it comes to man-boy sex and stabbing forks into partially born children. But a maid alleges that she bought Rush Limbaugh a few Percodans and suddenly the government has declared a war on prescription painkillers." Her attempt at satire reminds one of Jonathan Swift's essay, *A Modest Proposal,* in which he suggested that the children of the poor Irish be eaten to relieve the burden to their parents and to provide a benefit to the state. He wrote in 1729: "I have been assured by a very knowing American of my acquaintance in London, that a young healthy child well nursed is at a year old a most delicious, nourishing, and wholesome food, whether stewed, roasted, baked, or boiled. . . ." Swift was satirical. Coulter seems to mean every word she utters.

I'm loath to give this woman more attention, since that is her game. But in the name of science one can hold her up in the palm of one's hand and inspect her as one might examine a blind frog with thirteen toes and become interested in the nature of the environment that explains the creature. One cannot despise the frog. One can only wonder at it and hope that whatever virulent poison accounts for the mutation will not spread to the general populace.

3. Hate, the Road to Power, and the Elitists of Laura Ingraham

Of course, there's something more than hate available in the media. Witness the proliferation of sitcoms, mindless cartoons, nonviolent sports, adventure, environment channels, how to bake a gorgeous soufflé or where to buy a cheap diamond ring—whatever the viewing public wants, from preaching to pornography, is available today through the various media sources that find their way into America's home.

My premise is that for the several reasons we've encountered here and others we've yet to examine, the public is angry, often a smiling anger, often silent and repressed, but one that can be activated—something like a mob charging to the crazed beat and chant at a public lynching. And I argue that the media business is as conscious of this phenomenon as a cheap source of profit as any popcorn merchant at the movies.

When you get stuck in traffic and need your hate fix, there's Laura Ingraham on talk radio. A lot of hate is smogging the radio airways these days, something called "noise pollution." Ingraham is the host of a nationally syndicated radio program and author of *Shut Up and Sing: How Elites from Hollywood, Politics, and the UN Are Subverting America*, as well as another book that attempts to pillory Hillary Clinton.

Ingraham is the once blonde diva who clerked for Clarence Thomas and posed appropriately feline for a *New York Times Magazine* cover story in a leopard-print miniskirt, all the while hissing her hatred against elitists and feminists. She claims, in a backhanded way, that true Americans are white, southern, Christian, Republican—and own guns. She worked for a white-collar criminal defense firm, the kind that might defend the likes of the Enron chaps.

Ingraham worked simultaneously for both CBS as a commentator on the nightly news, and for MSNBC as a regular pundit. Her time with both networks was riddled with off-the-wall, often salacious commentary, such as a remark she made on MSNBC about Clarence Thomas's penis size. But her vicious killing instinct concealed behind a pretty face, her cruel and often outrageous offerings, raised ratings and the profits of her employers and made her a star. She is not timid about quoting the Bible, which, by the way, proclaims rich people (like herself) will not go to Heaven, and that money (which she has plenty of) is the root of all evil. She's the voice of corporate power that searches endlessly for one thing: money. Only money. *Only money, Laura!* But she still doesn't get it.

How can this woman, a set-in-concrete archconservative, compete for attention with the likes of Ann Coulter? They are touting the same tired message of hate against all but God, Bush, and the corporate King. But she's a clever one. She's created a new group to hate—those she calls "the elitists." And she spends 342 pages in her book telling us who they are and why we should hate them.

Now I am not an elitist and therefore, thankfully, she does not hate me. None of us want to be elitists, those snobbish, better-than-anyone-else bores. A standard dictionary definition of elitism is: "The belief that certain persons or members of certain

classes or groups deserve favored treatment by virtue of their perceived superiority, as in intellect, social status, or financial resources." By this definition Einstein, a person of superior intellect,
was an elitist, as were Karl Marx, Sigmund Freud, and Jesus
Christ, not to mention the Rockefellers and the heads of all of
those corporations out there who are rich and consequently are
not going to heaven.

An elitist, according to this lady, is someone who thinks that
"conservatives are stupid, that flag-waving is stupid, that having a
lot of kids is stupid, that driving SUVs is stupid, and that owning
a gun is stupid." According to Ingraham, the elitist also thinks
George W. Bush is stupid. This plows new ground for conservative argument. If we think that the intellectual base of any of the
above is suspect, then we are elitists, that is, we have refused to allow rightist political or religious dogma replace the normal functioning of reasonably operative brains. Ironically, according to her
definition of an elitist, a majority of the people of the United States
fit the bill, since they think that George W. Bush's brain got misplaced somewhere.

In short, Laura Ingraham's definition of the elitist is substantially identical to Coulter's definition of the liberal. According to
them, liberals are actually elitists, although many do not have a
college education or even high school diplomas and many are poor
and some are even on welfare. Thomas Jefferson, who didn't buy
all the Christian dogma available at his time, wrote: "The clergy,
by getting themselves established by law and ingrafted into the
machine of government, have been a very formidable engine
against the civil and religious rights of man." Jefferson was obviously an elitist. He was also a liberal and thought that church and
state should be separate. That made him an elitist for certain.

Indeed, Ms. Ingraham, the Founding Fathers were all top-
drawer elitists. Remember, Washington was the wealthiest man in
the colonies. All of our founders were gentlemen of means, if
means also meant they were owners of black human beings who
had been reduced to property. Of the fifty-five men who gathered

in Philadelphia in 1787 to draw up the Constitution, a majority were lawyers (but note: all of our women here are lawyers, including Ms. Ingraham); nearly all the founders were men of wealth in land, slaves, manufacturing, or shipping; half of them had money loaned out at interest; and forty of the fifty-five held government bonds. And yes, likely most of them would have thought that George W. Bush is stupid, which further qualifies them as elitists.

I suppose by the standard definition Ken Lay of Enron and WorldCom's CEO, Bernard Ebbers, along with Tyco's disgraced CEO, Dennis Kozlowski, are elitist because of their massive wealth, most of which was allegedly stolen from their shareholders, although they claimed to be part of the Bush conservative caucus.

We get confused by Ms. Ingraham's definitions unless we understand that she simply uses the term "elitist" to include anyone who disagrees with the proclamations of the conservative chip that has been transplanted into her brain. Again, perhaps David Brock, that born-again liberal who knew her intimately, explains it best of all. He says of her: ". . . She was the only person I knew who didn't appear to own a book or regularly read a newspaper."

At last the lies, the character assassination, and the hate became too much for Brock. He wrote for rightist publications and was one of the hard right's most loyal and active stalwarts. But his conscience finally caved in on him. In the preface to *Blinded by the Right,* Brock confessed that his book was about "what the conservative movement did, and I did, as we plotted in the shadows, disregarded the law, and abused power to win even greater power." In the preface to the paperback edition of his book, Brock said it even more clearly: "I was confessing to having been complicit in a propagandist campaign of lies against liberal targets—Anita Hill and the Clintons, among others."

Brock admitted witnessing and participating in all of the scandals of the era: Iran-Contra, the failed nomination of Robert Bork to the Supreme Court, the Clarence Thomas hearings, Paula Jones, Whitewater, including "the secret scheming that led to the impeachment of President Clinton." He called it a "tight-knit political movement" that socialized, schemed, and worked together toward the common goal and without a moral compass. He further confessed, "I worked for leading institutions of the conservative movement—*The Washington Times,* The Heritage Foundation, and *The American Spectator*—where I fought on the wrong side of an ideological and cultural war that divided our country and poisoned our politics." Some of that cadre's important members included several of the protagonists of this book, including two of our ladies, Ann Coulter and Laura Ingraham.

Brock observed that even in the grave national crisis that was brought on by 9/11, some of the hard right refused, even for a moment, to back away from what he called "a zealously intolerant, hate-filled, religious-based ideology." Referring to Ann Coulter, he said he was sickened to hear her call on America to "invade their countries, kill their leaders, and convert them to Christianity." Brock went on to painfully denounce the hateful scapegoating practices of purported Christian ministers such as Pat Robertson and Jerry Falwell, who blamed the terrorist attacks on gays, lesbians, and members of the American Civil Liberties Union. These religious leaders converted Jesus's love into the Christian Right's propaganda of hate.

But back to Ms. Ingraham. She further confuses us in her tirade against elitists because she labels some of them as "*limousine* elitists." These she accuses of being Communist subversives and Fascists. How can elitists be both Fascists and Communists? It doesn't matter. She wants to write a book about elitists, which really is a book libeling liberals. So she calls liberals elitists and gets herself a publisher. But she is top-drawer talent in teaching us to hate *someone* for *some reason.* She creates a sort of smorgasbord of hate.

Now about religion and elitism: she tells us that we must believe that "God exists, that God created human beings in His image, that God loves us, and that we all have an obligation to love, honor, and serve God," else we are elitists. That's why we brought on this war against all those elitists in the Middle East who do not believe in our God, right? If we work to keep church and schools separate, don't forget, God is watching. And those elitist judges who say the Constitution forbids us to interfere with the religious rights of others will go to hell. Hell is filled with elitists—and elitist judges.

Sigmund Freud, an elitist by Ms. Ingraham's standards, one who cared a great deal about the human condition, said, "Where questions of religion are concerned people are guilty of every possible kind of insincerity and intellectual misdemeanor." Whether one agrees with Freud or not, if one inquires into the truth of what he said, one would instantaneously be labeled by Ms. Ingraham as an elitist.

According to Ms. Ingraham, where you live determines if you are an elitist. If you live in New York, Los Angeles, San Francisco, or D.C., well, you are *prima facie* an elitist. These appear to be cities in which a majority of the people, mostly working people, voted Democrat, which is really the problem. If you shop at Wal-Mart you are saved. If you flew a flag before September 11, you are saved. All the rest out there are elitist or elitist suspects.

If you care about oppressed minorities you may be an elitist. If you think minorities should get a break in education—I suppose she means affirmative action—you obviously are an elitist.

And be careful. Do not support the UN lest she label you an elitist. If the world hates us, it is the world's fault, not ours. She says the Democratic Party "has reinvented itself as a cool hangout favored by Hollywood celebs, media yuppies, trial lawyers, multiculturalists, God haters, and the race-relations mafia who look down on the working people who once made up the backbone of the Democratic party."

One wonders if her leader, George II, is an elitist. This man ascended to the throne not with a red neck from having been exposed to a cruel sun for years while he worked his ass off to take care of his wife and kids. This fellow has soft hands, a swagger, and a built-in sneer. He is who he is because somehow George I and Barbara found each other on an occasion and behold—George II, the fruit of their loins! Some call him a spoiled brat, who never once came face-to-face with an honest day's work. I call him the simple victim of his birth, a case of primogeniture. Being the eldest put him in line for the throne.

None of this was George II's fault. One thing we suspect: he probably deserted the Air National Guard, and we know he was marvelously successful in manipulating the failure of one business after another. He is not really stupid. Not really. And he is not, I repeat, not, a hated elitist—else Ms. Ingraham, being intellectually honest, would have included him in her inventory of hated elitists.

Ms. Ingraham finally sums up who the true Americans are: "In other words, the kind of people who are the lifeblood of healthy, democratic societies—the kind of people most likely to send their kids to fight and die for this country—are now considered by their political elite to be the problem."

Give her words a second of thought. These Americans, the so-called "lifeblood of healthy, democratic societies," are, according to Ms. Ingraham, not permitted to think when beckoned by King George II, but eagerly send their kids off to be killed for whatever foreign frolic George II has in mind.

Hear what Walter Cronkite, obviously an elitist, said about the kind of people she is talking about: "We're an ignorant nation right now. We're not really capable of making the decisions that have to be made at election time and particularly in the selection of their legislatures and their Congress and the presidency, of course. I think we're in serious danger." It's called the dumbing of America, and, as we shall see, TV has had its hand in that from the beginning, and Ms. Ingraham speaks to those who have been its most obvious victims.

Ingraham attacks the media as left-wing, a worn-out mendacity as we all know by now, but she tips the hat to the same old party line. One thing's for sure: neither she, nor Nancy Grace, nor Ann Coulter, nor Bill O'Reilly, whom we shall soon meet, nor that fellow Hannity, nor Rush Limbaugh, all leading members of the

media who corral most of the talk, would ever tolerate being labeled left-wingers, much less elitists.

Then the woman says that the favorite place for elitists to hang
out is in the universities. Professors *are* a problem, I suppose.
Those in the universities presumably have been trained to think,
and those who think usually do not adopt the numb, dumb creed
the lady espouses. Still, give her credit. She's in line with the ideas
of Mao, who hated the intelligentsia as well. But Mao simply took
them out, stood them up against the wall, and shot them.

Next she attacks the "cultural elites." She says, "This is a broad
category encompassing not only the artistic and literary worlds,
but also the class of self-styled intellectuals." She adores Arnold
Schwarzenegger and Bruce Willis (both excel at pretend killing)
and Mel Gibson (who produced a blockbuster film about killing—
Jesus). She stomps around in this section, trampling over Virginia
Woolf, D. H. Lawrence, Aldous Huxley, H. G. Wells, and George
Bernard Shaw, who wrote books she probably hasn't read, authors
who are some of the most revered minds in literary history. But
once more she lives true to the ideals of Mao, who also despised
the artistic and literary worlds. The wall for them, baby, the wall!

She admonishes us to hate those who see themselves as citizens
of the world, to hate those who do not want our schools to become churches, and those who think gays should be left alone to
live in a culture that abstains from persecuting them. We should
hate those on welfare and those who support help for the poor.
And those who want peace. Yes, label those who do not agree with
you as liberals or elitists or Commies or Fascists or dopers or, or . . .
there is plenty of hate out there, something for everyone. This is
America. As Ms. Coulter said, we have a constitutional right to
hate. So please hate. Corporate power thanks you.

According to Ms. Ingraham we cannot trust the elitists, whoever they are. In vain we search for those we can trust. Can we
trust Mom? How about Dad? If we were betrayed as children, it
left scars on our tender psyches. Or we grew up innocent, and to
our horror discovered the world is filled with fakes and frauds. We

got hurt. But we still need to trust. We were jilted and lied to for something someone wanted from us. Our money. Our virginity, well, maybe something postvirginity, but they lied to get it. By now trust comes hard. But we still need to trust, and despite Ms. Ingraham, we try.

Who do we trust these days? The image of Daddy, the father figure, has, in ways, become the government—Big Daddy. Big Daddy sets the rules for the family—called laws—and goes about its business pushing other Big Daddies around, threatening, getting in fights called wars, killing, lying, and torturing, crimes that had our own daddy committed them would have landed him on the gurney awaiting the executioner's needle. But this big daddy is now *our* Big Daddy, and we have to support him, right or wrong. Something called patriotism.

Big Daddy puts us to work for him, like the farmer works his sons, gathers in the fruits of our labor, called taxes, and throws us into those wars where our sons get killed for Big Daddy, and it's just and it's right because Big Daddy says so. If you question him you are guilty of treason, or you may be called a liberal, a commie, a tree hugger, a faggot, or an atheist. Ask our bloodthirsty ladies.

In a democracy we're told that we can change, actually change, big daddies whenever we please. Our right. But we are children at our core, and the need to trust remains. We long to be secure, and down at the level of our first cell we must survive. It's hard for us to change big daddies. It requires us to change allegiances and to join new families and acquire new friends. It seems disloyal. Maybe unpatriotic.

I met a woman the other day who was stumbling to work as a desk clerk in a small-town Wyoming motel. It was late.

"You look tired," I said in a kindly way. I don't know why I say such things to perfect strangers. I'd been talking politics with the desk clerk then on duty, the clerk the woman was about to relieve. The tired relief clerk said she'd worked all day at school as a teacher, after which she'd gone home to grab a frozen dinner and do the laundry before she came to this second job that paid only the minimum wage. She worked at the motel until midnight. She was exhausted, but she had to hold both jobs because she was supporting herself and her mother, who lives in an old folks' home.

I asked another of my impertinent questions. "So what's your politics?"

"I'm a Republican," she said, as if she were making a confession. Most people in Wyoming are Republicans.

"How come? Is that party working for you?"

She shrugged her shoulders. "Always have been a Republican. My father was and his father. That's who we are."

"Where's your life?" I asked.

"I don't have one." Then across her heavy eyes, I saw the faintest flash of anger.

Still, who do we trust these days? Can you trust the preacher? How about the priest? What about the pharmaceutical companies that sell us their products, tell us they're safe, and then kill or cripple us? The doctors and hospitals whose negligence kills and injures more people than cancer and heart disease, and who want protection from suits for their wrongs—trust them? Trust the lawyers, who, we are told, are the most ruthless, money-hungry devils on the planet and should all be killed—first. Ask Nancy Grace about them. Do we trust her?

What about the newspapers? Most are owned by a few megacorporations—we'll see more about them later.

Do we trust the companies that denude our forests or the Department of the Interior, whose job it is to save them? How about trusting the chicken industry to serve us poultry that isn't foul and not full of hormones that cause little girls to need a bra at the age of ten? What about the cattle industry and our milk full of unhealthy crap and a nation suffering an epidemic of cancer?

I'm still asking, who do we trust? The insurance companies who insure our health, our homes, our crops, our lives? You buy an insurance policy, and you only buy a contract that a troop of insurance company lawyers wrote. The insurance contract—the policy you bought—has so many holes in it you could slam it over the front door and use it for a screen. If you suffer a loss, what the company may offer you is half of the loss you actually sustained.

You want to sue? You have a right to sue. You are an American. The courts are open. All you need is a lawyer who'll take on your case against one of the largest corporations in the world. You say you don't have the money to pay the costs, the hundreds, sometimes thousands of pages of depositions at five dollars a page, experts at a thousand an hour—costs totaling many thousands? And you're just trying to get the fifty grand that the insurance company owes you? You only have to wait two years to get your case heard, and then there are those appeals that take a couple more years and . . .

And whenever this trial takes place it's before a judge who, as likely as not, represented insurance companies before he was chosen for the bench, put up there by a corporate-owned governor or a corporate-owned president. Your case is one of hundreds in the judge's court. He needs to get rid of the damn cases that are piling up. And he has the power to dump yours—it's called "summary judgment." Surprise. You get no jury. But no one said you don't have the right to sue. I almost forgot my point. I'd rather trust the Mafia for full, honest protection than the insurance companies.

Can you trust the courts? I'm representing a former farm boy from Kansas who was wrongly identified by the FBI as having been involved in the mass murder of over two hundred people in Spain when a train there was bombed. Although the FBI now admits that they were wrong, and although this former farm boy suffered serious damage, when the young man wanted justice the government lawyers threatened him with delays with their appeals that could last, they said, as long as six years. He has a wife and family. Such delays are devastating. Yet no one tells him he can't go to court. The courts are simply the dysfunctional members in this family of justice.

What about the politicians? Can you trust them to represent you? Will you get anything but a form letter from Sen. J. Harvey Howmuch when you complain that the local poultry company is fouling your well so when you turn on the tap you get chicken-shit tea? The politicians are owned—lock, stock, and down to their go-nads, if they have any—by the corporate overlords who put them in office. You say the Democrats are different? If you take a close look you'll find that the Democrats are feeding from the same pig trough as the Republicans, a trough filled with corporate green.

And you hear these politicians on both sides yammering at each other with a slightly different set of adjectives. It's a show. But the corporations, who have no vote, who are not alive, who are not citizens, who should have no rights comparable to those of a human being, who, indeed, live on and on while we grow old and die—these monsters own our democracy, a government of, by, and for the corporation.

Back to Ms. Ingraham. Ask her if we should trust corporations and their CEOs, the kind her firm represented, the kind that are her employers. Do we trust good old Enron and World-Com and Tyco and all the others? Henry Pontell, a University of California, Irvine, criminology professor and a leading expert on white-collar crime, charges that "white-collar criminals cause more pain, death and financial loss than all common criminals combined. When you add up the impact of industrial accidents, environmental pol-lution, fiduciary fraud, unsafe products, and medical fraud, the ef-fects of white-collar crime are much greater than common crime." He shows that the price of bailing out just one corrupt financial institution during the savings-and-loan crisis exceeded the total losses of all the bank robberies in American history.

Corporations thrive on crime. Bloat on it. It's become an ac-cepted norm for corporations to cut corners, to lie, to cook the books, to engage in insider trading, to foul the environment, to bribe and cheat wherever it's profitable—and to end up owning both parties so they can continue their nefarious, unholy war for profits at the expense of workers and shareholders.

The FBI estimates all robbery in the United States costs $3.8 billion a year compared, for example, to between $100 and $400 billion for corporate health-care fraud, $40 billion for corporate auto-repair fraud, and $15 billion for corporate securities fraud. The 1980s' corporate U.S. Savings and Loan swindle alone is estimated to have cost up to $500 billion.

Take a look at some of our leading corporate citizens—Bayer, for example, who overcharged the U.S. Medicaid Insurance program and settled the matter for $250 million. What about Boeing (I'm picking a few alphabetically), which was charged with bribery, fraud, kickbacks, military-contract and export-law violations? They settled for a piddling $100 million. So, too, with Citigroup, the biggest loser of the ten major U.S. brokerage firms—it paid $400 million of the $1.43 billion in fines levied against these firms for misleading investors. And that good old company that claims, "Things go better with Coke," settled a race discrimination suit by black employees for $192.5 million.

These fines and settlements didn't leave even a bug splat on the windshield of these corporate giants. What they paid out in fines for their potpourri of malfeasance is merely a minor cost of doing business. Is there profit in corporate crime? Yes. Yet the CEOs who have not been charged personally with any crime, and this includes most CEOs of corporate criminals, continue on as accepted good citizens. They're welcomed in the finest country clubs; they are looked up to as the epitome of success; most go to church on Sunday and give heartily (and, of course, publicly) to charities—more to art museums than to soup lines for the homeless, more to music festivals than to homes for battered women.

How much trust does the average American vest in America's business? *The New York Times* says it's clear that disaffection is spreading. In a recent Roper poll, 72 percent of respondents felt that wrongdoing was widespread in industry; last year, 66 percent felt such was the case.

If we can't trust anyone, not even the local butcher with his finger on the scales, well, what are we going to do? Can we trust our spouses or favored other? Fifty percent of marriages go down the drink. You sure can't trust the kids if they're past fifteen. Who then do we trust? Maybe the Salvation Army. Maybe Mother Teresa, but she's now a saint. How about ourselves?

We've turned into a paranoid nation, but not without good cause. That's why we love dogs so much. At least most won't lie to us. We live in a frightening world populated with vicious human animals who want to devour us, a sort of social cannibalism. All of this corruption and abuse of decency makes us angry. And we hate.

The only effective voice the masses listen to is the television screen and talk radio and there, thank God, we can find someone who leads us in their latest hate rant. And it's cheap to the networks. Just put on a bloodthirsty lovely and some fool who will verbally word wrestle with her and you've got a program that sells—big-time—no actors, no production costs, just a couple of cameras, a couple of chairs, and the inevitable screams, snarls, and sarcasm. Hate.

It's as in Orwell's *1984*, where the party members were subjected to Two Minutes Hate every day, and sometimes Hate Week. Hate was the basis of Big Brother's control; hate and lies and the demand for unconditional, blind loyalty—remember, we call it patriotism—my country right or wrong, moral or immoral, honest or criminal. It doesn't make a bit of difference, it's my country even if all of this dementia, debt, and death supplies more profit for the corporate culture that already possesses most of the wealth, wealth that has been wrested from the lives of those who never had it and never will. So listen up to Laura Ingraham on hate radio, we'll all feel better.

4. For I Have Sinned

The Saga of Bill O'Reilly

I like this man, this Bill O'Reilly. He thinks a lot like I do. Even though he isn't one of the ordinary folks out there and never has been and says he, too, distrusts the elite—most of them anyway—nevertheless this multimillionaire many times over leaps onto common ground and embraces the working American. He adopts a definition of "working class people" as those "who do not have much control or authority over the pace or the content of their work and are not the supervisor or the boss." They account for 62 percent of America's labor force. And I don't blame him for being mad at Al Franken for putting a bad picture of him on the cover of Franken's book. Bill O'Reilly is a handsome guy and deserves better than a photo that makes his face look as green and mottled as an old dollar.

He's against a lot of things and a lot of people, without much original thought—none, as a matter of fact. But none of us can wander onto many paths that haven't already been packed down with the prior weighty stuff of the philosophers, the economists, the politicians, the pundits, and the talking heads. O'Reilly is predictable, but I think he's honest, as honest as a person can be considering who he works for and what his and his employer's agendas are. As we shall see, he is human. Very.

Here is a guy from the old school. Believes parents as a last resort should be able to administer corporal punishment on their kids although, as we know, by the time corporeal punishment is required the parent-child relationship has probably already failed. As most of us, he's sad that mothers have babies out of wedlock, but has no answer for that.

He thinks George W. Bush is honest, but maybe that's because, unsaid, he also thinks he's too mentally challenged to be successfully dishonest. I give Bush more credit than that. Bush is, as O'Reilly says, incapable of solving problems and "he is a child of privilege and brings a sense of entitlement to the job . . . a charter member of the power-establishment club that plays by its own rules." We agree on that. Still, except for his immigration policy, O'Reilly dutifully supports nearly the total Bush agenda, including that war. O'Reilly's politics are simple. He is an apologist for Bush, and he hates Clinton. He leans right just far enough that he does not fall out of his chair. In important ways he suffers a neoconservative mind-set. And oh, how he *hates* to have the conservative label pasted on him.

Well, Bill, you are a conservative—as are those who, in most ways, want things to remain as they were two hundred years ago. You say a person makes it or breaks it on hard work and good values. Yes. But if we aren't born with as good a set of genes as Bill, we'll have to join the rabble and thrash around in some cold river of misery, without an education, a good job, health insurance, and old-age benefits.

The good old American way lets those who are lucky (and those of us who enjoy a modicum of success are mostly lucky) go after the goodies and keep them, while those who aren't, the poor, the uneducated, the physically and mentally challenged, the children of whom he speaks without fathers, well, they just have to be obedient citizens and quit complaining, and not ask for help, and not demand a better salary, and not even suggest raising the minimum wage. Not good for America.

And by all means do not put a new roof on the Constitution. Bill wants to stick with the old one even though it no longer covers a nation that has expanded geographically, economically, scientifically a hundred times over and is now a nation of more than a quarter billion people of every race and creed. Our problems are different today, Bill. This is the twenty-first century. We go to the moon and do not struggle in Constitution Hall by candlelight.

And besides, as we know, our founders didn't recognize slaves as persons, nor did they recognize women or indentured servants or persons who owned no land. These folks were not given the right to vote. So when you talk about staying with the original construction of the Constitution, where does that leave you, Bill?

One other little point: Corporations had no rights as persons in those days. As we shall see later, they were not persons and the founders had no intent that they should enjoy the same protections as persons. If we applied the original intent of the Constitution today, corporations would never have the rights of living human beings as they now do. Rupert Murdoch's Fox corporations and all of their corporate advertisers who, with other corporate behemoths, control America—what would they say about that, Bill? Make you shiver? "We are a flag-waving network that looks to America's past for perspective," you say. Simple as that. But that's not a very helpful solution to the current problems most Americans face.

The chief reason that O'Reilly is a conservative is that like all conservatives he offers no solutions for the major issues confronting those he pretends to champion—such as better wages, workable health insurance, education for every deserving child, controls on the corporate thugs that are destroying our earth, an unfettered national voice for the ordinary citizen, reform of the election laws of this country that have permitted corporations to own the country and enslave our people. Here's a general rule: Conservatives do not have answers, only the same worn-out ideas—like cutting taxes for the rich, supporting ever-increasing power and profits for corporations, and playing a vicious game of politics that smears those who try to help ordinary citizens survive.

Part of the truth is, as he says it is: "Our federal government is not good at helping real people who have real problems, and it doesn't care about the money you give it as long as the revenue train keeps chugging along." Right. But he fails to state that the government is very good at aiding corporations. He says the government is good at "waging war" and among other things, "collecting taxes from individuals." Right again. But what about its inability to collect just taxes from your corporate sponsors, Bill? You forget to mention them. He even says that "the system is not designed to aid the individual," which, sadly, is still right on. What he fails to state is that the system is owned by the corporate King, which includes his employer and all of his employer's advertisers.

In most ways he supports the conduct and decisions of George II and attacks more liberals and Democrats than he does conservatives and Republicans. In the end, he is like most of us. He's a mixture of beliefs and ideas from both camps. But yours, Bill, end up leaning so far to the right that only you in deep denial could claim you are not a conservative.

O'Reilly admits he was once a registered Republican. That doesn't make him a bad person. So was I when I was young and inexperienced. When did he see the light? About the time he got going good on the media? Half his audience belongs to the Democratic Party. He's in tune with his network, which has also figured out that one simple proposition—ratings. You can't expect half your audience, which are Democrats, to listen to a man who admits he's a Republican. He has to be seen as a man of the working class, a man who takes up the cudgel for the ordinary Joe.

In ways he reminds me of one of literature's greatest comic figures—Don Quixote, referred to as that "muddle-headed fool with frequent lucid intervals who mistook windmills for giants." Of course we're all against the pollution of our young with the prurient junk on television. Of course we're not in favor of certain movie divas who suffer a paucity of morals. Yes, we despise individuals who cheat and lie, and he takes on plenty of them, ruthlessly. OK with me. Of course, we're distressed if some other pundit says unkind things about us. I know the feeling. Of course we are upset with the Catholic church, which is shamefully passive about its priests who have buggered little boys, and O'Reilly is a Catholic and openly shoves it back up the Vatican. And we do not like newspapers, especially *The New York Times,* if the paper doesn't agree with our conservative bent. All of those battles he takes on are understandable, and some I even agree with. But he never takes on the real dragon—the corporate King. No. Never.

Here is an essentially good man caught in a bad trap. As we've seen, he holds himself out as a friend of the workingman, but he cannot really befriend him. His trap is his work. He *works* for the said corporate King. Daily he lives with and takes orders from its henchmen. He cannot take on the corporate power structure, the advertisers, the car manufacturers, the drug companies, the mortgage Mafia. He cannot attack the banks and credit-card companies and the corporations that sell all the junk that a consuming public believes it must own. He cannot. And, except to hint at it from time to time, he does not.

His trap is worse than that. He knows the fear and anger and hatred that lie out there among the people, and he also shamelessly taps into it for ratings. He takes after, say, Jennifer Lopez or Whitney Houston or Bill Clinton or his own true love, Hillary, with a vengeance and perhaps with just cause. And the hate boils over in his voice, in his written words, and the people respond. Hate. God bless hate. And his ratings soar.

But we do not hear anything about the redistribution of wealth that Bush and his gang have accomplished to the unconscionable enrichment of the corporate King. It is like the child's trick: "Hey, look over there at that clown coming through the door!" and when the other kid looks, the first kid steals a big bite of pie off the kid's plate. Those in power play the same trick on the people. "Look at the gays. They want to marry. We have to stop them." "Hey, look at the abortionists, the child killers. We have to defeat them."

While the people look and hate and rail and fume and beat the walls, Bush is reelected and forthwith the corporate thugs steal the goodies of the nation and mortgage us and our grandchildren and theirs to the hilt to pay for it, and all the while the corporate King cackles and crows.

My friend O'Reilly does the same thing. He calls the little guy's attention, night after night, to whatever horror, crime, or outrage comes along. And while he is yelling about all those contemptibles, those despicables, those indictables, those shamefuls, which they may be, his master, the corporate King, the nonliving gang out there, remains untouched by him, but, and yes, here is the *big but*—he is simultaneously providing a fix for the masses who love their *hate*.

Now, Bill, you worry that people see you as a bully. Well, you are. But I understand. People who have power use it. You are not about to be beaten on your own program. You have the ability of a solid cross-examiner. You would have excelled as a trial lawyer. There you could have really fought for the rights of people. And anyone who comes on your program with a view opposing yours and expects to be fully heard is an idiot. If you were in court, a judge wouldn't let you interrupt or shout down the opposing attorney or tell him to shut up. But I understand. You are the big fish on your program. The people like seeing some poor bastard get his justly deserved comeuppance. And as we already know, a good brawl makes for good ratings, and you provide it. This does not make you a bad person, because you are not. But you *are* a bully.

You complain that people describe you as " 'contentious,' 'bombastic,' 'blowhard or bullying.' " You say, "While that assessment may be accurate, couldn't they throw in an 'incisive,' or 'courageous' or something like that once in a while?" Poor Bill. But let me be the first. I do think you are *incisive*. Whether you are courageous, as you see yourself, is another thing. You have to be afraid to be courageous. Courageous people do what must be done despite their fear. That is courage. What do you have to fear? You follow the party line of your bosses. For all of their shameless hypocrisy, you do not take on the real demagogues, the Pat

Robertsons and Jerry Falwells, because they are powerful within the party. You leave the real villain, the nonliving, nonbreathing master that is oppressing and enslaving the people and destroying their freedom, the corporate King, essentially untouched.

You take on the easy ones, those who are, at last, mostly the windmills of Don Quixote, individuals who are not as skilled as you in defending their positions—issues the solution of which will not change the status of the working class—and you have control of your shows. What appears to be courage, and it may seem courageous to you, is the dynamic that makes your shows sell. A lot of people think a lot like you and love to see those who oppose your views pilloried. Fun. Yes. Courageous? Well, I still like you.

You almost get there, Bill. Then you veer off just in time. Here is what you said about the corporate media: "The people who really run network news are money-men. Profit guys." You are right. "News is a major pain in the butt to them because news is expensive . . . also controversy is almost forbidden on the nightly news . . . the philosophy is don't rock the corporate boat . . . don't get anybody mad at you." I take it that you mean, don't get one of your advertisers mad at you. You are right again.

Then you almost reach the promised land of truth. Here is what you say next: "Since all of the network news organizations, including Fox, are run by huge corporations, and these enterprises are loath to criticize each other or themselves, you don't see consistent, incisive coverage of the damage [now watch how you suddenly veer off] that many media operations are doing to *the children of this country.*" (my emphasis) You almost said it, Bill. Almost! You were on the verge of saying that these huge media corporations don't cover the damage they are doing to *all* Americans, *period*—the consumerism you speak of, the enslavement to debt, the fear and hatred they sell. Instead you neatly narrowed your criticism to only hurting children.

Well, yes. They do hurt children. But the *national* hurt is that these corporations and their corporate advertisers control what the American people hear, what they see, and what they think. Collectively they become the voice of the King, the master, who also tells the people what to buy and how to pay for it, who to hate and against whom to go to war. But all you assert is that they *hurt the kids*. That is safe. Leaving out the ubiquitous damage caused by the corporate voice you work for is not courageous, Bill. It is quietly sucking up to the corporate King.

You take after Tim Russert (who in truth is a nice, passive fellow who you say gets his point across "while grinning like a likeable raccoon"), pointing out that "he [Russert] cannot hammer these people as I sometimes do on the *Factor* because NBC's parent company, General Electric, would not be comfortable with that." Well, yes. But tell me, when was the last time you hammered any of Mr. Murdoch's companies? And tell me when you hammered any of Fox's advertisers individually, by name? Maybe you have. If so, I know you'll let the people know exactly who they are.

Now you almost do it again. You are right on when you say, "From the time they are conscious of the outside world, American babies are bombarded with messages of consumption in a way that brainwashes them, sometimes permanently." You say this better than I have. You go on to rightly observe, "The buying power of the American consumer drives the country and is as addictive as nicotine." Worse. Try heroin. "Wall Street depends on it, and the government protects it." Right again, Bill. Then once more you *veer off*.

What is your solution? No one, especially you, is out there telling your listeners they are becoming enslaved as a result of the addiction you so rightly identify—consuming, that they are interest slaves, that they buy to satisfy their nearly insatiable craving for things. *Thingism* I call it and I will examine it later. But you remain utterly mute about the need of the people for a completely independent voice that will honestly educate the people or help the people educate themselves. Instead, the people turn to your program to hear your wisdom, to witness your courage, and to get their hate fix; and as a bonus they listen to all those endless, inane commercials. You know what I'm saying is true. You just can't say it.

Recently I listened again to one of Bill O'Reilly's hour-long extravaganzas of hate, holler, and howl. (I like O'Reilly better in his books than live on his TV show.) Anyway, here's how the show came off to me.

O'Reilly

He's baiting some barely articulate woman on something to do with Christians kidnapped in Iraq.

They're hollering. Really loud hollering.

Can't tell what her position is. He is hollering over her.

Can't tell what his position is. He is hollering louder now, shouting that her position is ridiculous. Re-dick-u-lous.

Never did get the point.

He cuts her off. Wham. He won.

Commercials
Get a Buick

Get Flonase, something for the nostrils

Get a mortgage at a good price, Lending Tree

Get a Gateway computer

Get a Capital One credit card

Conoco-Phillips—use natural gas

Get a Subaru

See boxing on *Showtime*

Watch something about *The Da Vinci Code* on History Channel

O'Reilly (finally back)

Pissed about a member of the Royal Family in Saudi Arabia who kills somebody as a repeat drunken driver and only gets a year in Martha's Vineyard, a jail like "a bed and breakfast." Victim's family member giggles. Her lawyer says it is unjust.

Commercials
Get a Ford

Get some kind of purple drug we should
ask the doctor about

Get a Panasonic Plasma TV

O'Reilly

The tragic death of Bob and Linell Shapiro's son from the drug Ecstasy mixed with alcohol. Shapiros going to establish a national awareness program.

Commercials

Something about Lucerne, Pink Lucerne, I think
Get an American Express rebate card
Get talking dolls of presidents, and one of Ann Coulter

O'Reilly

Some young guy says there are 850 lawyers out there who will fight free to keep nativity scenes. The ACLU lost. A black preacher wants stores to say Merry Christmas. People call in and some are against saying Merry Christmas.

Catholic schoolteacher gets fired because she gets pregnant out of wedlock. Does this violate her civil rights—not that she's pregnant but that she's been fired? A Catholic commentator says no because she works for the church, and this violates her contract and the religion of her employer. ACLU says men don't get pregnant and firing a woman for doing so violates equal protection.

Commercials

Ford again, the quiet Explorer
Lunesta or something. (I'm nearing exhaustion.)
A bank (red piggy bank)
Something about a Dell computer
Home loan lender
97.Biz.com about a scheme to make money

O'Reilly

Goes nuts about a newspaper that claims what the pregnant Catholic teacher did in getting pregnant out of wedlock was no different than what the Virgin Mary did. O'Reilly rages.

Screams. Appears to explode into a loud psychotic episode. Frightening. Says the paper is either anti-Christian or nuts. Takes the virgin birth as fact, and says the paper is lying about something sacred.

Commercials
Scottrade, a discount broker
Office Depot
Van Huesen shirts, drips all over them
Fox channel ad for itself

O'Reilly
Talks about his interview with Katy Couric and says we definitely have to see it. Go to O'Reilly.com.

Experiencing this hour I felt as if something uncivilized had exploded in me; I mean, at times I wanted to strangle the guy. Never saw a faster, nastier-talking human, a louder man, a more discourteous male—a bigger bully in my life—and POW! more commercials, and POW! here is O'Reilly again, pushing and shoving and getting his way on every issue—guests are mostly props for the man to proselytize, against which to push his opinion and to generate anger (he's said, "I guess I am one of the angriest journalists around these days") and POW! more commercials, one after another dumped in so fast I couldn't tell when one started and one ended.

I'm sure I didn't get it all. But he wasn't all wrong. And sometimes he smiles and is nice and thoughtful and charming. On some points I agree with him. I think Christmas should find its way back into Christmas. I know Bob and Linnel Shapiro and grieve for them. But when the show was over I felt agitated, and—as the master, O'Reilly, says is his goal—*annoyed*. More than annoyed—I felt like a balloon that had been blown up and then turned loose so that it went flying around the room with a great but short-lived gaseous sound. I was left with unattached anger, but I didn't know why; and after more than *twenty-five commercials* in an hour, I was *really* annoyed.

So how can this man ever tell the truth about the enslavement of the people in America to the corporate King? How? Roger Ailes is not his only boss. Ailes is merely the guy upstairs who is also a slave to the corporation that owns Ailes. He is not only employed by the Fox corporation; he is, in fact, beholden over the course of a year to hundreds of Fox's advertisers, which are mostly mammoth corporations. But O'Reilly is the ultimate slave.

Freedom of speech, Bill? You are free as your trap permits you to be free. Take on one of your sponsors sometime, like you take on Bill Clinton and the other public figures you emasculate. Then you'll be courageous. But you won't have a job.

I still like you. Sometimes.

If I were in your position, I'd be in the same trap. Al Franken got after you in his book—but I don't think you ever lied as Franken claimed. You may have said things out of context or you may have been mistaken about something or your memory of your "humble beginnings" may have been misrepresented, but I don't think you lied. To lie one must *know* he is telling a falsehood. You're above that. You might brag a little, and the truth is that every good story deserves a little embellishment, and you may embellish a little. But lie? No.

You say, "The so-called 'justice system' in America is not looking out for you, and you should write that down and read it every day of your life. If you are poor and you are arrested, things will get very bad, very soon. If you have money, justice might come around a bit quicker, but you will find yourself writing enormous checks on a regular basis. Lawyers charge by the hour, and at $400 per, just saying, 'Hi there, Perry Mason,' to one will cost you ten bucks. Generally speaking, any kind of legal problem is going to remove assets from your possession."

Yes, the justice system is broken. And again, you say it better than I: "Our justice system is overburdened, driven by money and connections, and [is] sometimes downright corrupt, and few in power seem to care." But once more you stop short.

The justice system for injured people, your workingman, Bill, and mine, is controlled by the insurance companies, your advertisers, and honest fellows like George II, who loads the bench with judges who have a deep love for the corporate King and some kind of genetic hatred of little people. As a whole, people cannot afford justice. The media, your playground, has so demonized trial lawyers that it is getting nearly impossible to find a jury that is impartial, jurors who don't distrust honest lawyers, jurors whose minds are not prepoisoned against their peers who have been maimed or killed by the corporate King's fraud or negligence. You pass that by with little more than your fine rhetoric that I admire and agree with. But bashing the justice system without holding out some hope of reform is to so undermine the system that it is of no practical or available use to ordinary people, all to the joy and profit of the corporate King, who—despite your occasional, careful criticism—loves you.

Now there is something else I admire about you, Bill. You are a human being who recognizes that you possess faults and struggle with weaknesses, and despite the fact that you may have "sinned," or will sin in the future, you are still willing to judge others. "Judge not lest ye be judged," the good book says, or something like that. And further, it says, "He who hath not sinned cast the first stone."

Well, Bill, if we all followed those rules we couldn't say anything about anybody, and this would be a very boring world and your show couldn't exist. The thing I like about you is that you recognize that truth about yourself. You know you are a hypocrite, but you are willing to admit it. That's a lot more than your evangelical brethren, the likes of Robertson and Falwell, are willing to do—two of the most accomplished hypocrites to have ever pitched their tents and passed their collection plates (and for shame that you've never taken after them for that).

But here's what you said on this subject: "I would not call myself a holy guy. I am a sinner but I do cast stones anyway." Now that you have confessed your sin, it's all right to commit the same sins over and over, show after show, again, right, Bill? I mean the entire format of your shows is to throw those stones. And you are so good at it.

Anyway, you go on to tell us about the admirable traits of your personality that have led to your success. You say, "My success is built on three foundations: personal discipline, education, and persistence." You then say, sounding like my Sunday School teacher, "In addition to developing discipline you need to keep your personal mistakes to a minimum. There is nothing more difficult in life to accomplish." Again I agree with this astonishing insight. Finally you say, "Most Americans, I believe, make most of their mistakes not in the workplace but in their personal lives." And in your own generous assessment of yourself, "At the same time, I made very few mistakes in my personal life." I got these statements from your book *Who's Looking Out for You?*, which I very much enjoyed reading. That book was published in 2003. Earlier, writing in your massive bestseller, *The O'Reilly Factor*, about sex— that was in the year 2000—you said ". . . You have to control this powerful force or it will control you, and maybe cause you to lose the things in life that are most important to you." So yes, Bill. You're doubtlessly preaching to yourself first and then to the rest of us.

One wonders if our friend, O'Reilly, saw this all coming—that he possessed some strange power to clearly warn himself against his own future by warning others about theirs. Was he suffering an overwhelming inner struggle all along, say, one like Bill Clinton's, which he's so often mercilessly ridiculed, or was this just one of those things that comes popping up in one's life like an uninvited carbuncle on the rear end? I am speaking of the unfortunate and devastating Andrea Mackris matter.

Following is just one of the many allegations made by Andrea Mackris, a *FOX News* producer, in her suit against Bill O'Reilly, which she filed October 13, 2004. In her complaint, filed in the Supreme Court of the State of New York, she alleged that O'Reilly called her on the telephone and told her he had been watching a porn movie and "babbled perversely regarding his fantasies concerning Caribbean vacations . . . when people shed their inhibitions, drink during the day, lay around and get lazy and after dinner come back and fool around . . . that's basically the modus operandi."

Then Ms. Mackris got specific in her complaint, claiming that during the course of his monologue, O'Reilly stated: "Well, if I took you down there then I'd want to take a shower with you right away, that would be the first thing I'd do . . . yeah, we'd check into the room, and we would order up some room service and uh and you'd definitely get two wines into you as quickly as I could get into you I would get 'em into you . . . maybe intravenously, get those glasses of wine into you. . . .

"You would basically be in the shower and then I would come in and I'd join you and you would have your back to me and I would take that little loofa thing and kinda' soap up your back . . . rub it all over you, get you to relax, hot water . . . and um . . . you know, you'd feel the tension drain out of you and uh, you still would be with your back to me then I would kinda' put my arm— it's one of those mitts, those loofa mitts you know, so I got my hands in it . . . and I would put it around front, kinda rub your tummy a little bit with it, and then with my other hand I would start to massage your boobs, get your nipples really hard, kinda kissing your neck from behind . . . and then I would take the other hand with the falafel [sic] thing and I'd put it on your pussy but you'd have to do it really light, just kind of a tease business. . . ."

According to *The Washington Post*, O'Reilly and his attorney, Ronald Green, never denied that O'Reilly had used such language, "but said he never broke the law and questioned whether Mackris was truly offended or was taking words and phrases out of context." What context?

The *Post* wrote that much of the criticism of O'Reilly centered on his role as a moralist who has lectured about too much sex in pop culture and had just published a children's book in which he warned boys against treating girls abusively.

The *Post* reported that Fox believed Mackris had tape recordings of the long, highly detailed conversations alleged in the suit, but Mackris's lawyer never confirmed that, saying only that they had concrete evidence.

On October 21, 2004, CNN reported, "O'Reilly referred to the legal dispute on his radio show, *The Radio Factor with Bill O'Reilly*. 'This is my fault. I was stupid, and I'm not a victim, but I can't allow certain things to happen and I appreciate your support, we get thousands of letters,' O'Reilly said."

"I am stupid, I am a stupid guy, and every guy listening knows how that is—that we are very stupid at times, but there comes a time in life where you got to stand and fight and I knew these people were going to do this, I knew they were going to do everything they could to try to destroy me and the channel and I just made a decision that I'm just going to ride it out, and I'm going to fight them."

But O'Reilly settled the suit.

The Washington Post observed, "The deal likely involves payment of millions of dollars to Mackris, since the two sides were discussing an offer of well over $2 million when negotiations broke down, say sources close to O'Reilly. Both parties agreed to keep the details confidential, according to the statement."

I do not judge the man. *He is presumed innocent.* All of the facts have not and will never see the light of day. Moreover, I doubt that there are many men of O'Reilly's stature and power who have not been so tempted. As he said a year earlier, "Once in a while that passionate feeling works out, but much of the time it does not. Infatuation is always temporary, often based upon nothing other than powerful attraction. Unfortunately, that kind of attraction often makes us do things we would not ordinarily do."

Given that he has, as he calls it, "sinned," the fact that he chooses to cast the first stone, such as the boulder he hurls at Bill Clinton, is remarkable. He *must* cast stones. That is who he is by his own admission—a stone-throwing sinner. Such brazenness hides the shame, yet I wish I could represent that O'Reilly is different from most of us. We hate most those things we despise most in ourselves.

Bill O'Reilly knows what respect is, and he cares about it more than all else. He defines it as "the state of being regarded with honor or esteem. All the money and fame and babes in the world can't beat respect. If the majority of the people who really know you respect you, you have achieved success. That's the truth."

Well, Bill, I can't speak for the majority of the people, but I respect you. Guilty or not, either way, it takes a lot of courage to go on throwing those stones and trumpeting family values and preaching to our kids after that infamous Mackris matter that you've suffered through. And once more I agree with you when you say: "If you are going to live a truly productive life, you have to forgive yourself. . . . Drop the guilt and strive to improve."

In the end, nothing changes. We are who we are. O'Reilly continues to bully his guests, to throw his stones, and to point his long, accusatory finger at the many sinners out there. No shortage of them, to be sure. He continues to bate those he considers liberals, continues to despise the ACLU and *The New York Times.* His take on the world hasn't changed. And he continues to play into that vast underlying hate that remains his crop waiting to be harvested. He asks, "Why are the most successful talk-show hosts conservative?" (Finally he has admitted where he stands.) He answers his own question: "Well, it's probably because liberals, whatever you think of their views, are usually nonjudgmental. . . . Liberals are just not easily annoyed unless they find themselves within earshot of Rush Limbaugh. He can get them ranting and raving."

What he's saying is that liberals have not yet learned how to siphon into that rich hate pool that lies roiling below the surface of the nation. Then he admits it—one of the major points of this book—that *hate sells.* "The best host is the guy or gal *who can get the most listeners extremely annoyed—over and over again.*" (his and my emphasis) That says it all.

As the most watched talking head in America, Bill O'Reilly understands, as do we, that producing hate produces those coveted ratings and profits. But on the other side of the equation, and there is always another side to every equation, lies *responsibility*. What none of these hate hawkers considers is where all this anger, this hate, this gathering fund of aggression in America is taking us. As we shall see, it is driving us into perilous places.

5. Hate, Hypocrisy,
and the Pimps of Power

So you see, from the standpoint of the corporate King, it really isn't a conspiracy out there with *FOX News* secretly joining the neocons—with Rupert Murdoch and Karl Rove taking over America—nothing as clandestine or ominous as that. (But give it time.)

It's simply the pursuit of ratings, nothing more sinister. If showing necrophilia to kiddies would spike their ratings, Fox would likely do it. But so would the other networks. Morality is never—I say, *never*—a consideration unless it is attached to ratings. Morality can be a talking point when it is useful, but there is no morality involved in the acquisition of profit.

None.

The networks show the people what the people want to see: the blonde, screaming divas, the hollering, hate-soaked talking heads of the other gender. The people's taste, their desires, are simply mined by the media. Follow that hate-filled vein of gold. Murdoch is thought to be a conservative, whatever that finally means.

But it does not mean that the man has a moral code elevated above, say, that of a common pornographer. His so-called conservatism is simple. If it pays, play it. I am trying to make clear that America's TV, conservative or otherwise, goes by the same mantra as the farmer feeding his hogs: "If they want it, feed it to them."

The faithful claim they are grateful to *FOX News*—their family conservative values, you know. The truth: *FOX News* is grateful to them. Hate is easy to play. Just tune in on the likes of O'Reilly, who, with his eyes foggy but his teeth bared, bawls out things like, "You want to have two guys making out in front of your four year old? It's OK with them. A guy smoking a joint, blowing the smoke into your little kid's face? OK with them. And *I'm not exaggerating here.* This is exactly what the secular movement stands for." (my italics)

Secularism, in philosophy, is simply defined as "the belief that life can be best lived by applying ethics, and the universe best understood by the processes of reasoning, without reference to a god or gods or other supernatural concepts." Hi there, Professor Einstein. Wish you wouldn't blow the smoke from your joint in my kid's face. Hello there, all you millions of decent Americans, you who don't blindly endorse right-wing, fundamentalist Christian dogma. Wish you'd kick those faggots out of the living room who are making out in front of the kids. Tune in, folks. This is The Hate Show.

O'Reilly, like our bleached blonde brigade, tells us over and over what sells. "Conservative people tend to see the world in black-and-white terms, good and evil. Liberals see grays. In any talk format, you have to pound home a strong point of view. *If you're not providing controversy and excitement, people won't listen, or watch.*" (my emphasis) So, Bill, we are not ultimately interested in the truth, in reason, in what is good for the nation, nor do we care about a thoughtful consideration of important issues. What we want is a screamer—controversy, anger smeared all over the airways like a toxic poultice. You want people hitting the walls. You want ratings and profit. That doesn't make you a bad person. But we need to know what this dangerous game is and where it's taking us.

The Fox Television Network, a network belonging to the same Murdoch media family, led the way in airing "the most offensive tabloid and sexually exploitative programming on TV," as one astounded and disappointed conservative put it. "Its strategy for cracking through the major networks seemed to be to out-sleaze them in showing degrading programs like *Temptation Island,* which sought to pull couples apart by getting them to cheat with virtual strangers; *Joe Millionaire,* which portrayed women as shallow gold diggers; and *The Swan*—a truly disgusting show in which women have their bodies carved up to gain self-esteem. All these programs have severely debased the culture and devalued women." But note: The other major networks followed suit with their own subtabloid programming that let us see women as promiscuous sluts.

Murdoch's Newscorp owns *The Sun,* the largest-selling paper in Britain, which posts a naked woman every day on page three. This is almost a "so what?" We are to scorch poor Murdoch as immoral when, in America, the adult entertainment business—a sweet euphemism for porn—is estimated at $12 billion yearly and goes essentially unchallenged? And these good, solid American companies like Liberty Media's On Command and Lodgenet Entertainment provide systems that invite hotel guests to take the same clicker that changes the TV channels and to tune in to every conceivable kind of raw porn that the sexually repressed minds of the American public can conjure up—group sex, cheating housewives, barely legal hot teens, husbands watching wives have sex with strangers, you name it and the great hotel chains have it—Hilton, Wyndham, Marriot, the others.

Porn is now as common as cornflakes, the XXX stuff that most of us have seen and, when asked, deny vehemently having ever seen. "Oh, porn on TV? Oh, really? I didn't know." And those lofty, good American corporations whose CEOs are counted among the best and the brightest in the highest echelons of society provide every sordid variety of porn that the twisted American libido can long for: Time Warner, Comcast, Cox Communications, Cablevision, and, of course, News Corp's *Direct TV* air open crotches, the shaved . . . well, the bowling ball–sized breasts and the humongous freakish male parts as large as baseball bats that threaten every man (and likely every female), all naked, glistening, and wet along with the endless, mindless action—something akin to one of those oil-well pumps out on our Wyoming prairies that monotonously lifts up and down, into and out of the substrata, but without the accompanying moans and groans and, "Oh God"'s, which count for the most original lines in these skin flicks that one will likely encounter. How do I know all of this? Did I see one of these in my hotel room last night? Of course not. The charge on my hotel bill, as promised, only says "movie."

So what is the point? We don't have to be too gifted to catch the game plan. Whether it's hate or porn or politics or any other current form of prurience—if the public wants it, even if it proves to be mental or moral poison, even if the dangerous dynamic will cause the democratic foundations of the nation to crumble—the corporate core will provide it, right up to the end. Freedom of speech.

Profit-seeking corporations are insane. With no mind at all, they are less than insane. They possess no moral governor, only that insatiable desire for profit. And one of these giants is no worse than the other. Look at dear, untouchable News Corp's *Direct TV* peddling porn like a common backstreet pimp. We never hear anything from O'Reilly about how News Corp, one of Murdoch's babies, is in the porno business.

That a voracious taste for porn—the largest on-line business in America—along with a claimed devotion to conservative family values, a love of God, and a belly boiling in hate can all be in full force in the same American citizen is a phenomenon that has escaped comment from the psychology crowd. But we are *whole* human beings. We love, we hate, we lust, and we honor moral codes we sometimes violate. Most of us are hypocrites in that we readily judge those who prove to be as human and deviant as we. Indeed, hypocrisy is a hole that most of us fall into.

The networks know of our foibles and exploit them. Still, it has proven hard for the hard right to acknowledge their humanness. And while the right's brightest stars—the likes of Bill O'Reilly, Rush Limbaugh, and William Bennett—keep harping about the sins of seculars and liberals and others, we have sadly seen O'Reilly himself exposed to factually unresolved claims of sexual harassment and Limbaugh and Bennett admitting their addictions to illegal drugs and to gambling, respectively.

Even before the revelation of Limbaugh's attachment to prescription drugs, David Brock was shocked by the hypocrisy of the leaders of the far-right conspiracy, as he outlined in his book, *Blinded by the Right.* He wrote: "Rush Limbaugh was not who he seemed to be on the air. . . . He denounced a lifestyle of liberalism, but himself is twice divorced and never goes to church." Rush Limbaugh introduced Rush Limbaugh to Rush Limbaugh's audiences as "your epitome of morality and virtue, a man you could totally trust with your wife, your daughter, and even your son in a Motel Six overnight." He told his audiences that the American people are more and more turning to what is called "traditional family values, rejecting what is abnormal or perverted" such as "commie libs," "feminazis," "environmental wackos," the homeless (whom he thought should be spayed), and gays.

Of Newt Gingrich, Brock wrote: "What I underestimated was Newt's capacity for hypocrisy: his ability to live his personal life as he wished, his embrace of his own closeted gay posse, while leading a scorched-earth crusade to have the government enforce right-wing political and social values—the very opposite of the ideals of liberty and limited government he claimed to espouse."

Our own diva of decency, Ann Coulter, while claiming that liberals "adore pornography," still, according to *The New York Observer,* seemed unconstrained to carry on a relationship with Bob Guccione Jr., scion of a fortune made in publishing pornography (*Penthouse* magazine), even while he was fending off a sexual-harassment suit of his own. I am happy for her. She seemed to be struggling with a life devoid of romance in Washington, D.C.

And the same lady, calling all on the left liars, seemed to condone lying to the FBI. On *Rivera Live* (where I jousted with her several times), she defended George II against allegations of cocaine abuse, saying, "In fact, it becomes a kind of joke that, you know, your friends you saw doing drugs constantly all the way through college were never, you know, not stoned. You always tell the FBI, 'No, never even saw them smoke pot.'" The last I heard, lying to the FBI is a felony. Ask Martha Stewart. And although Ms. Coulter wanted to leave her New York law firm "to get away from all these Jews," she dated Jewish neocon John Podhoretz. But so what? Well, Brock wrote that in his private conversations with Coulter he indulged her far too long in her virulent anti-Semitism.

As for Laura Ingraham, "whose stock-in-trade was the hateful, and politically incorrect sound bite," Brock says she once showed up for a TV interview in a full-length fox fur coat and immediately proceeded to mock "the squealing baby foxes which were cute when they were alive." Yet Brock claimed that she confided in him that "she didn't believe much of what she was saying on the airwaves." He characterized the Coulters and the Ingrahams and others as "this transparently empty right-wing circle."

The problem, of course, is not that America houses every assortment of bolts and nuts. These ostensible crazies, as we have seen, and as we shall further see, can be duplicated in any bar, on any given evening, in any city. America is that lovely conglomeration of idiots, loose screws of all walks of life, of all religions, of polar political beliefs from Nazis to stargazing atheists, of races colored from black to white and every shade between. In many ways this divergence creates a strong and vigorous country.

The danger is that these wingnuts within, who are at least marginally pretty and arguably intelligent, wield tart, tantalizing tongues, and, with a deluding intellectual veneer, are irresponsibly given power over the minds of the multitudes by the corporate profit makers. If these bloodthirsty hate peddlers—Ann Coulter, Laura Ingraham, and yes, our sneering curled-lipped avenger,

Nancy Grace, along with the men who match them—can command an audience of millions, the danger is that their virulent messages can finally madden the already angry masses beyond containment to the end that the people lynch themselves at the polls. And they have. How else does one explain the Bush dynasty?

Stranger and more alarming still is the willingness of conservative audiences to absolve their heroes. I think again of Bill O'Reilly, whose admitted hypocrisy has proven to be of little account so far as his ratings are concerned. Good Christians, I should say. They seem to forgive O'Reilly for whatever he may have done, clothing him, as they should, with the presumption of innocence. And they forgive Limbaugh and Bennett for their confessed sins as well. Still, these Christian audiences are not likely to forgive the poor for being poor, the common addict for his habit, or the single mother with a half-dozen starving, ragged kids for living off welfare.

But our said media heroes with their long, pointy white fingers—what if they're liars and weak and petty criminals themselves? What if their principal ability is staying blind to their own raging hypocrisy? These days we have too few heroes. We tend to overlook their flaws as the fans of these conservatives surely have—much in the same way that many Democrats have accepted Clinton's sexual peccadillo with Monica Lewinsky as a personality defect that should not destroy the whole man as a leader. We can accept our heroes' palpable fallibility, but we cannot extend such forbearance to each other. We are too angry. Too filled with hate.

Hypocrisy: Talking heads who judge their neighbors for the malfeasances that they, themselves, have committed; networks that advocate family values and sell hard porn; television news programs that claim to be middle-of-the-road but are sold out to their corporate advertisers—this is the *oppospeak* we have encountered before, the shameless double standard that has become a part of everyday life in America, in politics, in the business world, and especially in the media. Hypocrisy is a fact of life wherever money and power are involved. It always has been.

Let's take a look at the ultraconservative Pete Coors, the beer magnate whose hypocrisy ties him up like a steer in a roping contest. You could hear him gasping for breath at the last desperate moment of his campaign in Colorado for the U.S. Senate, where he was defeated, presumably because of his patent duplicity.

Coors claims to have those Christian conservative values (if, indeed, that hasn't become an oxymoron by now). But like Murdoch's sense of where the money is, Coors' beer commercials have been some of the most sexually explicit ads on television. Pete Coors found that those scenes of decent, sweet Pete Coors standing in front of a snow-covered Colorado forest and talking about his beer weren't selling beer. Who gives a damn about sweet Pete and the Rocky Mountains? We want fun. We want titties. We want girlies and frolicking and a promise of bedtime romps. If sweet Pete was to stay in the beer game he had to introduce some raunchy stuff, which turned out to be the Coors Beer Twins, who, by any standard, invited the libidinous attention of even old fogies in the nursing homes.

Shari Waxman wrote in *salon.com*: ". . . There is something uniquely off-color about Coors's latest advertising campaign. The commercial spots, which first aired during the 2002–3 NFL season, are responsible for Coors's highest-ever ad ratings, predicted increases in product sales, and a newfound relevance with twenty-one to twenty-five-year-old male consumers. . . . Besides being just plain hot, the aesthetically gifted twenty-six-year-old blondes featured in the campaign are twin sisters. Twin sisters whose four blue eyes seem always to be saying, 'Hey boys, anyone up for a three-way?' Sisters in a three-way? Gross."

The Coors Brewing Company has a long and tortured history with gays and lesbians that dates back to the seventies. Back then the company used to require those applying for employment to submit to a lie-detector test. One of the questions was whether or not the prospective employee was a homosexual. We are not going to have a bunch of fags filling up our beer kegs—something like that.

The outrage over that practice caused San Francisco supervisor Harvey Milk to organize a boycott on Coors. The gay-bashing position of the company soon had to give way. The brewing company started running full-page ads in gay and lesbian publications around the country trying to convince the gay community that the company had "straightened up," so to speak. The moral position had to give way to profits—the definitive corporate morality. Simple as that.

But back to Murdoch: Calls were made to the man to clean up his empire, to require his networks to conform to "his conservative values." But like all of us, his values are reflected in what he *does*. Murdoch does not join Jesus in blessing the meek, the humble, and the poor. Murdoch loves God. If you want to see God, take a look at George Washington. He's there smiling at you on the dollar bill.

Blind patriotism found its place in *FOX News*'s reporting of the Iraq war. Patriotism can and does color the facts, and in so doing takes on the dimensions of propaganda, not journalism. Propaganda simply consists of information intentionally biased. The Iraq war was a boon for *FOX News*. The British Broadcasting Corporation reported that *FOX News* saw its profits double during the Iraq conflict because of its "patriotic coverage of the war." At the height of the conflict, Fox gleaned a 300 percent increase in viewers, averaging 3.3 million viewers daily. Their viewership was said to be more than that of CNN and MSNBC combined.

Again, the issue is not what is *fact*, but what jumps profit; and in a time of war who wants to hear the ugly truth of innocent men and women on both sides being blown to hell, their arms and legs strewn all over the rubble-filled streets? Who wants to hear the crying of orphaned babies, of dying children, of old people rotting in filth because there's no room in the hospitals? We want to see Old Glory waving and the skies full of American bombers and the deserts vibrating with American tanks and our soldiers looking tough and brave and loyal and fighting for freedom against the villainous enemy, who, incidentally, probably never heard of the Twin Towers.

One might waste some amusement on the arguments between *FOX News* and the more centralist networks, which continuously demand that *FOX News* admit it is a tool for the Republican Party. But Fox refuses to own up to any right-wing bias. It claims it is in the middle, where it should be; and if the middle looks like the right to its lefty competitors, that's their problem. On the other hand, one might suppose that conservatives who claim the other networks are too liberal might hear those networks argue back that *they* are in the middle; and if the middle looks left, that's because their critics tilt unduly to the right. Truth is, they've all turned right, and they all know it.

Fox demands to be seen as "Fair and balanced, as always," the *FOX News* slogan. But one Internet encyclopedia states: "Although most critics do not claim that all *FOX News* reporting is slanted, most allege that bias at *FOX News* is systemic, and implemented to both target and build a right-wing audience." It goes on to observe: "The channel is often regarded by international audiences as primarily being a propaganda vehicle for the Bush administration, as it not only promotes advocacy of such things as the U.S. invasion of Iraq, but also attempts to explain and advocate the broader neoconservative worldview behind those actions."

The network was founded by its president, Roger Ailes, who for years was among the most aggressive Republican politicians in Washington. He was a longtime strategist in the Nixon and Reagan campaigns. With Ailes's help, Daddy Bush turned a double-digit deficit in the polls to a win, which, of course, included the now legendary Willie Horton incident, which among other campaign smears, did Dukakis in.

A few other facts: *FOX News* anchor David Asman was formerly on the right-wing editorial page of the conservative Manhattan Institute. The host for *FOX News Sunday* was Tony Snow, a former chief speechwriter for the first Bush administration and at this writing, Bush's new press secretary. How about Eric Breindel, formerly editorial page editor for the right-wing *New York Post*, who, before his death, was senior vice president of *FOX News*'s parent company, News Corporation? And then there's Brit Hume, a contributor to the conservative *American Spectator* and *Weekly Standard* magazines, and FOX's leading talk-show host, Bill O'Reilly was a columnist for the conservative *WorldNet-Daily.com* and, as we've seen, formerly a registered Republican. Ann Coulter has appeared on the various *FOX News* talk shows so often that her seat before the camera is said to bear the permanent imprint of her posterior.

But at last, none of the above reflects any intent of *FOX News* to carry the laboring oar for conservatives, for the Republicans, or for the Christian Right without the advantage of profit. Ailes denies being biased toward the Republicans. He told the *New York Daily News*, "They [his critics] hate the idea that there is a huge niche for fair and balanced news." He went on to say, "We're not programming to conservatives. We're just not eliminating their point of view." They did, indeed, find a huge niche, and they've been exploiting it ever since. Ailes found that the network's conservative slant *sells*. If it wasn't selling, if its ratings took a nosedive, Ailes would be tilting the programming in the other direction or he'd probably be long gone.

The credibility of all news agencies would be greatly enhanced if they would only *admit their bias*. Then we could defend ourselves. We'd have a base against which to judge their news, their statements, their opinions that are daily laid out as truth. I think of Hugh Hewitt, who is styled by *The New Yorker* as the "Most Famous Conservative Journalist Whom Liberals Have Never Heard Of." He is a columnist for the online edition of *The Weekly Standard* and the evangelical magazine *WORLD*, and he is a syndicated radio talk-show host. His employer owns 104 radio stations covering twenty-four of the country's twenty-five major markets. Salem Communications, the owner of this mass of conservative noise, hires eight talk-show hosts, five of whom are said to be conservative and three mainly Christian. God Bless Salem, the home of the first American witch hunts. Hewitt has an audience of seven hundred thousand on 112 stations. His guests have included Karl Rove and Dick Cheney. The man is honest to this extent: *he admits he is biased,* and he stands for the idea that "fair and balanced" journalism is old-fashioned and stale.

The New Yorker says, "He is so deeply conservative that it is almost impossible to get him to accept the liberal point of view of the world on any point." You can trust your own opinion of what you hear from him because you understand where the man's coming from; just as when one of your kids is hollering about his brother, you know you're hearing only one very lopsided side of the issue.

However, some are so overt in their bias that no confession is necessary. It screams at you. Example: We hear Ann Coulter say, "Time and again, in all crucial maters of national self-defense, the Democratic Party has shirked the honor of leading this country in war, be it cold or hot." We know who she is. She is too young or blinded to remember Franklin Roosevelt and Harry Truman, who led us in World War II, and what about John Kennedy and his stand against the Russian missile threat? Any leader of any political persuasion would be a better hero to mankind if he did not lead us to war, but to peace. Ms. Coulter, by such statements, has declared herself a conservative (if not a dingbat), and we are given the opportunity to protect ourselves from her empty-headed volleys if we haven't previously abdicated our power of reasoning by allowing the conservative dogma chip to be substituted for our brains.

My mantra: *Hate sells.*

In point: Matt Gross, who left *FOX News* in March 2001, after working as a web journalist and editor, wrote: "Let me just say that the right-wing bias was there in the newsroom, up-front and obvious, from the day a certain executive editor was sent down from the channel to bring us in line with their coverage. His first directive to us: seek out stories that cater to *angry, middle-aged white men who listen to talk radio and yell at their televisions."* (my emphasis)

Gross went on to write in October 2003: "To me, FNC (*FOX News Channel*) reporters' laziness was the worst part of the bias. It wasn't that they were toeing some political line . . . it was that the facts of a story just didn't matter at all. *The idea was to get those viewers out of their seats, screaming at the TV, the politicians, the liberals—whoever—simply by running a provocative story."* (again my emphasis)

The cat escaped the bag when on May 20, 2005, Scott Norvell, the London bureau chief for *FOX News*, published an op-ed piece in the European addition of *The Wall Street Journal* in which he was criticizing the alleged left-wing bias of BBC: "Even we at *FOX News* manage to get some lefties on the air occasionally, and often let them finish their sentences before we club them to death and feed the scraps to Karl Rove and Bill O'Reilly."

The actor and liberal Sean Penn said, "There's a long history of people who capitalize on the lowest common denominator of people's impulses, Adolf Hitler being one of them. Not everybody wants to hit the wall in a violent rage and break their knuckles, so he [referring to O'Reilly] does it for them. . . ."

Here are a few examples of the kind of hate that *FOX News* promotes with their conservative yodeler, Bill O'Reilly. On his September 17, 2001, broadcast, O'Reilly said that if the Afghan government did not extradite Osama bin Laden to the United States, "the U.S. should bomb the Afghan infrastructure to rubble—the airport, the power plants, their water facilities, and the roads."

O'Reilly went on to declare: "This is a very primitive country. And taking out their ability to exist day to day will not be hard. Remember, the people of any country are ultimately responsible for the government they have. [Might that include American citizens as well?] The Germans were responsible for Hitler. The Afghans are responsible for the Taliban. We should not target civilians. But if they don't rise up against this criminal government, they starve, period." O'Reilly added that in Iraq "their infrastructure must be destroyed and the population made to endure yet another round of intense pain. . . . Maybe then the people there will finally overthrow Saddam."

And again, if Libya's Muoammar al-Gadhafi did not relinquish power and go into exile, O'Reilly said, "we bomb his oil facilities, all of them. And we mine the harbor in Tripoli. Nothing goes in; nothing goes out. We also destroy all the airports in Libya. Let them eat sand." The last I heard, the bombing of civilian targets and using starvation as a weapon are war crimes under the Geneva Convention. What we observe from O'Reilly here is a call for reciprocal U.S. terrorism, which, in the end, legitimizes the terror of our enemies.

I've said that hate is a valuable commodity. Numerous companies are selling it in the form of clothing, CDs, music, and dolls that glorify hate. That hate takes a concrete form in physical commodities tells us that hate, real and raw, can and is being sold as such—for immediate cash.

Recently the eleven hundred Target stores across the land were selling shorts and baseball caps decorated with a neo-Nazi hate symbol and yanked them when they were discovered. Are we so naïve (I was) not to recognize that the symbol 88 is the neo-Nazi shorthand for HH, which stands, of course, for Heil Hitler? These products were withdrawn by Target when they discovered what they were selling. Beneath the eyes of the general public a thriving business of hate has emerged. It could not exist but for the fact that hate sells. We knew that already, but did we think that manufactured and selling elsewhere in America is a T-shirt that reads,

RACE MIXING IS DEATH.
WARNING

Under which is a horrid skull with the Star of David implanted in the middle of its forehead and below the skull the words:

ASSOCIATING WITH "ZOG"
AND WELL-KNOWN RACE TRAITORS
IS HAZARDOUS TO YOUR HEALTH.

ZOG is, of course, the acronym for "Zionist-occupied government."

Chip Berlet, senior analyst at Political Research Associates and a longtime scholar of hate culture, says, "All successful social and political movements develop these accompanying cultural items and accessories." I suppose that the same dynamic, the longing to be identified with something, permits the National Football League to sell its caps and jerseys to the public in what has become a multimillion-dollar industry.

Berlet goes on to observe: "There seems to be a culture that's sustaining the movement through its current crisis," adding that the emerging subculture is "a sign that the movement has reached a certain level of maturity and organization." Hate is there. Profit seekers from all sides work it.

Many conservatives have preached the language found on a shoulder patch that sells for seven dollars. It reads, "If you can't feed 'em, don't breed 'em." But the vile and hateful illustration that accompanies it falls below the lowest standard of decency. It shows the cartoon of a black person, just big eyes, teeth, and a huge slice of watermelon.

Children are brought into the hate culture with a pretty white teddy bear bearing the infamous numbers 88. It sells for fifteen dollars. And the hater's girlfriend can buy an Aryan Nations thong, white, of course. The seller says that by purchasing their merchandise "you will be contributing greatly to the *cause of Christ* by enabling us to continue the mission for which we are annointed [sic]." Again, I was taught that Jesus loved us all. I must have missed something somewhere.

When defending Randy Weaver of Ruby Ridge, I was first introduced to the hate culture, and these hate peddlers were little more than a pitiful sideshow. Today National Alliance head Erich

Gliebe says that his neo-Nazi group grosses more than $1 million a year from Resistance Records, its music-and-merchandise label. Four years ago an Interpol study showed that white power music had become a $3.4 million-a-year enterprise. One company manufactures a fully decorated, dressed Hitler doll. The company claims it does not sell it as a hate item but as a part of collectors' World War II memorabilia. Remember, this is America. We are all free to say what we wish and buy and sell what we want. But along with our freedom goes that troublesome thing called responsibility, responsibility for the consequences of its exercise.

The problem, as seen by the Southern Poverty Law Center, is its effect on the young. "Kids love the in-your-face quality of this stuff," says Kathleen Blee, a sociology professor at the University of Pittsburgh. And, as with the sale of sportswear bearing the emblems of the professional teams and their players, there is a sense of camaraderie that comes with joining a subculture. Yes, instead of joining Bronco fans you've joined the Skinheads. Suddenly you have friends.

One white supremacist recently bought a publishing house. He proclaimed: "We hope to become a major corporation as a means to an end—ensuring the survival of the white race." At their Web site one can buy neo-Nazi propaganda and paraphernalia. The site assures, "Your money stays within the movement and aids us in our ultimate goal. White Power!"

The hate theme has invaded the colleges. In a recent convention of college Republicans the group was selling shirts bearing homophobic and racist themes. One of the shirts depicts Rosie O'Donnell and her partner, Kelly, and reads, MR. (?) AND MRS. (?) O'DONNELL. Another says, THE CLINTON LEGACY, and shows a photo of the Twin Towers exploding on September 11. A third has a picture of African-American filmmaker Spike Lee, and says, BRING BACK THE BLACKLIST, and still another reads, NO MUSLIMS NO TERRORISM.

Some Republicans expressed outrage over the shirts and condemned their sale. The director of public affairs at the Log Cabin

Republicans said, "The reason we Log Cabin Republicans exist is because there is intolerance in the Republican Party, and the party is not where it should be." Free enterprise works both ways. Because of pressures eBay has banned the sale of hate items such as Nazi battle flags and Ku Klux Klan cloaks.

But all hate is not focused on just one side of the political landscape. One site offered a Tom DeLay T-shirt suggesting he commit suicide with the caption, WE CAN DREAM, CAN'T WE? And another offered a T-shirt saying KILL BUSH, as its theme was adorned with splattered blood.

Hate and violence are a nasty married couple that ironically are in love. That America has always been a violent nation is difficult to deny. We go to church, yes. Yes, we have a nonviolent side to us, our charitable open hearts that bring on uncountable and unheralded acts of kindness toward each other, especially in the face of tragedy. Thousands of charities reflecting the goodness and caring of our people abound in this country. But our charitable side does not mitigate the proposition that, in sum, we are a violent nation, that we were established by violence, laud it, sing about it, teach it, are enthralled by it, support it, and hold it close to our hearts in patriotic fervor.

How all this hate pertains to the future of America remains the critical question. That hate can be reduced to something concrete and can be sold evinces its inherent appeal. We do not display on our bodies clothing which repels us. And we do not stay tuned to radio or television programs that cause us to retch. That large segments of the nation are drawn to, not repelled by, the hatemongers we have met in these pages confirms the dangerous attraction hate creates.

The danger becomes alarming when the backroom decisions governing the content of what we daily see on television, the quintessential tool of propaganda, are founded, not on that which is true or moral or for the benefit of a people or the good of a nation, but on how the networks' ratings, and thus its profits, can be elevated. As usual the people become their own victim.

This is not a new or startling insight. We have always been admonished to follow the dollar. But we experience today networks not committed to ethical journalism but to an unabashed mollification of the demands of their audience, programming that plays into and expands their darkest, primal urges, the most dangerous of which is hate. And, as we shall see, hate, and its underlying causes, are leading us toward the eventual annihilation of our cherished freedoms.

6. The Noxious Garden

The Cultivation of Hate in America

W e continue to ask, what is the source of all this anger in America, this greatest nation in history, where there is plenty for all, and all are for plenty? How is it that these gentle-looking mothers and solid, hard-working fathers who walk around smiling and nodding, these good citizens who go to the Parent Teachers meetings, host their friends at those Sunday tailgate parties before the game, help out with the Boy Scouts, those soccer moms with the kindly eyes, and the family praying and singing hymns to Jesus—how is it that hidden beneath their benign exteriors lies a lake of molten hate, one not even recognized by them or by *you,* my friend. You are angry? Well, so am I. So is everyone except Pollyanna. But why?

Hate is a virulent virus and is seeded like an entity sprouting on the breath of a noxious wind.

We teach our innocent children to hate. We infect them with that horrible disease. We teach them to hate other innocent people, those of different races, of other religions, of another class.

We, as innocents, have been taught to hate blacks and Muslims and Jews. We hate the rich, and the rich hate the poor, and the poor hate themselves. We hate criminals who may be only victims, and we hate politicians and priests and perverts. Some hate women and some hate men and some gays, even though men and women and gays have had no choice in achieving their status. But we may hate them nevertheless. We hate those we fear. We hate those who seem more powerful than we, more beautiful, more intelligent. Jealousy and hate are fraternal twins and adore each other's company. We hate our fathers or our mothers if we have been abused or think we have. Ah, an endless supply of hate—more contagious than the flu, more deadly than anthrax—awaits every member of the species who has taken its first toddling step.

While a bird has the ability to fly and thus escape most of its enemies and the groundhog can dig deep into the earth and thus foil most predators, the creator has played a cruel joke on Homo sapiens. It has endowed this species with a self-destructive specialty—the will to hate. Thus gifted, humans can kill millions of their own. They firebomb whole cities, killing hundreds of thousands in a single pretty, starry evening. They pollute the air they breathe and the water they drink. They denude the earth of its forests, poison its fish, and will intentionally nuke entire nations—all without so much as a whimper. And, as we have seen, hatemongers know how to turn hate into love—that is, they are specialists in a sort of emotional alchemy. They can transform hate into money, which, in this strange world, has become love itself.

This is a divided country, one engaged in a civil war of ideas. And a financial war—let's call it, "I got it and you ain't, and you ain't gonna get it because God loves me"—also divides us. We label the far right with hard names, like "neoconservatives," which carries with it nasty connotations, such as those who love war, are closet racists and homophobes, those who drown each other in the baptismal tubs and pray to Jesus to kill all who disagree with them, especially the liberals, who, according to the conservative lioness, Ann Coulter, are those who "nearly went stark raving mad at having to mouth patriotic platitudes while burning with a desire to aid the enemy."

Treason!

It might therefore be useful to give consideration to the kind of world that has produced Team Hate and their disciples. At the outset one can see that it is a cold and impersonal island where the inhabitants are preprogrammed with a mind-set that leaves little room for understanding, for caring, for human compassion, for learning, or for advancement of the species beyond the brutal Stone Age. The inhabitants of the island are detached from the reality that constitutes the lives of Americans. Ethics are defined by those in power in accordance with the need and greed of power and, according to Coulter, liberals have no ethics—none, which is a strangely unethical judgment. Hypocrisy is a perk of power. In this world virtue is a sentimental nuisance. Theft of workers' lives, their retirement, and their dignity is virtue in the corporate culture. Business fraud, robbery, and cheating are all virtues if in the end they lead to the ultimate virtue—profit.

In Team Hate's world the worker no longer sees what he's done with his life as worthy. The virtue he once knew as a child is an anachronism. The wealth of self-development has been replaced by a quest for things. When his things are soon depreciated, he is angered, for once more he's been cheated.

But our political and philosophical differences don't provide an accurate explanation of why we're so angry. It's easier to crunch each other about gay marriage, and maul each other about abortion, than to discover the root cause of our anger. Safer to rant about Michael Jackson and Scott Peterson and all of the other public hangings than to ask with caring, "Hey, pal, how come you are so angry?"

Today our ideas of success are fame, power, and money. Most Americans have none and can hope to have none. Parents who rear their children to become useful citizens are not deemed as successful as the wealthy business brute who has wrested a fortune off the backs of these parents. How a person has grown and bloomed is not as important as how much money one has made, even though the original self may have become shrunken and shriveled. Politicians and the wastrel heirs of some patriarchal fortune are marketed by their publicists in the same way that cars, beer, and shampoo are sold. The average American is left out.

After black slavery, the worker, black and white, became the new slave who was left to fend for himself, to feed and educate his children, and to see to his own burial. At the beginning of the Industrial Age the workingman was transformed into another commodity, an item of energy that could be converted to money.

Nothing has changed.

The worker is told that he is free, but—as we shall see in a later chapter—in ways important to human fulfillment, he is not, and he knows it, and he is angry. He senses his loss of belonging, and he joins a television church or become a fanatic fan of a sports team. His anger is sometimes expressed in random violence and is recorded in the acceleration of the crime rate. His need for alcohol and drugs and at last an escape into the "plug-in-drug," television, has become endemic to the country. Indeed, we've entered the new Prozac Age.

From what I've observed, most people take their anger as a part of their personality—like one accepts one's total body makeup without considering its parts. On the other hand, talk to the guy who's given his life to a corporate employer, a guy who's been dumped just before his pension accrues, and he can't find a lawyer to take his case, can't get into court, can't be heard, and we can see why he joins the likes of Nancy Grace in saying that lawyers are a bunch of pigs and the Constitution is a political ball batted around between politicians. He knows from his own experience that justice does not exist for him, and that all this leftist noise about freedom and rights is part of the great American myth. Sadly, he's right. Dead-on.

Talk to the woman who can't get her deserting husband to pay child support and who can't get a job because her skills have been outsourced to somebody making twenty-three cents an hour in

New Delhi and we'll begin to understand something about anger. Talk to the mother who's lost her children to her drunken husband, who could buy a better lawyer, one who just happens to be friendly with the judge. People feel helpless. Lost. Forgotten. Unimportant. And you begin to understand how, when Ms. Coulter says that women should never stray from the home, it angers a woman who is worrying herself sick about how she's going to take care of her kids and keep the bank from foreclosing on her little house.

This generalized hate often has a narrow base. It's easy to hate gays if one can't find a job that pays more than the minimum starvation wage. It's easy to jump on the patriotic bandwagon to blow the hell out of half the innocent people in Iraq if one has, in effect, been blown to some sort of economic hell and is equally innocent. When people feel hurt they hurt back.

I'm talking about something we all know. We just don't bring it up. We don't talk about ourselves, our feelings, or our sense of being excluded. Anyway, who would understand? Besides, to talk about it is to confess a sort of failure. Instead we talk about the Jackson and Peterson cases and the current hellish hurricanes because we can deal with those more comfortably than with the storm from within.

We don't talk about not being loved by our spouse or our other because we're afraid of rejection, or we want to avoid that unpleasantness, or because our own inadequacies may be thrown in our faces, or we'll have to finally look at theirs and wonder what the hell we're doing in this relationship. We've been taught not to express our feelings—a social prohibition against that touchy-feely stuff that supposedly betrays manliness and turns women into whiny neurotics.

Passion is seen as immaturity and not to be trusted. Be cool, man. Cool! Caring about another is opening one's self to injury. People have turned cold on the outside, cold like an eternally smiling death mask. We convert the most serious matters into jokes and get our news from comedians. Somebody said, "Laughter is the politically correct way of crying." We no longer know how to sing. We cannot write a poem. But inside the rage is seething and growing and craving to be expressed. Then along come these bloodthirsty women and their male counterparts. And millions of people are glued to the tube. There's that wonderful detestation floating across the networks that says we are not alone after all.

But something else is going on here. The world has become mechanized. We find ourselves admiring the machine. We tend to imitate it. In so doing we've become so machinelike, so attached to computers, so driven by music in our ears produced by music-making gadgets, so devoted to automobiles and video games and television voices, and the radio with its eternal noise pollution, that we have lost ourselves.

We gloat over our intelligence, hold ourselves superior to every other living creature. Who are we? What have we become? Who knows? Who cares? How often we hear the neighbors of some guy who has just shot his wife say in shock that he was "a nice, peaceful, quiet man who was never known to cause any trouble."

The society we live in is touted as the best on earth. Americans tend to take for granted that we have the greatest democracy ever devised by man. We have to believe it or we are not good Americans. People are always saying to me, "So you think this and that and the other is wrong with this country, right, Spence? Well, ain't that just too bad. Tell me, Mr. Smartass, where there's a better country, and if there is one, then read my bumper sticker: LOVE IT OR LEAVE IT."

I am not in the business of comparing America to other countries—although the United Nations ranks our standard of living tenth, with Norway first, followed in order by Iceland, Australia, Luxembourg, Canada, Sweden, Switzerland, Ireland, and Belgium. Iceland? No, I do not want to move to Iceland. No, Norway is not inviting to me—we have our own mountains and an eternity of snow in Wyoming.

I am not comparing America to Iceland although every child

there is guaranteed a free college education. I am talking in a general way about what our corporate-industrial state does to people, without their realizing that the culture itself creates stress, disappointment, and a pesky anxiety that keeps the pharmaceutical stocks popping.

In times past we possessed individual skills, most of which have now been surrendered. What's happened to the shoemaker—even the shoeshine boy? If we took from our lives every imported item, we'd run around naked, shoeless, and be without TV sets, most of our cars (the good ones), our cameras, our electric toothbrushes, our computers, our cell phones—nearly everything we own is made elsewhere. The nation is like its parts, the people. We are mortgaged to the last nickel, and our grandchildren's last penny. Our debt to China leaves that nation owning our taxes, therefore the income of our people, therefore their labor. Lord help us if China decides to foreclose. Perhaps we should be teaching our children Chinese.

And what do we export? We don't export brains anymore. The brains have gotten corroded on Wall Street. If anything will calcify the brain, it's the hustle in the stock market or in banking, where the greatest human talent is to squeeze the unfortunate. These people produce nothing, just as America has become a nation that produces little. A vague sense of overall worthlessness prevails, and it makes us angry. We get used to it, like one gets used to a pervasive bad smell.

Since the revolution that propelled women out of the home, presumably in search of their freedom, men and women can no longer raise their children without the help of nannies and overcrowded day-care centers. Both parents are separated from their children at their formative ages. We don't send our puppies off to a boarding school, if ever, until they've gotten over their puppiness. We want them bonded to us, to become part of the family, to adopt our ways. But children? Well, Mother has to work. Father too. Such does not bode well for independent, self-reliant, well-adjusted offspring. A nanny of twenty or fifty kids becomes Mom.

Why, in good times, is looking after one's own children a privilege only for the rich? Should women really delegate child care to a television set and a nanny? And sadly, too often the organized sport circuit for children is a stand-in for Dad.

Something isn't right, and when something isn't right—even if we can't exactly identify it—anxiety takes over like a fever; and bliss, whatever it used to be, becomes a distant memory. We get angry with one another, and ourselves, and escape into television, where we can be doused with today's murders and horrified with today's rapes, and we turn on some cop show where the scum of the earth are out investigating and prosecuting the scum of the earth, and on another talk show we hear Ann Coulter snort her little snort and tell us that we are guilty of treason because we don't support the war. Then if you throw the brass candlestick at the TV set the Japanese have another sale and your wife says you have to get anger therapy or she's going to leave and take the kids.

Individual attention to Junior is impossible in the commercial household that has taken the place of the family home. Parental time has been sold to the system, however you see the system. Individual love, although garnered on the run—"love on the run" as it is called—has been in large part sacrificed. Love has been replaced with things of every imaginable sort. How can you say I don't love you when I bought you a new convertible and those worn-out jeans that cost more than a dozen pair of new ones? How can you say I don't love you when I worked my ass off to pay for your straight teeth?

Yes, love is money.

People feel cheated, and when they feel cheated they get angry.

Most people work simply to feed themselves and their families, to pay the mortgage, to pay off the credit cards, and, in short, to survive in this age in which a man cannot earn enough by his own labor to provide for his family. My father worked six days a week. He rode a bicycle to work to save gas that sold for twenty-five cents a gallon, and he hunted and fished on Sunday. We lived on wild meat—deer, elk, antelope. Never tasted a piece of beef until I was sixteen. Mother stayed at home, washed the clothes on Monday, ironed on Tuesday, made our shirts and coats, tended the garden, canned for winter, and we rented my room out to tourists in the summer. I slept in a tent in the backyard. I never knew anything but happiness. Never really appreciated it.

It is standard knowledge the American worker makes less today, the dollar adjusted for inflation, than he made in the 1970s. We have tried to be good parents. We still have those shoved-in hours together at the kids' football games and the Christmas plays. But we have lost the ability to converse with our children. They don't want to talk to us either. They are too busy talking to their friends across town on their own private cell phones, even at dinner. The family has been taken over by the TV family—what's his name that "everybody loves," yes, *Raymond,* after which Mom and Dad are glued to *The Apprentice,* where some older asshole fires a younger one. No one talks about the issues that prepare children to embrace the reality they must face. We don't need to. They're in their rooms playing some TV game where they kill a hundred space gooks a minute.

The world is going to hell. Thank God, there's no room for us, we say. Hell is sold out.

And the talking heads of hate prove it—it's the liberals, you know. Annie'd eliminate the liberals if it wasn't such a waste of time, blast 'em with the gun she says women should tote.

It's a murderous, bloody mess out there. People kill you as you're driving to work, people you never met, never spoke a word to—they will poke a pistol out the window of their passing car and kill you.

Go to the shopping mall and some guy and his adopted kid will shoot you with a big game rifle from a hundred yards away—kill you because you happen to walk in front of their sights.

Here's what the conservative Democrat Sen. Joseph Lieberman wrote in the conservative publication *Policy Review.*

Consider a few facts. There are 95 million households in America with televisions, which means more households own TV sets than telephones. Sixty-five percent of those homes have at least two TVs, which on average are turned on seven hours a day. The typical child watches 25 hours of television every week. That is more time than most of them spend attending religious services, talking to their parents, reading books, or even listening to their teachers. Many kids spend more time watching television than any other activity except sleeping.

No one can seriously deny the potential influence that kind of constant exposure carries with it. Whether they want the responsibility or not, they [the TV programmers] are influencing our values. . . . Consider this passage from a stunning article Adam Walinsky wrote last year in *The Atlantic Monthly*, in which he warned of a coming generation of "superfelons" who, when they mature, will likely make the cities of today look peaceful:

"These young people have been raised in the glare of ceaseless media violence and incitement to every depravity of act and spirit. Movies may feature scores of killings in two hours time, vying to show methods ever more horrific. . . . Major corporations make and sell records exhorting their listeners to brutalize Koreans, rob store owners, rape women, kill police. . . . These lessons are being taught to millions of children as I write and you read."

But for Mom and Dad, click to MSNBC. Ann Coulter is on. If what she says is true, we are in a lot of trouble: "Liberals choose man. Conservatives chose God." We're suddenly confronted with a nation where only God counts and people can go to hell? Or she may say, "Whether they are defending the Soviet Union or bleating for Saddam Hussein, liberals are always against America. They are either traitors or idiots. . . ." Or out of the blue she'll proclaim, "We've got to attack France." I repeat: I've heard more rational ravings from a street-corner lunatic in San Francisco. And I am out of brass candlesticks to throw at the TV.

I am not against two cars and two TV sets. I just wish the cars could drive us back to the family, and that TV could provide us with insight on how to live rather than how to become Desperate Housewives or, in a Schwarzenegger movie, how to kill fifty-three people in the first thirty-second segment, all with the same level of caring as shooting ducks at a carnival booth. There he stands, our hero, his muscles flexing like the pistons on a twelve-cylinder engine, the guy who can kill with either hand and never sheds a tear, the dead cluttering Hate Street.

Deep down some feel like we should change the Constitution so that a citizen not born in this country can be elected president, so that finally we can put someone in the White House who's skilled in flexing muscles and pulling off heads instead of those imposters who claimed they were war heroes, or who skipped the war altogether. We *need* heroes; and Arnold, a God-fearing man, God bless him, could be our man.

It's hard for us to recognize what's happened to us. We don't have time to reflect. We don't have time to live. We don't have a life except on the breathless run. We've forgotten how to walk. We don't have time to be close. We don't have time for the quiet emotions. We don't have time to create, to invite growth. We don't have time to love. Love takes time. And somehow all of this, nothing very specific mind you, builds this sort of amorphous cage in which we exist, beating breathlessly at the bars, yes, in which many of us were born. And it tends to piss us off.

At whom are we angry? We're not mad at Grandma or the next-door neighbors whom we do not know because we haven't had time to make their acquaintance. We've been told that it's our parents' fault. That's the latest diagnosis for the millions of perturbed psyches who crowd the couches in the dim-lit rooms of our psychoanalytical surrogate parents who charge I don't know how much an hour and whose most urgent desire is to appear normal themselves. We all grew up in those dysfunctional families, and if there are problems out there it is not the fault of the system or the discontent of a money-driven nation. It's obviously the fault of Mom and Dad.

We are not mad at the capitalists who own us or the idea of a free enterprise system that drives us into the milking stanchions like dairy cows. We are not angry at McDonald's, even though the fat is hanging off our bones like half-full gunny sacks. How can we be angry at Wal-Mart? They hire good Americans, don't they? And wring the last cent out of their employees so they, too, can join those who live under the poverty level. What difference does it make that the minimum wage worker earns $10,500 *a year*, while last year the CEO of Wal-Mart earned $3,500 *an hour* (and the CEOs of Hallibutron and ExxonMobil earned about $8,300 and $13,700 *an hour* respectively)? But Wal-Mart passes the savings on to us, doesn't it? Yet we gnash our teeth—even in our sleep. We have to wear those night guards in our mouths so we don't wear out our molars.

We float in a historical vacuum without any recognizable connection to our past. We've forgotten the men, our grandparents, and theirs, who died in the streets and in the mines—the laborers who provided the flesh and blood that was converted to cash by the robber barons of a past century. Again, nothing changes. In those days when the industrial nation was being formed, the moneyed men saw workers as little more than beasts of burden. Frederick Taylor, the father of scientific management in the days of Henry Ford, wanted a man "of the type of an ox." We've forgotten the children in the factories and the black slaves in the fields and later in the ghettos and poor farm shacks who've been segregated from us as if they suffered a leprosy of the soul.

Today the Revolutionary War and George Washington and his soldiers without shoes in the wintertime are but boring required reading in the eighth grade. We are unattached to the hideous slaughter of the great Civil War, which took the lives of more Americans than all the other wars we've fought put together. We've lost contact with our deep historical roots. We are alone on this time line. We have no understanding of ancestry. We have no clear sense of the suffering and sacrifices of countless past generations who brought us here. We love the Broncos and the Saints and the Yankees. USC vs. Texas is more important than the plight of workers who haven't had a job for five years, and whose unemployment has run out. We feel separated because we've lost the vision of who we were, and we have no idea about who we are about to become. Without that—call it a historical common connection—we feel abandoned. And anger comes easy.

We can no longer relate to the miles of pretty white markers at Arlington Cemetery, graves that stand in the stead of the sons and fathers who gave their lives for freedom. We have mostly forgotten them, except on Memorial Day. Ann Coulter says, "Liberals malign the flag, ban the Pledge, and hold cocktail parties for America's enemies; but no one is ever allowed to cast the slightest aspersion on their patriotism." Tears come to my eyes. Her myopic hatred. The emptiness. But I end up being angry.

Neither Ms. Coulter, nor the others, ever define "a liberal" except in the most slanderous of terms, such as, "Whenever the nation is under attack, from within or without, liberals side with the enemy." So perhaps we should define the term *liberal* for her: Any dictionary will define the word as meaning those who are marked by generosity, bounteousness, openhandedness, and are not narrow of mind. They are, instead, broad-minded. Look up the word. Liberals are emancipated from convention, from dogma, and seek to advance the lot of the average citizen. They are supposedly free from bigotry.

Liberalism is an ideology that sees itself as striving to maximize the well-being and liberty of each *individual* through a democratic system of rights under the law. The rights of the individual, the living, are preferred to the rights of the nonliving corporate oligarchy. The belief systems of most Americans are founded in liberalism, an idea that *people come first*. Indeed, liberals believe in an open, competitive economic process, the free exchange of ideas and of political expression, a system that promotes the life, liberty, and happiness of the individual American. In that respect, our founders were liberals. Those who lie buried at Arlington would rise up in support of that kind of America, the kind they fought and died for.

Still survival remains the only issue. Having destroyed the earth, we begin to consider moving to another planet, to outer space, to join Buck Rogers, or whoever will whisk us away from the garbage heap we're making of our earth. As Ms. Coulter says, conservation is "the explicit abnegation of man's dominion over the earth. The lower species are here for our use. God said so. Go forth, be fruitful, multiply and rape the planet—it's yours. That's our job. . . . The gas guzzling cars with phones and CD players and wet bars—that's the Biblical view."

Rape the planet.

To quote the conservative hero James Watts, the former Secretary of the Interior, "If you've seen one tree you've seen them all." He once told me personally that every session of the cabinet under Reagan was begun with prayer. (What they prayed about I do not know.) Perhaps their prayers were answered. Yes, we know we are as destructive as rats in the pantry. We *are* rats. Lost rats. And unless we understand our rodent instincts and begin to change them (if we can) we stand little choice except to die of our own stupidity.

Why not despoil the environment as our blonde hater argues? The earth belongs to us to pillage and rape. Besides the end, as the fundamental Christians believe, is near. You do not save that which will be useless. As Mark Twain once remarked, if you have a nickel in your pocket when you die you wasted it.

I remember the tales about my old grandfather on my mother's side. He'd been taken in by a fundamental Christian sect in Illinois and the congregation had been promised that if they just believed, and all of them did, they would be taken up to heaven at a given time and place. The time came and the place was Peach Tree Hill. So off they climbed, and there they waited and waited. One need not save the environment or anything else if the end of the world is upon us. My grandfather also believed. Yes, deeply.

Except my grandmother confided to my mother that when they left the house for Peach Tree Hill grandfather locked the doors, securely.

Who are we? Maybe we're NIKE or GAP or CAMELS. We must be. Our T-shirts say so and so do our baseball caps. We provide corporations free advertising of a myriad products ranging from whiskey to monkey wrenches. We've become so devoted to the corporate core that, as a culture, we've finally agreed to give them free endorsements by wearing their corporate labels on our bodies wherever we go. We willingly *pay* for the right. We wear Exxon's baseball cap, sometimes backward (to show our independence)— backward so we can sell its product to those people coming up on us from the rear. The pelicans and the ducks and the countless miles of coastline in Alaska that Exxon destroyed are just oil under the bridge. But deep inside we know we are merely ciphers. And our impotence makes us mad.

How do you express your anger to anyone? If you start talking the way I'm talking here, your fellow workers are going to remind you that you must be very grateful to the companies because they provide you with jobs (although they are outsourcing most of them these days) and, besides, they must be all right because they control all those honest men and women in Congress who *they chose* and we elected to represent *us*. Reminds one of what Boss Tweed of Tammany Hall once said: "I don't care who does the electing so long as I do the nominating." And if we keep on talking that way Big Brother's little friends over in the FBI will open up a file on us, and then what?

Hate is a terrible thing. It is dangerous. Hate kills. If a competent psychologist (perhaps another oxymoron) were to analyze this mob of citizenry as if it were a single individual, that person would be diagnosed as dangerous to himself and others, as a person on the edge of violence, as someone on the order of a paranoid schizophrenic who might next be encountered on the top of the post office blasting away at passers-by with an AK 47.

So people hate? So what? We've hated from the beginning of

time. The single most authentic trait of the species may be its ability to hate—and to slaughter its own.

But the antidote for hate is, of course, *caring*, something that has to do with fairness, with inclusion and simple social decency, something the Christians used to know called "love," an idea that people are valuable, and that we should, as a nation, support them in their struggle for betterment and enlightenment—in their "pursuit of happiness."

The question, therefore: What can we expect for the future? Is the danger as real as I suggest? Why doesn't our collective consciousness realize the danger? Perhaps it does, but the realization is slow to seep to the surface. In the following chapters we shall begin to see where all of this is taking us.

7. Freedom of Speech

The Unheard Voices of People

In May of 1831 Alexis de Tocqueville, a young Frenchman no less, wandered into this new nation of ours to see what he could see. He was here when Jefferson was pushing Adams and his cohorts around, claiming that Adams represented the uppity rich (Laura Ingraham's elitists) and, as Jefferson called it, "the well born." When Jefferson's party of the people took control, de Tocqueville was there to make his observations in his *Democracy in America*, a book that proved to be an important influence on the new nation, one read by nearly every politician, including Abraham Lincoln.

He wrote of man's separation from his tribe, his community, an alienation that he understood during our earliest times, one that virulently persists today in America, although we're often crowded together in cities of millions. We're estranged from our families— a son, Tom, in Seattle, working for Boeing; a daughter, Julia, in New York, laboring as a computer programmer for Citibank.

Mom works at a job away from home. Dad, well, he's at the other end of the city in a different inner community.

As we've seen, our surrogate family has become the television screen. First thing in the morning it speaks to us before we've scoured our teeth. At night the stars of various shows become our family. We take them into our bedrooms. They do not know us, nor we them. But we know them more intimately than we know Mrs. Grasser, who lives in the apartment down the hall. We have more familiarity with the pigeons that light on our windowsill and leave their white calling cards in exchange for bread crumbs than with our neighbors. From this alienation, de Tocqueville saw the loss of the country. How could that be? Wouldn't the citizens rise up to take it back?

I think again of George Orwell's *1984*, in which the protagonist, Winston, longs for some kind of a revolution. Orwell wrote: *"Until they [the proles—the common man] become conscious they will never rebel, and until after they have rebelled they cannot become conscious."* (his italics)

Little doubt that the proles of America could, if they willed, rise up and throw corporations out of government easier than Jesus threw the money changers out of the temple. They could lock the doors against the politicians that pimp for the corporations, just as cops occasionally sweep the streets of pimps on New York City's Tenth Avenue. They could, if they wished, recover the airways that belong to the people and install voices of truth, as we shall see, conditions precedent to our return to a life in a democratic state.

Early on de Tocqueville correctly observed that this democracy was one in which "men are seldom forced by it to act, but they are constantly restrained from acting. Such a power does not destroy, but it prevents existence; it does not tyrannize, but it compresses, enervates, extinguishes, and *stupefies* a people, 'til each nation is reduced to be nothing better than a flock of timid and industrious animals. . . ." (my italics). In a democracy do we become nothing more than benign, stupid workers living pointless lives except as breeders of the species?

Back in the 1830s de Tocqueville was arguing for a free press. He was right again when he wrote: "I think that men living in aristocracies may, strictly speaking, do without the liberty of the press: But such is not the case with those who live in democratic countries . . . servitude cannot be complete if the press is free: *the press is the chief democratic instrument of freedom.*" (again my italics) So do we have freedom of the press, or does the profit industry, the new King, own it, and if so, what sort of revolution is possible to retrieve it?

The idea of a free press in America is just that—an *idea*, one long ago abandoned in practice. James Madison, hailed as the father of our Constitution, warned us. He said, "A popular Government without popular information or the means of acquiring it, is but a Prologue to a Farce or a Tragedy or perhaps both. Knowledge will forever govern ignorance, and a people who mean to be their own Governors, must arm themselves with the power knowledge gives them." Madison was talking about an unrestrained, informed, active press.

But A. J. Liebling, a hero to some of the "new journalists" of the sixties and seventies, said, "Freedom of the press belongs to the man who owns one." Corporations, not men, own the media, corporations without souls, a condition as frightening as if we left a sociopath to make our nation's moral decisions, for neither the corporation nor the sociopath possesses a conscience.

How do our present leaders feel about freedom of the press? George II didn't want anyone snooping into his papers as governor of the state of Texas, so he moved them into his father's presidential library, where they are clothed with certain protections. And his father, George I, said in a speech to some roofing contractors that the press was a group "which I now confess I hate."

Freedom of the press, its sister, freedom of speech, and the firstborn, freedom of thought, are all children of Mother Liberty. We see her standing in New York Harbor and say to ourselves, "Ah, there she is, our dear Mother Liberty." But the truth is that freedom in America is more a fable worshipped from afar than the truth, and Mother Liberty is, in important ways, as unalive as her symbol standing there, cold and motionlessly holding her torch on high.

We take our freedoms, including freedom of speech, as we take religion, as an article of faith, as part of a belief system that tends to camouflage the truth. Ms. Coulter will call me treasonous for suggesting that freedom of speech is an illusion, and she and her cohorts will again point to the bumper sticker "Love it or leave it." Ironically, we are not totally free to deny we are totally free.

Yes, we are free in certain blessed respects. We are free to vote. But only 54 percent of eligible voters cast their ballots during the last four decades of our presidential elections. Compare that shameful number to Italy's 90 percent, Germany's 80 percent, France and Canada's 76 percent, Britain's 75 percent, and Japan's 71 percent. We, who preach democracy, rank thirty-fifth in voter turnout among the world's prominent democracies.

And why don't we vote? Most say, "What difference does it make?", which is another way of saying, my rights, whatever they may be, are ineffective in changing my life for the better. Besides, if you have voted with the majority for the president of the United States, the U.S. Supreme Court will take your vote from you. Right?

Right.

Let's suppose we're visitors from another planet assigned to report back whether these humanoids in America who claim to actually enjoy freedom of speech and press do, indeed, enjoy them.

First we see that the author of this book is able to write and publish it if he can secure a publisher who thinks it may provide a profit. Otherwise the manuscript will curl up in a closet and yellow, and one day a grandchild, cleaning the closet out for the storage of old skateboards, will toss it without even a sigh.

As a visitor from another planet we would observe that Americans' freedom to discuss critical issues in any mass gathering such as is provided by national television or radio is subject to the will and control of a corporate master. A corporation? Yes, a corporation is a strange phenomenon. It is something that controls everything but cannot be seen or touched. Yet a visitor from another planet, confounded, would at last understand these gigantic non-palpable "nothings" actually control the nation and its 290 million people.

Five of these monsters (two of them foreign) control half of all book publishing. Bertelsmann, a German corporation, owns Random House, the Bantam Dell Publishing Group, Crown Publishing, Doubleday, and Knopf, forty or more imprints in all. Another German group, Holtzbrinck Publishing, owns companies in the United States held by Verlagsgruppe Georg von Holtzbrinck, based in Stuttgart, Germany. The U.S. publishers include my publisher, St. Martin's Press; Farrar, Straus and Giroux; Henry Holt and Company; and other imprints.

Time Warner recently sold its book group to a French publisher. It owns *Time* magazine, CNN, HBO, *Court TV,* Warner Bros. Studios, and Lord knows what else. Viacom owned Simon & Schuster, which includes, among others, Scribner's and scores of television stations and cable networks including CBS, Showtime, the Movie Channel, and MTV. Minor publishers and self-publishing exist, but unless the author is published by a major house with a staff of sales personnel and the resources to buy space in several major national retailers, his book will sell few copies.

As visitors from another planet investigating what Americans call freedom of the press, we might conclude that this is a freedom mostly reserved for profit-making corporations. People are only free to consume news, information, art, and entertainment as the corporations offer them.

I remember my amazement years ago that an early book I wrote, one published by a leading house, actually sold something like thirty thousand copies. But my excitement soon waned when I realized that's not half the audience that attends just *one* National Football League game on any given Sunday. The following Monday try to find one of your friends or neighbors who, in person, actually attended the game, say, between the Colts and the

Giants. Try to find one of the thirty thousand who read that earlier book of mine? Hello, I am so glad to finally meet you!

Joseph Goebbels, Hitler's minister of propaganda, said of
books: "As long as the book remains the privilege of a small, elite
class and does not find reception by the people, one will not be
able to speak of real benefits to the nation through the book."
Book readers are *elitists,* Laura.

In a recent article in *Harper's Magazine,* its pithy editor, Lewis
Lapham, brandishing his trademark neon satire, was bemoaning
that America was already a Fascist state. As defined by Benito
Mussolini: "Fascism should rightly be called corporatism as it is a
merger of state and corporate power." Lapham observed: "We
don't have to burn any books. . . . We can count it as a blessing
that we don't bear the burden of an educated citizenry. The publishing companies can print as many books as will guarantee their
profit (books on any and all subjects, some of them even truthful);
but to people who don't know how to read or think, they do as little harm as snowflakes falling on a frozen pond."

Scores of books by important authors are stacked up in my
study. Most are published by major houses. Most have sold mod-
estly, say, ten to fifty thousand copies. These books remain chiefly
unread, unheralded, mostly unquoted, in fact anonymous to most
citizens. Worse, the percentage of the U.S. adult population reading *any* book has declined by 7 percent over the past decade. This
decline has accelerated from minus 5 percent to minus 14 percent
since 1992. And a 10 percent loss of readership amounts to twenty
million people!

I remember when I would ask prospective jurors to tell me the
last book they had read, and I was always staggered at their responses: Most couldn't remember a single book. A few had read a
Reader's Digest abridgment; some piously, their eyes glazed over,
said the Bible.

Not surprisingly, the steepest decline in literary reading (novels, short stories, poetry, plays) is in the youngest age group. The
rate of decline for adults between eighteen and twenty-four is 55

percent *greater* than that of the total adult population. Not surprising, nonreaders watch more television than do readers. A 1999 study showed that the average American child lives in a household of 2.9 televisions, 1.8 VCRs, 3.1 radios, 2.1 CD players, 1.4 video game players, and 1 computer. Perhaps we should alter Ms. Ingraham's definition of "the elite" to those who read *anything*. As you read this you are perhaps among the truly elite in the country. (My hand extended. "Glad to meet you!") However, you would equally qualify as an elitist if you read one of our ladies' libelous diatribes.

What about newspapers? So you feel like the local zoning ordinance is taking your property without due process and you want to be heard? The corporate newspaper boss does not care if you wrangle about that. It only increases his readership. Write a letter to the editor—usually not more than a hundred words. It gives readers the idea that they have a say and are heard. But don't forget: *80 percent of daily newspapers are owned by corporate chains.*

Want to get on television and tell the world something you think is vital to America? Take your bedroll and camp out on the doorsteps of NBC in New York. And tell your next of kin where to pick up your body when you die of old age or exposure. You have the right to say it to every soul who passes by so long as you aren't jailed by the police for disturbance or vagrancy or as just a plain nuisance. But if you want to speak to the masses, a corporation controls *to whom* you say anything.

Well, there's radio. There are thousands of radio stations across the land. We are OK with radio. Workmen listen to the radio while they frame up our houses and multitudes, perhaps most of Americans, listen to the radio as they go to and from work. Radio is the savior of free speech. All right. But the Federal Communications Commission (the FCC) has allowed four behemoth corporations to buy up radio stations nationwide so that those four control 90 percent of all radio advertising revenues. What do we think that does to "free radio"?

But let's get real here. Who actually enjoys free speech in this country? And to what extent? Certainly those who would dare advocate a tepid, somewhat socialist program are not heard except as fodder for the likes of O'Reilly and that fellow Hannity. If liberals wish to argue that foreign countries supporting social reforms for their people should receive the assistance of the United States while dictatorships should not, such humanists, let's call them, will be sparsely heard. We don't hear much nowadays from those who want to increase the minimum wage or think that a state-operated health-care system might be in order.

Conservatives on television enjoy more freedom of speech than liberals. And why shouldn't conservatives be the favorite child of the corporate King? They favor the positions of their corporate sponsors. Do we think that NBC, owned by General Electric, is going to get behind a movement to take corporations off of corporate welfare? What about ABC, owned by Disney? Disney owns so many media outlets that it would take an entire book to discuss them all: major publishing houses; countless television and radio stations in the major markets; nearly a score of magazines; movie production and distribution companies; a wide distribution of Internet enterprises; music production and distribution organizations, and theme parks, of course. And who owns CBS, "the most watched network in America"? It should be. It was the property of Viacom, a prime beneficiary of White House pressure to allow a single media conglomerate to own enough television news outlets to reach 39 percent of the nation. Viacom owned more than a hundred television and radio stations across the nation, as well as book publishing and film production and distribution companies.

What about magazines? Only three corporations control "most of the business of the country's 11,000 magazines." Further, today, despite more than twenty-five thousand outlets in the United States, twenty-three corporations control most of the business in daily newspapers, magazines, television, books, and motion pictures. This is the kind of media control that would have caused Hitler's Goebbels, the propaganda czar, to swoon. "Ah, Gott in Himmel!"

So freedom of speech has snuck in the back door through the Web. Right? Here we go again. The research company Jupiter

Media Metrix reported, get this—that just four corporations own the Web sites that more than 50 percent of Americans spend their time viewing. Thom Hartman says in his carefully researched book *Unequal Protection:* "Although many Internet users think of the World Wide Web as a commons of ideas, it's a commons whose access is now almost entirely controlled by a small number of very large corporations."

Do the corporate media kings censor? CBS refused to run MoveOn.org's thirty-second spot during the Super Bowl, an ad that opposed the war in Iraq. It was *too political.* The ad opposed the Bush administration for running up the national debt to all-time-high levels and showed small children laboring away in some factory to make the point that our great-grandchildren will be saddled with an enslaving burden of debt. A pity the producers of the ad couldn't have worked in something about the sale of beer with babes in scanties or new cars—which, of course, would have made the ad perfectly acceptable. Right?

And the administration will not permit us to see the caskets of our own soldiers being shipped home—a jaw-clenched secret—or display the crippled, their legs blown off, their arms now stumps, their brave faces smiling from their wheelchairs. Remember that the estimated more than a hundred thousand innocent Iraqi people, including women and children, who have died in this war "for freedom," this "collateral damage," are also not fit subjects for viewers on these corporate-controlled American networks.

Censorship? A poll conducted in 2000 by The Pew Research Center for the People and the Press found that "sixty percent of investigative reporters thought corporate owners influenced news decisions, and forty-one percent of reporters could list specific examples of recent times they themselves had avoided stories, or softened their tone, to benefit their media corporation."

And hear what Bill O'Reilly says about freedom in the newsroom. "Everyone in network news can tell you stories of betrayal and deception. For many good journalists the atmosphere becomes so poisonous that they pack up and leave. Not too many capable reporters relish playing office politics. So you, as a viewer expecting to get an accurate news broadcast, are not being informed by the best and brightest. In many cases they've gone off and left the newsroom to the least and the most ruthless." And, Mr. O'Reilly, who would the least and the most ruthless be?

Still another ominous fact: Most Americans now feed on news from the right-wing media. According to Pew, 30 percent of Americans say that their primary news source is talk radio, which is 90 percent dominated by the right. Twenty-two percent get their primary news source from *FOX News*, CNBC, and MSNBC, all dominated by the right. Another 10 percent get their news from the Sinclair network, which is the mother of all right-wing news sources. Its owner requires all seventy-five of his affiliate television stations "to take a pledge to not report critically about this president or about the war in Iraq." Freedom of the press.

The majority of Americans are still getting their news from electronic corporate-owned media, and as Robert Kennedy Jr. said in a 2005 speech he delivered to the Sierra Summit in San Francisco, the said corporate-owned media has "no ideology except for filling their pocket books and many of them are run by big polluters. All of them are run by giant corporations that have all kinds of deals with the government and are not going to offend public officials."

We all know that advertisers exert control over the media's content. But Ben Bagdikian, a well-known and respected media watchdog, has noted that although local television stations have long been subject to the interests of local advertisers, by the turn of this century it has "become acceptable in national newsrooms for business chiefs to dictate to editors about content."

What's more, a great portion of the news comes from press releases authored by public relations firms working for their corporate employers. And big companies often provide ready-made video news releases (VNRs), ready to be dropped into the evening news—

most often provided by the pharmaceutical and food industries. You probably see them nearly every evening on the news, stories that tout medical breakthroughs of one kind or another. News channels favor these VNRs because they look as if the news people—you know, the "ones you can trust"—went out themselves and did that meticulous job of reporting. And you never hear a disclaimer by the station advising you that the VNR was not their reporting but, in fact, constituted free promotion for one of its advertisers.

So if corporations now control the news, well, don't they therefore also have a lot of power in the political arena? Another embarrassingly obvious question. Jamie Court, a nationally known and award-winning consumer advocate, says in his book, *Corporateering:* "The awesome power of today's media is harnessed to focus on *individuals and their morals,* rather than the *corporation and its values,*" which is a polite way of saying that corporations use their nearly absolute power to expose and degrade people—after all, it's wondrous entertainment as well—rather than laying bare the shameful epidemic of corporate crime that people must silently endure. Hello again, Nancy Grace and your harangue against all, guilty or innocent. But we *never* hear you take on the crimes of your corporate sponsors.

And hello, again, Ann Coulter, and your bitter menu of hatred against individuals. Here is what Coulter said about a Nobel Peace Prize winner, former president Carter. "Carter is so often maligned for his stupidity, it tends to be forgotten that he is also self-righteous, vengeful, sneaky, and backstabbing." On the other hand, she lauds the late senator Joseph McCarthy. She claims that "Soviet spies in government were not a figment of the right-wing conspiracy. McCarthy was not tilting at windmills. He was tilting *at an authentic Communist conspiracy* that had been laughed off by the Democratic party." (my italics) These right-wing tongue waggers of both sexes clearly enjoy unbridled freedom of speech to libel and defame whomever they please—but rarely does a corporation come under their fire and, of course, rarer still one of the media's corporate sponsors.

And so as good law-abiding, tax-paying Americans, we can surely rely on our government to protect our sacred right to freedom of speech, can't we? We have the vaunted Federal Communications Commission to keep things in balance. Right?

First off, the airways were not owned by the networks. We, the people, owned them. Originally nothing was paid by ABC, CBS, or NBC for their takeover of that which belonged to the people. During the 1980s our precious property was auctioned off to the highest bidder by region and frequency. But auctioning off the airways permitted the successful bidders to say we, the people, have no voice in what goes out over the air. The networks *own* them.

Michael Powell, Colin Powell's son, was appointed FCC chairman by George II. Powell declared that the public-interest standard for broadcasters was "dead on arrival." The standard that had long governed media action "is about as empty a vessel as you can accord a regulatory agency and ask it to make meaningful judgments," said Powell.

The Public Broadcasting Service (PBS) holds itself out as the independent voice of the people. But it, too, has been overtaken by corporate sponsors, and its content controlled indirectly by a conservative Congress that limits its financial support depending on how displeased, from time to time, Congress has become with the network's content. At most, PBS provides the appearance of a public voice, but sadly not much more since it faithfully adheres to the standard corporate line—a sort of underlying shrug of the shoulders that says, What's good for the corporate state is good for the people.

I say that the right-wing free speechers, such as Limbaugh, O'Reilly, George Will, Bill Bennett, Bill Buckley, and the Hannity fellow—together with our own blustery bloodthirsty brigade—enjoy a lot more time on the tube speaking to the masses than, say, Ralph Nader, Jim Hightower, or William Greider. Here is the way fair and balanced Rush Limbaugh answers the criticism that he does not have liberal guests on his program: "I'm not guaranteed," says Limbaugh, "the liberal guest is going to be honest about what he believes." Instead, to provide balance he provides us his own rendition of the opposing views, for example: "If it were up to you people [liberals], we wouldn't exist as a country today. You would have given in to the Soviets long ago, you would have appeased the Soviet Communists. You would appease Iran right now. You probably wouldn't have cared about the war on terror or the bombing on 9/11."

Sounds suspiciously like the party line. Ann Coulter in *Treason* says:

> What the country needed was Joe McCarthy. His appeal was directed to a sturdier set—the mass of ordinary Americans. It's interesting that Democrats [liberals] keep claiming to speak for the working man, but somehow it's always right-wing Republicans who make a direct connection to the workers. (What liberals mean by "working families" is "non-families in which no one works.")

And the lady knows that despite the destructive comedic content of what she says, many people will believe it. She admits, "Any statement whatever, no matter how stupid [and the foregoing is an example of dazzling stupidity], any 'tall tale' will be believed *once it enters into the passionate current of hatred.*" (my italics) She has understood one of the themes of this book: lie, make the most outrageous, hurtful, stupid charges, and people will believe them, first because they are spewed out over the airways. Therefore, they must be true, at least true in part, at least true enough that she can't be sued, and the ugly flower of hate comes blooming out of this right-wing manure.

Liberals like Michael Moore and Al Franken see conservatives as liars and fops and laugh at them, but their satire and humor leave that massive underlying hatred in America untapped, and the millions who are addicted to hate, unsatisfied. The likes of

Moore and Franken feed the angry multitudes humorous Pablum when they are hungry for the raw, bloody meat of hatred.

One writer claims that the masses are listening to the hard right because they are so available. Michael Parenti, an internationally known author and lecturer and self-acknowledged progressive, says, "Availability is the first and necessary condition of consumption . . . supply *creates* demand."

Yes, liberals and conservatives can sit down to dinner and talk to each other without fear of being arrested–not yet (although their FBI files may now include memos setting out what they said at last evening's dinner party). Some liberals seem to think their phones are being tapped—likely their paranoia—until we were all stunned to discover that Mr. Bush II had some time ago secretly authorized tapping the electronic communications of our citizens *without a warrant.*

At the request of the government, the shocking story of warrantless snooping was withheld from the American people for a year by *The New York Times.* The government claimed that the revelation of such a wholesale attack on our freedoms would compromise its fight against terrorism. But this infringement on our constitutional rights had required the cooperation of some of America's great corporations. *The Times* reported: "But the N.S.A.'s [National Security Agency's] backdoor access to major telecommunications switches on American soil with the cooperation of major corporations represents a significant expansion of the agency's operational capability, according to current and former government officials"—a sweetly put understatement.

Bush's edict that the government could and should tap citizens' electronic communications without a warrant violates the requirements of the Fourth Amendment and is illegal. But while the tapping was going on, George II, as is his wont, lied about it. Here is what he said *before The Times* finally ran its story:

Now, by the way, any time you hear the United States government talking about wiretap, it requires—a wiretap requires a court order. Nothing has changed, by the way. When we're talking about chasing down terrorists, we're talking about getting a court order before we do so. It's important for our fellow citizens to understand, when you think Patriot Act, constitutional guarantees are in place when it comes to doing what is necessary to protect our homeland, because we value the Constitution.

Thoughtful persons inside and out of Congress have called for Bush II's impeachment. Lewis Lapham, editor of *Harper's Magazine,* observed: "We have before us in the White House a thief who steals the country's good name and reputation for his private interest and personal use, a liar who seeks to instill in the American people a state of fear, a televangelist who engages the United States in a never-ending crusade against all the world's evils, a wastrel who squanders a vast sum of the nation's wealth on what turns out to be a recruiting drive certain to multiply the host of our enemies. In a word, a criminal—known to be armed and shown to be dangerous." Lapham said, "I don't know why we would run the risk in not impeaching the man."

Rep. John Lewis (D., Ga.) reminded us that Bush II is not king, and that he would sign a bill of impeachment if he had a chance. John Dean, who had hands-on personal experience with impeachable offenses during the Nixon administration, said that "Bush is the first president to admit to an impeachable offense," referring to Bush's admission that he ordered the bugging of citizens without a warrant, and John Conyers Jr. (D., Mich.) has introduced a bill to investigate the administration for possible impeachment.

One remembers that lying about a wayward penis led to the impeachment of President Clinton, while Bush has lied us into the horrors of war that are responsible for the deaths and maiming of hundreds of thousands of innocent people. Now he has blatantly and arrogantly snatched from us our sacred constitutional protections, for which thousands of American men and women have given their lives.

Even under the so-called Patriot Act almost no showing is required before the government can launch its secret snooping. But at least to begin with, a court was at hand. At least there had been some slight nodding in the direction of constitutional government. Now Mr. Bush feels he's not subject to even the almost limitless powers granted the government by the "Patriot Act" but that he can, as he pleases, junk the Constitution.

Ann Coulter, of course, is not so demure. Our rights, yours and mine, to be safe from government intrusion are trumped by her blindsiding hyperbole. Here is what she said: "Which brings me to this week's scandal about No Such Agency spying on 'Americans.' I have difficulty ginning up much interest in this story inasmuch as I think the government should be spying on all Arabs, engaging in torture as a televised spectator sport, dropping daisy cutters wantonly throughout the Middle East, and sending liberals to Guantánamo."

"Daisy cutters" are fifteen-thousand-pound fuel-air bombs that explode just prior to hitting the ground at a height of from one to six feet and are designed to kill everything within a square-mile radius of the impact point. These are the largest conventional bombs the United States military has in its deadly arsenal.

If Ms. Coulter's desire to wantonly dump these bombs throughout the Middle East is humor, then save me. If it is not, then save her. It gets attention like a nasty kid in the grocery store, who flops himself on the floor screaming, to the desperate humiliation of his mother. But he does get the coveted attention.

As we proceed in this work it becomes easier to understand why both Coulter and O'Reilly despise *The Times,* which finally revealed the scandalous story, one that plainly foretells the willingness of the right to grasp all power and settle in comfortably to an electoral dictatorship. She wrote: "My only regret with Timothy McVeigh is he did not go to the New York Times Building." And O'Reilly, as well, experiences frequent and heinous joy in kicking *The Times* (that liberal rag) around at any given opportunity. But in the far distant past we hear Thomas

Jefferson lamenting, "An elective despotism was not the government we fought for."

And some citizens feel they must fly the flag and paste a yellow ribbon sticker on the back of their SUVs lest they be seen as unpatriotic Americans. If you're a Muslim, well, you already have your very own personal FBI file. If you're an Arab you'll likely be profiled at any airport. If you're a blonde with blue eyes but do not smile at the airport security people who run you through the chutes and X-ray machines like cattle on a Wyoming ranch, if you complain or say anything slightly sideways to these folks with large power, you may miss your plane and have a lot of foreign hands all over your body. They might even confiscate your baby's shoes. And if you object to your congressman, you'll get one of those friendly form letters saying how much he's shocked by all of this, but this is a time of war and you're being saved from being blown to hell by some devotee of bin Laden, wherever he is.

In times of war freedom of speech is severely curtailed. And it's mostly voluntary because one does not want to be perceived as an enemy sympathizer, or even a liberal, because, as Ann Coulter charges: ". . . Liberals side with the enemy." By her logic half the people of this country must be traitors.

Today freedom of speech means you can say what's on your mind, and so long as it's not a threat against anyone or anything you'll likely not be arrested. Your phone may be tapped and unidentified individuals may shadow you, but you probably will not be arrested. If you speak of a revolution to overthrow the corporate master you must hasten to add that you are speaking of a *peaceful, nonviolent* revolution. You can speak of this to your neighbors and friends, but if too many people become interested in what you're saying and offer to lend their assistance, well, you may have a conspiracy going; and if one of them suggests that the government should be overthrown by violence, you may be charged as part of that conspiracy whether or not violence ever entered your mind, after which may come an unwelcome knocking on the front door, and when you look out the window you may see jacketed men (perhaps along with a woman or two) with FBI in large white letters on the back of their flack jackets. And for the first time you may find yourself on national television—wearing those pretty, shiny bracelets. But one thing for sure: Do not make any statement whatsoever to them or you may be charged with lying to the FBI, a felony.

This kind of freedom of speech, this benign complaining and whimpering, this ineffective sort of speech-making at peace rallies and my writing here, in fact, are encouraged by the system. This sort of freedom permits the energy of discontent to be expelled, like the gaseous content of an unhappy stomach—as in the town meeting where the irate citizens appear, holler a lot, the councilpersons listen and nod, everyone goes home, and things go on as usual. Not only does this tepid sort of speech, let us call it *nothing-speech*, release hostilities against power, it also validates the myth that we enjoy these freedoms in America; and, in the end, assists those in power to retain power.

Even the Founding Fathers never intended that freedom of speech should be used as a weapon for the masses to overthrow them—not really. Remember, too, that the Bill of Rights, which includes the First Amendment guaranteeing free speech, was not a part of the Constitution. When a gentleman from Virginia, one Colonel Mason, suggested that a Bill of Rights be included, he was unanimously voted down. Massachusetts abstained.

But a lot of unhappy people descended on the founders. Mortgage foreclosures, riots over food, popular protests, the ragged debtors invading the Capitol Building and threatening the men of property, these events conspired so that during the ratification process a Bill of Rights was reluctantly adopted as a concession to the protesting rabble, the price paid for the Constitution's ratification.

One wonders about that new elitist gang sitting up there in their black robes, their judicious scowls properly in place, who now interpret what the original mob intended when it demanded the Bill of Rights. I speak, obviously, of the United States Supreme

Court, some justices of which are said to be the lapdogs of corporate power, while others are intellectual wanderers who have too long been removed from the people. Only occasionally does a justice come into view who has retained a remembrance of the work, suffering, and sacrifice experienced by the citizens. In short, this court of last resort stands guardian of the Constitution, which is often a euphemism for preserving the rights of the corporate King.

Freedom of speech and the press was originally an instrument to ensure open debate over vital issues encountered in this experiment called democracy. In those days the nation was little more than a large town meeting. Men could gather and speak, listen, debate, be heard, and, with intelligence and thought, attempt to resolve the issues of the day.

Today, of course, debates continue to be aired in the town halls of television. But the meeting places, the media, are owned by the corporate master; and corporate advertisers dominate the scene. Can we imagine what might have happened at Constitution Hall if hanging from all the walls surrounding the room were seen ads for Miller's, McDonald's, State Farm insurance, and Citibank credit cards, not to mention the car company ads, and if every five minutes or less someone came bursting through the door hollering at the top of his lungs the advantages of a new sex-enhancing drug?

We often hear sorrowful regrets expressed that we can no longer produce the quality of men who founded the nation, that somehow a God-sent miracle occurred that such great minds could have gathered at one time in one place to construct such an instrument as our Constitution. However, it might be remembered that the total population of the thirteen colonies at that time was comparable to the number of people living today in Cincinnati.

The genius of the founders grew out of their experience—their indentured lives under the dominance of a distant king who was impinging on their wealth. That burdensome tax on tea! Their genius was the product of a small number of men with the will and opportunity to sit down in one place and intelligently communicate with each other. They were not conditioned by the six-second sound bite. Their most cherished pastime was lively conversation rather than dumbing out on a high-definition screen. But they had no intent to relinquish power to the populace. The common herd were not going to rule the polls, not in this new republic.

We who claim to be a democracy and who seek to impose our way of government on the rest of the world, preaching, always, about *our democracy*—well, we are *not*. Most of us know that but forget it. The word comes from the Greek *demokratia*, and is made up of *demos*, meaning "the people," and *kratein*, meaning "to rule," hence, rule by the people.

We begin to laugh (or cry) when we ask ourselves, do *people* rule in this country? A country ruled by the people? In reality it is this strange, almost nightmarish scene, a country ruled by nonpeople— let us call it a *corpocracy*— something like that.

Madison was afraid of "the superior force of an interested and overbearing majority," and saw as a safeguard against it the representative republic we enjoy. In the *Federalist No. 10*, published November 22, 1787, he wrote, "A religious sect may degenerate into a political faction in a part of the Confederacy. . . . A rage for paper money, for an abolition of debts, for an equal division of property, or for any other improper or wicked project, will be less apt to pervade the whole body of the Union than a particular member of it. . . . In the extent and proper structure of the Union, therefore, we behold a republican remedy for the diseases most incident to republican government," all of which simply meant a few "responsible" citizens representing the horde so that the perceived idiocy of the horde could be restrained.

For the election of the president, the founders, of course, created an "electoral college," so that a presidential candidate receiving a plurality of those voting would not necessarily obtain the presidency. Think of poor Gore. The candidate who gets the plurality in any state also gets that state's total electoral vote. Therefore, the candidate receiving the most popular votes may not win after all. But this small technicality is not what makes America's claim that it is a democracy such a shameful farce. The candidates who win are those who sell out to money. Quick example in passing: It takes over $50 million to get elected to the Senate in California. This, of course, ensures that we enjoy in our "democracy" the best candidates money can buy. Oh, my!

Here again let us ask Ms. Ingraham about *elitism* in America. Laura, aren't the true elitists the corporations, the ones that hire you and control the rest of us? Our candidates have become the toadies of the corporate King, who then storms into the world with "shock and awe" bombs and kills innocent men and women *and* children (don't forget the uncounted children) hollering "Democracy! Democracy! Give the people democracy. Our boys and girls are fighting and dying that they may have a democracy. God bless America." In, say, Iraq, shall we call it an oilocracy?

Back to our founders: Genius usually arises out of a community of thought, one idea from one person generating ideas from others—what we call "brainstorming." But fifty-five men and women who might meet today in Cincinnati to overthrow the corporate King and to be led by the likes of a George Washington and his ragtag army of rabble-rousers would be hastily dragged off to a federal prison somewhere and labeled traitors despite the admonition of the Bill of Rights that observes:

> That to secure these rights, governments are instituted among men, deriving their just powers from the consent of the governed. That whenever any form of government becomes destructive to these ends, *it is the right of the people to alter or to abolish it, and to institute new government,* laying its foundation on such principles and organizing its powers in such form, as to them shall seem most likely to effect their safety and happiness. (my emphasis)

But please, I want my FBI file to clearly show that I am *out of any such conspiracy if one exists, and that I do not promote, agree to, or sanction the violent overthrow of our government!* Put that in my file. *Now!*

Our corporate King, as reflected in the dogma of the far right, is not threatened by an armed takeover. Not in the least. In fact, the conservatives fight for the right of the people to own guns, even "assault weapons" (rifles, of course, that fire only single shots. Those that fire multiple bursts are outlawed.). If people can own guns, their possession of such comparatively innocent weapons tends to allay their fears of the government's storm troopers descending upon them with machine guns.

Can we visualize the reality? There stands good old Joe Citizen waving the Constitution in one hand and stubbornly brandishing his fully legal .38 caliber, six-shot revolver in the other. He is standing off the FBI's assault team armed with tear gas, submachine guns, and grenades, and I don't know what else. We've seen it all too often already. Those so-called classic Americans are either dead or in prison. How can I forget my client, Randy Weaver, whose unarmed wife was standing in the doorway of their makeshift little home in the mountains of Idaho with her baby in her arms. Then she was shot and killed by the FBI. And before her, the Weavers' little boy and his dog were also shot and killed by the ATF. The conservatives say, "Keep your guns. Have fun. Kill each other, or your guns may be an excuse for us to kill you."

As we've seen, the profession of journalism is not entirely sold out, and occasionally, here and there, a protest is heard, albeit of little consequence in changing the corporate stranglehold on free debate. You will probably remember the Natalee Holloway missing person story. Natalee Holloway was an eighteen-year-old girl from Alabama who vanished on May 30, 2005, from the island of Aruba, where she was vacationing with some of her classmates to celebrate their high school graduation.

The case was, of course, devastating to the girl and her parents. But what made the case so critical to America that we became more concerned with crime in Aruba than with the raging corporate crime in this country that is slowly gutting the nation? Why does the media focus us on the piteous story of this one girl but not on Congress's refusal to deal with our own pathetic health care system, which abandons millions to unconscionable risk? And our wars? Now watch *FOX News.*

For undisclosed reasons Fox focused on the Holloway story and broadcast hourly updates on the case. Every soul in Aruba, including the garbageman, was interviewed. Struggling to discover a reason for the story's importance, at first O'Reilly wanted to make this a lesson to America. "See, this is what happens when you vacation outside of America in nations with swarthy peoples." And not to be outdone, the other networks, MSNBC and CNN, mindlessly piled on.

The story grew into a monstrous distraction, which is in line with Orwell's "thought police." Big Brother tells us what we should be thinking about, the missing girl in Aruba, not the missing morality in the system. In panic the Dutch sent three F-16 fighter planes to search for the body, the other networks called in all manner of so-called experts to guess what happened and who might be fingered. Fingers were pointed in every direction, and innuendos of conspiracies and cover-ups, including nasty diatribes against the Dutch authorities, proved to be mostly the products of the networks' empty-headed competition looking for blood and gore and horror—and, of course, ratings.

First, two former security guards were arrested, men whom O'Reilly called "slugs." In this case O'Reilly (who is against the death penalty) thought it unfortunate that Aruba didn't impose the death penalty so the Dutch authorities could threaten their suspects and get the information they sought. But it turned out that these two "slugs" had nothing to do with the abduction, and they were released, *without* any apology from O'Reilly and that Hannity fellow and the others who'd held them up to the world as possible murderers.

None of the TV-talkers bothered to put this story in perspective for their American listeners. No one on the networks rose up to protest that aside from the tragedy to the parents, the newsworthiness in this story could hardly justify the feeding frenzy of the media that was devoting thousands of hours of television and radio coverage to the case, especially in view of the fact that in the United States alone, *more than a million people* are reported missing each year, mostly minors. As one thoughtful blogger asked, what about Reyna Gabriella Alvarado-Carerra? Few have ever heard of her. She was a thirteen-year-old Hispanic girl who is believed to have been abducted by a stranger in Norcross, Georgia—Nancy Grace's home state—and just shortly before the Holloway case. Ever hear of Reyna's case?

About this time Bob Costas had signed on to be an occasional substitute for Larry King. But when he was told that the subject of the evening's program was the Natalee Holloway missing person case, Costas balked and refused to do the show. Few can afford to exercise such independence, but Costas is not an employee of CNN and has wide discretion as to whether he will take part in a given program, especially one that has no major intrinsic newsworthiness except that created by the talking heads themselves.

When Costas said no, CNN immediately covered itself. Jonathan Klein, president of CNN's domestic operations, piously observed, "It's important that we never have an anchor doing a story he does not believe in." Right. But Matthew Felling of the Center for Media and Public Affairs told The Associated Press that the Holloway coverage amounted to "emotional pornography," and CNN's own Nancy Grace was spread out all over the story for days.

Try as it has, CNN has not been able to get it right: CNN's Klein jumped on Fox's Greta Van Susteren, who was in Aruba on the Holloway story the night fourteen marines were killed in a roadside bombing in Iraq. "Fourteen Americans dead and they [Fox] have Natalee Holloway on. And they're supposed to be America's news channel?" Klein charged.

But what about CNN's own *oppospeak?* Fox executives, of course, pointed to Nancy Grace on CNN prime time, claiming that she had done almost as many hours on Holloway as Ms. Van

Susteren had. How do you answer that? Well, you say, as Klein said—"I do not supervise the Nancy Grace Show." And as for Larry King's show, which had also found reason to snatch at ratings by piling on to the Holloway case, Klein says, well, he doesn't supervise King's show either.

Fox accuses CNN of being holier-than-thou because of CNN's continued plummeting ratings. And Fox has a point. Fox's margin in viewers over CNN's grew 57 percent since Klein took over last December. Strangely, Klein says CNN has to stop "obsessing over this trivia stuff," like the Holloway case. I agree. But he knows what sells, and more and more it becomes apparent that it is not cold, hard, honest news.

So what is CNN really saying? It's saying, we want to be seen as a network that gives the public important news and at the same time we want to enjoy the ratings and profits that tabloid journalism produces. We want it both ways.

The American Civil Liberties Union is one organization that over the years has attempted to cleanse itself of the hypocrisy we have so often encountered here and to fight for the rights of Americans, even those with ideas that seem repulsive to us. The ACLU says, "If the rights of society's most vulnerable members are denied, everybody's rights are imperiled." It points out in clear language the proposition that is lost to the right wing: "The American system of government is founded on two counterbalancing principles: that the majority of the people governs, through democratically elected representatives; *and that the power even of a democratic majority must be limited, to ensure individual rights.* (my italics)

The ACLU says that the majorities' power is limited by the Bill of Rights, which consists of the original Ten Amendments ratified in 1791, plus the four post–Civil War amendments (the Thirteenth, Fourteenth, Fifteenth, and the Nineteenth Amendments) the latter adopted in 1920. "The mission of the ACLU is to preserve all of these protections and guarantees." Among those, of course, are "Your First Amendment rights—freedom of speech, association, and assembly. Freedom of the press, and freedom of religion supported by the strict separation of church and state . . .

★ Your right to equal protection under the law—equal treatment regardless of race, sex, religion, or national origin.

★ Your right to due process—fair treatment by the government whenever the loss of your liberty or property is at stake.

★ Your right to privacy—freedom from unwarranted government intrusion into your personal and private affairs."

The ACLU goes on to say, "We work also to extend rights to segments of our population that have traditionally been denied their rights, including Native Americans and other people of color; lesbians, gay men, bisexuals and transgendered people; women; mental-health patients; prisoners; people with disabilities; and the poor."

We can see why this guardian of our individual rights is so hated by the conservatives and utterly loathed by Bill O'Reilly, Pat Robertson, Jerry Falwell, and, of course, the genteel Ann Coulter.

On *The Radio Factor* O'Reilly said, "The ACLU is the most fascist organization I have seen in decades. . . . They're intellectual fascists, and they use the courts as their Panzer divisions." He rages on: "[T]here is no question the ACLU and the judges who side with them are terror allies."

Yes, Bill, they go into court, and, say, you don't like it that gays have rights equal to your own, that your ideas of God ought not be imposed on others in a public school, that black people have an equal right to employment and education, and that the poor have the same right to unhampered access to the courts as we, yes, and that even Nazis have the right to speak freely in this country—and fighting for those rights makes the ACLU comparable to Hitler?

But what about your pal, Rush Limbaugh, when his butt was up against the blaze because of his alleged illegal use of prescription drugs, and the government seized his doctors' medical records as part of a criminal investigation involving "doctor-shopping." Here, Bill, is what the ACLU said about that in court: "While this case involves the right of Rush Limbaugh to maintain the privacy of his medical records, the precedent set in this case will impact the security of medical records and the privacy of the doctor-patient relationship of every person in Florida. . . . *If the state can do this to Rush Limbaugh, then the privacy rights of every citizen in Florida are in jeopardy.*" (my italics)

The ACLU, which is seen as the Antichrist by the guns and Bible crowd, was suddenly, but only momentarily, redeemed when it filed its brief on behalf of Limbaugh. In an interview with *Time* magazine, Limbaugh now declares himself a longtime fan of the ACLU, but his declaration came *after* they filed their brief on his behalf: "In a situation like this, I think it's safe to say I welcome its support, and I don't find it hypocritical at all, because I am not anti-ACLU. If the ACLU wants to go after, say, nativity scenes or this sort of thing, I may take issue, but there are other areas where I've supported things it has done." As always, what is right and what is "American" seems to depend on whose ox is being gored.

Vigorous and fair debate involving ugly issues is an essential and often painful exercise that is obligatory for a free nation. Without it the collective wisdom of a people remains stunted and wasted. Television that transcends the six-second sound bite is the most effective gift that technology has delivered to the species for the preservation of its freedom. But when it is captured by the nonliving King, the corporate master, the right of the people to be informed and to be free vanishes like tears in the desert.

Simply stated, we do not enjoy freedom of speech as envisioned by the Constitution. Free speech was meant to be *effective* speech by a people free to debate the issues among themselves. Justice Hugo Black, in the famous 1945 *Associated Press v. U.S.* case, said, ". . . The First Amendment rests on the assumption that the widest possible dissemination of information from diverse and antagonistic sources is essential to the welfare of the public, that a free press is a condition of a free society." Yes, Justice Black. Your words were a warning about the impending complete corporate takeover of our airways and the print media as well.

Despite the staggering power of the mass media—the magic of television and the plethora of books and newspapers—our people remain chiefly uninformed except as to what they are told they should buy, how they should pay for it, and how the corporate overlord wishes them to think concerning matters that threaten corporate interests. On all other issues crucial to a free people, our attention is diverted by the likes of our blonde blasters and their male ilk as to whether Michael Jackson molested boys and Scott Peterson killed his wife—tabloid stories that should occupy the back pages of the media as marginally newsworthy.

At home our attention is diverted from the struggle of ordinary people attempting to survive and to educate their children. First-line stories are not that over seventy human beings died in a suicide bombing in Iraq, with such suicide killings that have become nearly a daily occurrence after George II declared, "Mission accomplished," but that Natalie Holloway is missing and the authorities in Aruba are incompetent, and one should shun vacations among dark-skinned people.

The new King disguises its media lies with kindly-looking faces, with compelling voices, and with promises of all earthly pleasures. Operating behind the touted religion of the right is a new religion. It espouses an ethic without moral boundaries. It is an ethic that uses up people as a machine burns fuel. And it exercises its constitutional right called "freedom of speech" to lie to us about what is good for our health, our families, and about how we should spend the fruits of our labor—which, at last, is to provide more profit for the King. Where all this is leading us is perhaps too frightening to consider. We shall see.

8. The Ghost of Goebbels, Propaganda, and the Rock-Hard Right

Hate was the principal fuel of the Nazi power machine. Hate.

Hate the Jews. For, as the Nazis proclaimed, even a forgiving God hated them! Jews became the scapegoats for all evil in Germany and the world. They were the cause of all of Germany's setbacks on the battlefront, the reason for every economic woe that Germany faced, the cause of war itself, even of prostitution and disease. There was no end to the evils and suffering that were attributable to the Jews.

Alexander Kimel, a holocaust survivor, writes: "Hitler adopted the crude simplistic outlook on life: the Jews are the source of all evil in this world. Hitler found a purpose in life, cleansing the German race from the clutches of the Jews. Hatred of the Jews became his obsession, his creed, faith, and religion."

Of course, Joseph Goebbels was Hitler's Propaganda Minister. One of the principles of Goebbels's propaganda machine was that "propaganda must facilitate the displacement of aggression by specifying the *targets for hatred*," in other words, before hatred erupts into overt violence, the Nazi leaders should direct that smoldering hate toward the enemy—again, in Germany, the Jews. When 9/11 came we were provided with an objective of our hatred. We could hate bin Laden and Muslims and Arabs and anyone with a darker complexion. In the meantime our love of the president, the police, and Congress skyrocketed. Hate was, and still is, in its glory days. In Mesa, Arizona, a forty-nine-year-old Sikh Indian wearing a turban was shot down in front of his gas station. In Dallas a Pakistani Muslim was found shot to death in his convenience store. In Huntington, New York, a Pakistani pedestrian was nearly run down by a motorist who had threatened to kill her. In San Gabriel, California, an Egyptian Christian was killed in his grocery store. In Somerset, Massachusetts, a group of teenaged boys threw a Molotov cocktail onto the roof of the Olde Village convenience store owned by a family from India, and in Boston, a Saudi Arabian man was stabbed as he left a Back Bay nightclub, all unprovoked acts of hate.

So here lies America with a mass of preangered citizens who were already hating for nearly every conceivable reason. Suddenly they have a target, one that is alive, one they can actually see. And we agree to a war against Iraq, where, but for our well-founded contempt for their leader, we have no basic quarrel with the Iraqi people.

Scapegoating has always been a way of life in America, one, for example, in which black Americans have been the target for the pent-up aggressions of the white population. Native Americans got plenty of the poison and were essentially exterminated.

By employing pure scapegoating, the rock-hard right has pushed forward its own agenda. It addresses the honest complaints of parents over inadequate resources for schools and scapegoats a curriculum of sex education and AIDS-awareness programs. By focusing on the nation's confusion over the changing roles of the sexes, it scapegoats the feminist movement and those who support free choice. The nation is suffering from unemployment and job outsourcing to other countries, and the scapegoats become those who seek to correct the injustices of race discrimination.

In point, I had long questioned the claim of Hillary Clinton that her husband and his administration were the victims of a vicious right-wing conspiracy and that flat-out hate-based scapegoating was rampant. What else was there to say in defense of Clinton after the blue dress? But already we've forgotten the hate charges that eventually proved mostly empty, the right's suggestion that Vince Foster was murdered, the so-called Whitewater affair, which amounted to approximately nothing, the shrill viciousness of Troopergate, Travelgate, and the other gates of hate. Mostly we were unaware of this tight, ultraright-wing legion of haters dedicated to grabbing power and destroying the Clinton administration, a conspiracy that is now well documented. Even Ann Coulter described the Paula Jones case "as a small, intricately knit, right-wing conspiracy."

The Clinton years brought on a tragic, hate-filled division of the nation. Leaders found it acceptable to lie and to disseminate lies in the cause of power. Again, David Brock said, "What I didn't see then was that a politics built on *hatred* of those who were not straight, white, God-fearing men in nuclear families would, as a matter of logic, turn against me and mine." (my emphasis)

An entire nation became victims who were fed this diet of hate to the end that the people blindly voted against their own interests. Because they hated gays, and voted that single issue, the poisonous side effect of their vote was to elect candidates who were enemies of labor and the poor. Because they hated free-choice advocates, and voted that issue alone, they elected candidates who also fought against fair wages, decent health care, and an environment already staggering under the poisonous sludge of corporate pollution. These hatemongers, through the dark dynamic of hate, delivered power to the right wing, who thereafter used their power against the fundamental interests of the people who elected them.

Hate, like love, can be taught. Hate is a product of the environment in which people find themselves, be it an all-white, gated community or an all-black ghetto. But hate is also taught on the television screen and over the radio waves. Most haters learn to hate early in life in the same way they learn a particular religion, to become blindly patriotic, or to be intolerant of their neighbors. Children are a part of a society that hates, and children adopt its hatreds. When they are grown we simply say they're prejudiced.

As a lawyer I try to discover the prejudices of prospective jurors because prejudices that have become absorbed as a part of the juror's personality structure can never be dispelled. This hate sits at the heart of the individual like the sprout that started the tree is still a part of the towering pine.

I am not arguing that we are beyond redemption. But the cure for prejudice is to uncover it, to be aware of it, and to keep it at a conscious level, to print it on the billboard of the mind so that it is always in sight. The demagogues who berate and hate on television do the opposite.

All violence is not physical. The verbal abuse of spouses of either gender, of parents toward their children, of Hitler railing against the Jews, yes, of a leader of one nation passing judgment on the leaders of others as "the Axis of Evil," are forms of violence. We see it at the extreme end of fundamental religions, from the killing of "infidels" by the Crusaders to the suicide bombers who kill their own identified "infidels." Nancy Grace and her need to verbally destroy those who come to her attention—the innocent as well as the guilty—are driven by a heart that was broken by an original violence.

Countless millions of people are asking, "How do I get ahead? Everybody else is making it except me. I work as hard as I can, but there's always somebody getting what I'm entitled to; and the boss doesn't give a damn for me no matter how hard I work. I have these kids and my wife is working herself to the bone. We're tired. Very tired."

Then along comes Team Hate saying this country is threatened by a bunch of elitists or liberals or God haters called "seculars" or "baby killers." The liberals support all those lazy unmarried mothers on welfare, and you're supporting them with your taxes. Those liberals want to raise taxes so everybody can have sex and kids and lie around while you work yourself to death. Scapegoating. The working guy has always felt like a loser, but he turns on the TV and there his prejudices are validated by Team Hate. It all makes sense to him.

Team Hate is smarter than it is intelligent. The unfunny antics of Coulter are remarkable only because they are intentionally outrageous, tasteless fabrications that evoke anger—which pays. Ingraham reminds me of a child swinging blindly at a piñata and constantly missing. And Grace continues to drum on her tragic past as an excuse for injuring people in her angry present. O'Reilly and Limbaugh and the Dukes of Jesus drown themselves in sentimental nonsense and are so entangled in their own hypocrisy and often so shook-up over trifling issues that they've lost any concept of who they are and require someone to introduce them to themselves. But they excel in creating hate—mostly against liberals.

Such an energy of hate spills over at the polls. We elect a president who, himself, embraces violence and shifts his rationale with the same dexterity as he changes his shorts. Violence and its threat are the mother of political power. People rally behind the hating leader. Patriotism. And patriotism garners our leader further power. Unless we can recognize this dangerous dynamic, this plague of hatred will surely bring on the darkest times for America.

Very civilly Goebbels said, "There are two ways to make a revolution: One can fire at the opponent with machine guns until he recognizes the superiority of those who have the machine guns. That is the simplest way. One can also transform a nation through a revolution of the spirit, not destroying the opponent, but winning him over. We National Socialists have gone the second way, and will continue on it. Our first task in this ministry will be to win the whole people for the new state. We want *to replace liberal thinking* with a sense of community that includes the whole people." (my emphasis)

Replace liberal thinking? Create a sense of community?

The abhorrence of liberals in America by Team Hate has become pathological. Liberals have criticized the nation's treatment of prisoners at Guantánamo Bay, Cuba. Here O'Reilly espouses ideas that set the heart to trembling. Regarding the treatment of these "detainees," O'Reilly said that Americans "must know the difference between dissent from the Iraq war and the war on terror and undermining it," and that "any American who undermines that war . . . is a traitor." But finally he makes no distinction between "dissent" and "undermining the war." Indeed, if you do not support the war, both O'Reilly and Coulter will charge you with treason.

It is a strange aberration of logic from which these haters suffer. They mouth support for American democracy, an ideal that argues for the humane treatment of the species. Even those convicted of the most heinous crimes are protected against cruel and unusual punishment by our Constitution, not because they are citizens, but because they are human beings. But what about persons of a different religion, imprisoned without lawyers, without charges, and without trials, those "detainees" at Guantánamo Bay, or in Abu Ghraib prison, or in the recently discovered gulag of secret CIA prisons in Eastern Europe? Should they suffer the loss of basic human rights, including their right to be protected from torture at the hands of those who themselves espouse democracy?

Prisoners who after years of incarceration have been released (and without charge) complained of ongoing torture, sexual degradation, forced drugging, and religious persecution. One prisoner said he "witnessed two people get beaten so badly that I believe it caused their deaths." Some of these prisoners are children.

That these humans have no rights, no right to a lawyer, no right to a fair hearing, no right to be held only when there is probable cause to hold them, does not bode well for how democracy is seen in operation by the rest of the world, especially as the world witnesses how America thumbs an arrogant nose at the Geneva Conventions. As of this writing more than two thousand five hundred Americans have died and many thousands have been maimed in this war to bring a window dressing of *democracy* to the Middle East. Is something wrong here?

Recently the United Nations led the world in condemning our conduct in the torture of prisoners and depriving them of simple due process at Guantánamo Bay. The United Nations demanded that Guantánamo Bay be closed. At the same time further acts of torture at Abu Ghraib prison were revealed by Australian television, pictures that show even worse abuses and degradation than those broadcast in America several years ago. We have squandered our standing as a leader in democracy. In its place we have become the epitome of hypocrisy across the earth, a nation that preaches to other nations concerning human rights and that secretly commits unconscionable acts of torture itself. I love my country. But I am ashamed of what my country does under the rubric of national security. We can never be secure by becoming the world's most blatant hypocrites.

The authority for torturing both the guilty and the hapless, who happened along at the wrong place at the wrong time, comes down from George II himself and from his Goering counterpart, Donald Rumsfeld. They have been advised by a new, cocky, power-bulging generation of lawyers who appear bereft of any knowledge of the Geneva Convention, a treaty that denounces torture and that is the law of our land. These rogues in power who, worldwide, espouse democracy and decry the violation of human rights in other countries seem ignorant to the core. Have they never learned of the Nuremberg trials or the Uniform Code of Military Justice, which characterizes "cruelty," "maltreatment," "threats," and "assault" as felonies? Have they even become peripherally acquainted with the U.S. Constitution?

The Nazi view of "war crimes" is reflected in the attitude now adopted by the GOP itself. As the Nazis argued then and as the

United States now argues, no international convention binds this country since it constitutes a violation of U.S. sovereignty. Have we forgotten it was the United States that, from a higher plain, insisted upon fair trials for Nazi war criminals (who were treated humanely), and it was the United States that supported the Nuremberg Principles. Specific U.S. law binds our citizens (which would include George II and his gang) to the Principles of Nuremberg, a violation of which could result in penalties as severe as life imprisonment or, if death results to the victim, the penalty of death. Little wonder that this administration refuses to ratify the treaty creating the International Criminal Court with international jurisdiction over war criminals.

Legal minds diseased by power have gone so far as to suggest that the military might get advance authority—some call it "advance immunity"—from their superiors and thereby avoid the criminal penalties prescribed by the Uniform Code of Military Justice for torture. Such a request might sound like this: "We are about to torture a captive. We know it is illegal (and immoral). Even though we know we will be criminals if we do so, will you agree, in advance of our crime, that we will not be prosecuted?"

Under the auspices of such mental and moral aberrations, our government has subjected a Muslim prisoner to "a hundred and sixty days of isolation in a pen perpetually flooded with artificial light. He was interrogated on forty-eight of fifty-four days, for eighteen to twenty hours at a stretch. He had been stripped naked; straddled by taunting female guards, in an exercise called 'invasion of space by a female' [such humiliation to the Muslim mind-set is the most degrading and the most painful], forced to wear women's underwear on his head, and to put on a bra; threatened by dogs; placed on a leash; and told that his mother was a whore." He was "subjected to a phony kidnapping, deprived of heat, given large quantities of intravenous liquids without access to a toilet, and deprived of sleep for three days . . . his heart rate dropped so precipitately, to thirty-five beats a minute, that he required cardiac monitoring."

One military official declared that he was "appalled by the whole thing. It was clearly abusive, and it was clearly contrary to everything we were ever taught about American values." That there have been no protests in the streets of Washington, D.C., against such conduct by our government is disturbing. One trusts it does not reveal a callus of the American soul and its disregard for human rights. In the Third Reich the citizens were also silent and had similarly amended their values.

Not long ago voters in San Francisco opposed military recruiting in the city's public schools, including colleges. This was shameful, O'Reilly decried in his column (carried unashamedly in our local paper in Jackson Hole, Wyoming). "It is outright disrespectful to the American Armed Forces. . . . Men and women sign up to protect their country and they do their duty. Yet they are not welcomed in San Francisco's schools." O'Reilly blames the problem not on the obvious—that the military ought not be allowed to invade our schools with their propaganda in a program that smacks of the methodology of Hitler's Youth. Instead, O'Reilly says this is the fault of liberals, and that San Francisco is the haven for liberals, across the land. What do you expect from these traitors?

Listen to O'Reilly as he turns his hate-liberals sights on Air America. "So, all those clowns over at the liberal radio network, we could incarcerate them immediately. Will you have that done, please? Send over the FBI and just put them in chains, because they, you know, they're undermining everything and they don't care, couldn't care less."

That O'Reilly is somewhat familiar with Hitler's Goebbels is tantalizing. He writes, "Nobody should begrudge any American the right to an opinion, but, hey, Rosie [O'Donnell], come on, let's think out your flaky liberal agenda a little. Are you making sense, or are you spouting propaganda? I mean, *a guy named Joseph Goebbels* did the same thing on the *far right* during World War II." (my italics)

In a report prepared during World War II by the U.S. Office of Strategic Services in describing Hitler's psychological profile, one that seemed to echo the teaching of Goebbels, the primary rules were: "Never allow the public to cool off; never admit a fault or wrong; never concede that there may be some good in your enemy; never leave room for alternatives; never accept blame; concentrate on one enemy at a time and blame him for everything that goes wrong; people will believe a big lie sooner than a little one; and if you repeat it frequently enough people will sooner or later believe it."

O'Reilly considers himself a moderate. Goebbels considered himself a moderate Fascist. These self-characterizations have served them both. But by claiming he's a moderate, O'Reilly's employer, Fox, can hang up its sign that reads, "Fair and balanced as usual," and his claim that he is a moderate seems to make his immoderate postulations somehow more acceptable.

Goebbels employed mass mind control for evil ends. But corporate propagandists have learned much from the man: they adopt his same techniques to turn the people against their own interests. O'Reilly's method—I am speaking only of *method*—on health care is a parallel example. People suffer and die in the richest nation in the world because they cannot pay for crucial health-care needs, while there is ample money to conduct illegal wars? Consider how O'Reilly turns the people against their own interests.

O'Reilly: Here's my problem with the government's paying for all of our health. Some people smoke. Some people overeat. Some people take narcotics. Some people don't take care of themselves. Do you think that I, as a taxpayer, have a moral obligation, when their health collapses, to pay for them?

Dr. Steffie Woolhandler (Harvard Medical School): Well, as human beings, we have an obligation to take care of each other when we get sick.

O'Reilly: Even if you're irresponsible?

Of course we don't want to pay for the follies of others. But by directing the argument to the "irresponsible," O'Reilly turns us against the majority of responsible people who *need* health care— a first-rate Goebbels method.

Both Goebbels then, and corporations today, employ the *doublespeak* of George Orwell, a method devised to capture the minds of the masses in support of propositions against the people's own interests. So we hear today's spinners telling us that polluting corporations are nature's pals, that weapons-manufacturer General Electric "brings good things to life," that spreading shitty sludge on farm fields is "beneficial use," and that the killing and mutilating of thousands of innocent human beings in that war are merely "collateral damage." We haven't forgotten, have we, Ann Coulter's admonishment to rape the earth because it was given by God to rape?

As we've seen, in America the corporate-government marriage (which Mussolini called "fascism") already controls the principal means of communication: radio, television, and the newspapers. The new King has no need to confiscate the media as was necessary in the Nazi takeover. In America, control of the people's voice has already been accomplished under the shell game played at the table of the Federal Communications Commission, where, as we have seen, "public interest" was "dead on arrival." The Fascists have not entered by force through the front door, but by stealth and wealth through the back door.

The propaganda of the Third Reich would pale in face of the eloquent science of today's advertising, which, indeed, is nothing less than commercial propaganda. The techniques of corporate advertising are not substantially different than the propaganda that served to capture a nation for Hitler. He took over a nation that was mostly literate, a people that allegedly thought for themselves. His challenge was to convert an intelligent population into a committed force behind the goals and methods of the Third Reich, and he succeeded through propaganda.

I remember the days when our own propaganda against the Soviet system included the horror that in Russia mothers had to work outside the home and that the state was rearing their children. I'm not here to judge whether the family is better off with mothers working. I fight daily for the freedom of the species, male and female. I only point out the radical changes in the national attitude we've witnessed in little more than a generation and that these changes have been brought about by intransigent propaganda that has linked women's freedom with certain imperatives: what *things* the modern family must buy and what both men and women must do to acquire the means to buy them.

A painful example of how far the nation's propaganda machine has gone by way of flattery and seduction: It has told women, "You've come a long way, Baby," which is to say, you have been freed by taking up the tobacco habit, which, of course, offers you death by cancer in return.

Goebbels opined that it made no difference whether what was said was true. It only mattered if what was said sounded true. Hitler agreed: "If you wish the sympathy of the broad masses, you must tell them the crudest and most stupid things."

Advertising not only educates the people about products that prior to their brainwashing they had not known they needed, it also creates an insatiable desire for new experiences, the thrills of a holiday in Hawaii or a clandestine rendezvous in Las Vegas, where "What happens in Las Vegas stays in Las Vegas." Moreover, advertisers have become the keepers of the people's life goals, and people's goals change from time to time as the advertising manipulators on Madison Avenue find it to their advantage to change them.

Goebbels recognized that when pro-Nazi or anti-Semitic propaganda spewed from the mouth of a popular German movie star instead of from Goebbels himself, the public was more likely to respond favorably. In the same way, today's PR firms use fake front groups or "third parties" to speak for corporations. To sell their shoes or their clothing, today's advertisers habitually use star power, endorsements by superstars or celebrities who are paid fortunes to promote a product. Think, in passing, of Michael Jordan and Nike. The major cost of the product is often not the labor of thousands of tired, sometimes underaged workers in shoddy conditions in Third World countries, but the holy word from a worshipped celebrity who may possess little wisdom but a wondrous ability to throw a ball to some designated place.

Goebbels enjoyed a communications monopoly in Germany and, like Mao, denounced "intellectualism" and encouraged book burning. Today, as we've seen, U.S. corporations have a Goebbels-like grip on all forms of communication. Book burning is not necessary. People are addicted to the masters to be, the corporate propaganda machine. In 1934 Goebbels proclaimed in a speech at Nuremberg: "Propaganda is a means to an end. Its purpose is to lead the people to an understanding that will allow it to willingly and without internal resistance devote itself to the tasks and goals of a superior leadership. . . .

"In the end, such propaganda miraculously makes the unpopular popular, enabling even a government's most difficult decisions to secure the resolute support of the people. A government that uses it properly can do what is necessary without running the risk of losing the masses . . ."

The master propagandist goes on to observe: "The effective propagandist must be a master of the art of speech, of writing, of journalism, of the poster, and of the leaflet. He must have the gift to use the major methods of influencing public opinion such as the press, film, and radio to serve his ideas and goals."

He saw the common man as dull and stupid. We hear our counterparts call the guy who comes home, opens a beer, and turns on the television a "couch potato." Goebbels went on to say, "The rank and file are usually much more primitive than we imagine. Propaganda must therefore always be essentially simple and repetitious." He emphasized, "the most brilliant propagandist technique will yield no success unless one fundamental principle is borne in mind constantly . . . it must confine itself to a few points and repeat them over and over."

Consider the eternal repetitions of the ad campaigns of Coca-Cola—"things go better with Coke," suggesting that life is enriched by drinking water plus a small amount of flavoring, caffeine, and sugar; or the endless "This Bud's for you," telling us we've earned and deserve the reward of a hard day's work. How about Fox's "Fair and balanced, as usual," and CNN's "The world's most trusted network," and the government's daily assurance, echoed and mouthed by all the corporate media, that promises us we are fighting to make America secure and to spread democracy across the world? As Hitler once remarked, "How fortunate for governments that the people they administer don't think."

William L. Shirer, author of the standard work on Nazism, *The Rise and Fall of the Third Reich*, recalls: "I myself was to experience how easily one is taken in by a lying and censored press and radio in a totalitarian state." He had daily access to foreign papers and listened regularly to the BBC. Yet, he said, "it was surprising and sometimes consternating to find that notwithstanding the opportunities I had to learn the facts, and despite one's inherent distrust of what one learned from Nazi sources, a steady diet over the years of falsifications and distortions made a certain impression on one's mind and often misled it. No one who has not lived for years in a totalitarian land can possibly conceive how difficult it is to escape the dread consequences of a regime's calculated and incessant propaganda."

Shirer tells of meeting well-educated and intelligent individuals and hearing them mouth the most outlandish assertions. "It was obvious they were parroting some piece of nonsense they had heard on the radio or read in the newspaper."

"Think of the press as a great keyboard on which the government can play," said Goebbels. He saw to the manufacture of cheap radios so that every German family had the means to receive his propaganda. The corporate King has been even more clever, for nearly every family in America owns one or more television sets and radios, which have been sold to the profit of the corporate King's company store.

Herbert Krugman, a researcher who became manager of public-opinion research at General Electric, undertook to discover what happens physiologically in the brain of a person watching TV. He ultimately concluded that as real-life experience is continuously replaced by the viewer's experience on the screen, politicians and corporate advertisers can cause the desired responses to be triggered so that the *TV "world" becomes the real world*. The mass mind takes shape, the people believing they are operating out of their personal volition, out of their needs and desires. He concluded that whoever controls the screen controls the future, the past, and the present. We remember that GE owns NBC and that it produces devastating weapons of war.

The New York Times recently reported how the federal government has taken to prepackaging news—nothing more than propaganda. The people see it, believe it, and govern their lives by it.

"It is the kind of TV news coverage every president covets," The *Times* writer observed. "'Thank you, Bush. Thank you, U.S.A.,' a jubilant Iraqi-American told a camera crew in Kansas City for a segment about reaction to the fall of Baghdad. A second report told of 'another success' in the Bush administration's 'drive to strengthen aviation security': the reporter called it 'one of the most remarkable campaigns in aviation history.' A third segment, broadcast in January, described the administration's determination to open markets for American farmers.

"To a viewer, each report looked like any other 90-second segment on the local news. But *the federal government produced all three.* The report from Kansas City was made by the State Department. The 'reporter' covering airport safety was actually a public relations professional working under a *false name* for the Transportation

Security Administration. The farming segment was done by the Agriculture Department's office of communications." (my italics)

The *Times* reporter claimed that at least twenty federal agencies, including the Defense Department and the Census Bureau, have made and distributed hundreds of television news segments in the past four years. But more alarming, these appear on television without any attribution. The viewer is watching political propaganda in the guise of news.

The Times wrote: "An examination of government-produced news reports offers a look inside a world where the traditional lines between public relations and journalism have become tangled. . . . It is a world where government-produced reports disappear into a maze of satellite transmissions, web portals, syndicated news programs and network feeds, only to emerge cleansed on the other side as 'independent' journalism." TVA Productions, a video news release company, acknowledged, "No TV news organization has the resources in labor, time or funds to cover every worthy story. 90 percent of TV newsrooms now rely on video news releases."

In attempting to gain support among black families for its education reform law "No Child Left Behind," the Bush administration paid Armstrong Williams $240,000 to promote the program on his nationally syndicated television show and to urge black journalists to promote it as well. The deal required Williams to regularly comment favorably on the Bush program and to interview Education Secretary Rod Paige for TV and radio spots. So if you want the public to go with you, you pay some shill to support it. Again, who do we trust?

The Williams contract was part of a $1 million deal with Ketchum INC., a public relations firm that produced "video news releases" made to look like news reports. The Bush administration also used similar releases to support its Medicare prescription drug plan.

The U.S. General Accounting Office (GAO) called this an illegal use of taxpayers' dollars. Obviously. It reported: "The failure of an agency to identify itself as the source of a prepackaged news story misleads the viewing public by encouraging the audience to believe that the broadcasting news organization developed the information. The prepackaged news stories are purposefully designed to be indistinguishable from news segments broadcast to the public. . . . The essential fact of attribution is missing." This boast of Goebbels seems somewhat relevant today: "We have made the Reich by propaganda."

Consider how daily we are reminded of our want of security. People across this land are fearful of some looming act of terrorism. Since the masses of people live in large cities, we are constantly bathed in fear. We are at war. Terrorists are among us. We must be forever vigilant. We can no longer trust our neighbors. People of different races and religions may be the enemy. We cannot get on an airplane without our shoes being examined. Therefore we surely must face critical danger. Television keeps us informed of impending jeopardy. We give up our rights to the government in the form of legislation such as the Patriot Act that pulverizes our constitutional guarantees to be secure in our homes.

Such an unyielding assault of propaganda that creates a sense of impending catastrophe furnishes the executive branch cause to expand its power and, yes, to flood us with additional propaganda and to withhold from us facts that are necessary for a free people to conduct the affairs of our government. Now our leaders, responding to the climate of danger, present themselves as ready and able, yes, as heroes who can and will protect us, who will resort to gallant and resolute acts in these times of terror, and we hasten to follow.

After 9/11 and in rapid succession, the administration reversed the presumption of openness underlying the Freedom of Information Act, and arrested and deported thousands of persons by means of secret evidence and secret hearings. With barely a peep from the populace, the so-called Patriot Act was passed permitting a secret court on secret papers to issue secret warrants that allowed government agents to secretly steal into our homes, to secretly search our files, records, and computers, to install secret listening devices in our homes and offices, and to secretly tap our phones.

Since 9/11 thousands of government Web sites have been removed from the Internet on the grounds, of course, of national security. In 1998 Daniel Patrick Moynihan called America a "culture of secrecy." In 2004 more than 15 million documents were classified, almost triple the number of which Moynihan had complained. We have recently been told that fifty-five thousand previously open, declassified pages in the National Archives have been removed from public access. The restoration of classified status was secretly begun in 1999 when the CIA and five other agencies objected to the information that had been declassified by President Clinton. One marvels at how easily history is obliterated.

And as we've seen, secrecy is especially a precursor of torture. One cannot torture under the open eyes of a horrified population. The CIA knows this. It has established secret compounds, "black sites" in Eastern Europe, where prisoners are held secretly and dealt with in secret ways, including torture. The torture must be kept clandestine else, knowing of it and not raising our indignant voices, we would have to suffer our own hypocrisy. One celebrated political philosopher, Edmund Burke, remarked back in the eighteenth century, "The only thing necessary for the triumph of evil is for good men to do nothing."

The problem is simple. We no longer own our own minds. They already belong to the corporate-government oligarchy. We have been thoroughly propagandized. We do not know our frontal lobes have been so tinctured with propaganda that we—all of us—will vehemently deny to our last breath that we have lost our ability to think independently.

The myths of our freedom and our way of government, our ideas of justice for all when there is little justice for any, our sense of right and wrong, which has been perverted to accommodate our greed for profit—all of these transformations have changed us into a different species, one that will murder countless numbers of its own over a variant idea of God, one that will destroy its own home on this earth for money, one that will let its own children starve and deprive its fellow members of the species of the most fundamental human rights because of the color of one's hide. This evil transformation of the species is the result of propaganda. We are its victims.

9. Hate for the Love of Christ

Pat Robertson and the Christian Right

As I was taught by a devout Christian mother, Jesus loved us all, even us sinners. Yes, especially us sinners. One might argue that Christ was a liberal.

Today I'm stunned by the phenomenon that permits a self-proclaimed Christian clergy to pervert the teachings of Christ—an enlightenment brought about by love, one now forsaken by the Christian right for hate. In short, how can these born-agains claim to be followers of Christ, the champion of love, when their primary offering is hate?

It's not that we are born without the capacity to hate. Freud showed that hate is the expression of a deep, unrelenting instinct of destructiveness against which love, also a profound and nascent instinct, offers a response. "Die we must," says the psychoanalyst Karl Menninger, "but in the meantime we can live, if we can love." These two instincts abide in the same house.

But why those of the Christian right have attached themselves to the dark side, the side of hate and destructiveness, rather than the enlightened side of love as espoused by their acclaimed "savior and Lord, Jesus Christ," seems a mystery couched in hypocrisy, ignorance, and an insidious and malevolent agenda.

The attack against liberals by such nationally known evangelists as Pat Robertson, founder of the Christian Coalition, is a case in point. Robertson is a partisan of the Republican Party and campaigned to become the party's candidate in the 1988 presidential election. In an interview with Molly Ivins, Robertson said, "Just like what Nazi Germany did to the Jews, so liberal America is now doing to the evangelical Christians. It's no different. It is the same thing. It is happening all over again. It is the Democratic Congress, the liberal-based media, and the homosexuals who want to destroy the Christians. Wholesale abuse and discrimination and the worst bigotry directed toward any group in America today. More terrible than anything suffered by any minority in history."

It is easy to label one's enemies with the Nazi tag. I, too, have discussed some *methods* in argument and media manipulation in America that parallel the techniques of propaganda in Nazi Germany. But to compare liberals, a major segment of the people in the country, with the Nazis is thought that plunges into the great abyss. The statement is hysterical, hateful, and half-witted, and cast, in the name of Jesus.

Robertson clearly possesses functional intelligence. After graduating magna cum laude with a bachelor of arts degree from Washington and Lee University, he received a juris doctor degree from Yale University Law School and, in 1959, a master of divinity degree from New York Theological Seminary. How can a lawyer and a man of sufficient intelligence to graduate with honors from a leading university concoct such a hate-filled, lame-brained demagoguery in the name of Christ?

Robertson undoubtedly understands that what he says has consequences. He is a leader in the mighty Christian Coalition and the host of *The 700 Club* on television. What are his goals? He claims in his mission statement: "I want to be part of God's plan of what He is doing on earth, and I want to bring Him glory."

This lawyer, preacher, businessman, and propagandist surely knows that the Constitution mandates a separation of church and state with the simplest language: "Congress shall make no law respecting an establishment of religion or prohibiting the free exercise thereof. . . ." Yet in an address to the American Center for Law and Justice, Robertson proclaimed, "There is no such thing as separation of church and state in the Constitution. *It is a lie of the left* and we are not going to take it anymore." (my emphasis)

Jefferson was one of those "liars of the left." In an 1802 letter to the Danbury Baptist Association, Thomas Jefferson, then president, declared that the American people, through the First Amendment, had erected a "wall of separation between church and state."

Madison, considered the Father of the Constitution, was another of those "liars of the left." He said, "The number, the industry and the morality of the priesthood, and the devotion of the people have been manifestly increased by the total separation of the church and state." In an earlier, undated essay (probably early 1800s), Madison wrote: "Strongly guarded . . . is the separation between religion and government in the Constitution of the United States."

Supreme Court Justice Harry Blackman was one of those "liars of the left" when he wrote in *Lee v. Weisman*, 1992: "When the government puts its imprimatur on a particular religion it conveys a message of exclusion to all those who do not adhere to the favored beliefs. A government cannot be premised on the belief that all persons are created equal when it asserts that God prefers some."

And Sandra Day O'Connor was one of those "liars of the left" when she wrote in the Texas Ten Commandments case in June of 2005: "Those who would renegotiate the boundaries between church and state must therefore answer a difficult question: Why would we trade a system that has served us so well for one that has served others so poorly?"

Robertson has lost his way. Surely a man of God wouldn't lie. But perhaps God wished him to lie—this time about homosexuals. Here is what Robertson said on that subject: "Many of those people involved with Adolph Hitler were Satanists, many of them were homosexuals and the two things seem to go together." All good bedfellows, right?

Those who purport to know tell us that the death rates of homosexuals and Jews in the Nazi camps were approximately the same. Homosexuals did not survive long. They were required to wear their pink emblems and were exterminated within the first few months of their camp experience.

And what about Robertson's Christian views on race? This godly fellow, talking about apartheid in South Africa, said, "I think 'one man, one vote,' just unrestricted democracy, would not be wise. There needs to be some kind of protection for the minority which the white people represent now, a minority, and they need and have a right to demand a protection of their rights."

If we can bear it, let's take one more look at Robertson's views. Here is what he said about women's rights. "I know this is painful for the ladies to hear, but if you get married, you have accepted the headship of a man, your husband. Christ is the head of the household [what domestic household did Christ head?] and the husband is the head of the wife, and that's the way it is, period." To my knowledge Christ never held himself out as the head of anything. As for women he, the humblest of men, washed the feet of the prostitute. And Pat, when you arrive at the Pearly Gates and discover Rosa Parks is relieving Saint Peter at the watch, what arguments for admission are you going to make to her?

One of Robertson's latest pilgrimages into the screamy-jeebies of biblical psychosis was his judgment that God is punishing Ariel Sharon, prime minister of Israel, with a stroke, because of the prime minister's new policy of withdrawing from the West Bank and Gaza. "God considers this land to be His," Robertson harangued, his finger pointing. "You read the Bible and He says 'This is my land,' and for any prime minister of Israel who decides he is going to carve it up and give it away, God says, 'No, this is mine.'"

It is all right with me that such as Robertson be free to say what he pleases. And that one who purports to follow Jesus, Robertson, should make such profane judgments sadly represents the lost and the pitiable.

I refuse to review the murky business history of this "man of God." If you're interested, look it up. Find out about his total wealth in multiple millions, how he sold the Christian Broadcasting Network, which bore the gifts of many donors, to whom he sold it, and who profited from it. Recently he sold the Family Channel to Rupert Murdoch, another man who brandishes elastic ethics. It is all a money-mad mess to which I wish to devote no more space.

But what are we missing here? The so-called Christian right and the far-right wing of the Republican Party are dancing together. Why? What do Jesus and greed, Jesus and power, Jesus and the hatred of homosexuals, Jesus and the oppression of women, Jesus and the rejection of the black race have to do one with the other?

It's been over two thousand years since Christ said anything—at all. When he was preaching, he spoke about greed and the rich. As a child I remember hearing in Sunday school about how a man came to Jesus and asked, "Good Master, what must I do to have eternal life?"

Jesus answered, "If you want to be perfect, go and sell everything you have and give the money to the poor, and you will have treasure in heaven; and come, follow me." But when the young man heard this, he went away sadly, for he was very rich.

Those who purport to be students of the Bible have been transplanting words into the mouth of Christ for centuries—the holiness of the Crusades, which were little more than exploitations for riches and power undertaken in the name of Christ; the inhuman torture and death of countless "heretics" on the church's racks; the burning of a million women as witches—all in the name of Christ. More recently evangelical preachers have claimed Jesus spoke disapprovingly on:

* card playing (I didn't know they were playing bridge or Texas Hold 'Em poker in Christ's day)
* music in church (early on music was confined to brothels and saloons)
* ice cream Sundays (Christians required that such a heavenly treat have its name changed slightly to "sundaes")
* masturbation (obviously Jesus didn't approve of masturbation since none of his followers was blind)
* homosexuality and abortion (neither were considered by Christ in the Scriptures)

Scour the Bible and find any such admonitions of Christ and the untold thousands of other judgments made in his name. Did he approve of slavery and segregation? The slave owners who beat their slaves, raped their slave women, and sold their slave children taught their slaves Christianity. Christian slaves were said to be more obedient and worked harder. Their conversion had nothing to do with saving their souls.

And who was this character named Jesus? We seem to have forgotten. In describing himself he said, "The Spirit of the Lord is upon me; he has appointed me to preach Good News to the poor; he has sent me to heal the brokenhearted and to announce that the blind shall see, that captives shall be released and the

downtrodden shall be freed from their oppressors." (Luke 4:18)
And when someone asked, "Sir, which is the most important
commandment in the laws of Moses?" Jesus was straight about it.
"This is the first and greatest commandment: 'Love the Lord your
God with all your heart, soul, and mind.' The second most impor-
tant is similar: 'Love your neighbor as much as you love yourself.'"
(Matt. 22:36–40)

I woke up the other night wondering what Pat Robertson
would do if his neighbor was black, gay, and a Democrat.

When this man ran for president in the late eighties, he claimed
to have seen combat duty in Korea. Those who called him a liar and
a fraud, among them former GOP congressman Pete McCloskey
of California, who served in the same unit as Robertson, claimed
that Robertson had relied on his father to save him from combat
duty. Robertson sued McCloskey and Andy Jacobs, an Indiana
Democrat, for a total of $65 million, ostensibly to quiet them.
Robertson dropped his lawsuit, possibly concerned that the line of
decorated marine officers who were ready to testify against him
would ruin his presidential aspirations. Some claim that Robertson saw no combat in Korea. So what? This may be endemic to
the far right. We remember that George II, lost somewhere on his
way to duty, suffered from the same problem.

No doubt if a liberal believes in charity toward the poor over the
greed and power of the rich, such is in line with what Christ
taught. But there's ample hypocrisy to go around. Liberals, both in
and out of the church, have their hands as deeply in the pockets of
corporate America as the right, and they bow as fervently to the
dollar. Some of the richest men I know are Democrats who made
their fortunes squeezing the last penny out of the hides of their
poor workers.

A fellow by the name of Tim LaHaye has had a powerful and,
in some ways, an unheralded impact on America. He's another
evangelical preacher, a man in his midseventies, who graduated

from the way-out-in-right-field Bob Jones University. Along with Jerry Falwell, he cofounded the Moral Majority, whose fund-raising letters warned Americans that they were faced with doom by secular humanists, militant homosexuals, and "baby killers." Of course, their message was that their flocks should be saved, to send money, a lot of it, to register and to vote Republican. Jerry Falwell claims it was LaHaye who inspired him to get involved in national politics.

But this fellow LaHaye is interesting because, along with the man who really writes his novels, Jerry Jenkins, he is the best-selling author in America (the *New York Times* Best Seller List does not include all of LaHaye's massive sales). For the first time since 1994, the bestselling novel in this country wasn't written by a gentleman named Grisham, but under the name of this retired evangelical preacher.

What's going on here? So far 17 million copies of the Left Behind series have been sold. Through the Left Behind series of twelve books, fiction no less, LaHaye is reaching more people than through the Moral Majority. The pitch in these stories is that Jesus will return and take with him those who believe in him. They will joyfully ascend into the sky, and those who refuse to worship Jesus will remain behind and suffer horribly and die—the Christian fundamentalist belief in the Rapture. At the sound of a trumpet, Jesus will make his appearance in the clouds and magically lift up the believers, and they will thereby escape the horrible calamities at the hands of the Antichrist, all as promised in the Book of Revelation.

Woe unto those who do not believe. They'll be left to battle against Satan's horrors alone. And there is hope for the Jews who will suffer Great Tribulation. Some 144,000 Jews will come to accept Jesus as their savior. And remember, the Jews must be in control of Israel before Jesus will come. Is the time upon us?

Fear of the end seems to be the propelling force for sales of LaHaye's books. Again, I have nothing against commerce, but money and profit seem to be the most powerful motivator even for the likes of our Christian clergy who somehow have forgotten the admonition of Christ, which, in plain language, was "Give it up, Baby. Give it to the poor and follow me." Somehow the churches themselves have overlooked this troublesome detail.

I was taught that Jesus is forgiving. The Jesus I learned of as a child would certainly understand and forgive if we didn't rush out to accept the fiction of LaHaye as His word, or if we were skeptical of the messages delivered to us by the likes of Robertson and Falwell. At last, we create our own gods in our own images and, whatever their motives, the evangelical right have created theirs.

The Catholic church was the first corporation, and remains the richest in the world. Other churches, each with their spin on what Christ said, follow with their own bulging purses. One such church comes quickly to mind, the Church of Jesus Christ of Latter-day Saints (Mormons), which is per capita the fastest-growing church in America. It claims a minimum of $30 billion in assets and annual gross income of $6 billion—more than Utah's state budget this year.

The Church of Jesus Christ of Latter-day Saints is only the seventh largest in the United States. Its holdings include the world's largest beef ranch—the 312,000-acre Deseret Cattle & Citrus Ranch outside Orlando, Florida. The ranch's land alone is worth $858 million. The church also owns America's largest producer of nuts, as well as Bonneville International Corporation, the country's fourteenth-largest radio chain, and the Beneficial Life Insurance Company, with assets of $1.6 billion. That it does good work is undisputed. But a side effect of its beneficence is the preaching of its dogma, which includes the idea that the church and its membership must submit to the authority of the state—even an evil state. Where is the resistance of good men to the wrongs of a nation?

Theodore Dreiser, the great American novelist, raged against the wealth of churches. In 1931 he wrote:

I decry the power of the Church and its use of that power, in America in particular! Throughout the world, as all know, the churches are so organized as to have the wealth, size, and formation of a great corporation, a government, or an army. And in America, the wealthy individuals who rule in corporate affairs appear to be attracted to the church by reason of its hold not only on the mind but the actions of its adherents. . . . In short, it makes for ignorance and submission in the working class, and what more could a corporation-minded government or financial group, looking toward complete control of everything for a few, desire?

And so we see those who claim to be devout followers of Jesus, those who champion the most unloving belief systems—a shrug of the shoulders at minorities and women, an abhorrence of persons with different lifestyles and different religions—we see those who pervert the language of Christ to suit their agendas, an assortment of mammoth ecclesiastical lies and slanders of the teaching of Jesus—we see them (shall we call them the "non-Christian Christian right"?) not as money changers in the Temple but as the *owners* of temples dedicated to the creation of wealth and power, both institutionally and individually.

But be frightened further. We observe this powerful movement entering into a strange marriage, one that would have likely shocked Jesus, one that mocks His words and His suffering, a marriage not with the spirit of Christ but with the rock-hard political right that is controlled by corporate power and money and that faithfully serves the nonhuman corporate King.

The power for such a perversion—the love of Jesus joining with the love of money—the forgiveness of Christ joining with the hate preached by the religious right—the humbleness and peace of Christ joining with the arrogance of a lying, warring administration—is a staggering phenomenon of the most cynical and cruel contradictions. How could this happen?

First, most of us are fearful of death. If we had no more fear of dying than driving to McDonald's for a hamburger, most of us would already be dead. Most want to live *forever,* and religion promises that we can if we just side with the right deity and give its emissaries our power and our money.

Second, as we've already discovered, there's great power in availability. Television puts these "ministries" at the fingertips of millions. I knew a woman in the small town of Dubois, Wyoming, who had the Christian Channel running full blast in her café twelve hours a day. People came for her good cherry pies and her hamburgers, but even the old hard-assed cowboys listened to the TV evangelists because people are attracted to the tube, to the sounds, and, at last, to the charismatic carryings-on of the evangelical preachers who gasp and scream and, near swooning, "Paraaaaaise the Lord!"

Third, these television "ministries" have credibility, mostly because they're on television. Such is the power of TV sales—to get thin, to get wrinkles gone, to get the belly marbled with muscle, to get hair, to get the new potato peeler, to get an erection, to get . . . yes, to get religion and eternal life.

Fourth, we've been taught to abdicate our authority to those who claim to have authority over us. evangelical preachers present themselves as commissioned by God to tell us how we must think (the insertion of the Christian hard-right brain chip) and what we must do, including our duty to deliver our hard-earned money to these "ministries," and thus guarantee ourselves a reserved seat in heaven. You have to pay to get through any gate. Doesn't everybody know that?

Fifth, perhaps the most important reason these "ministries" succeed is because they mine into that molten lava of hate. Hate "faggots," hate "child killers," hate blacks (despite their assurance that they love them), hate liberals, hate feminists, hate those who hate the Christian right, and hate those who do not hate those who hate the Christian right, in short, hate everyone except the haters, in the name of Jesus!

Hitler founded his movement on the idea that Christ approved of the pure white race and hated his own, the Jews. Such is a towering insanity to begin with. But here's what he said in a famous speech, and the German people, not unlike our own, listened:

"Today Christians . . . stand at the head of Germany. . . . I pledge that I never will tie myself to parties who want to destroy Christianity. We want to fill our culture again with the Christian spirit. . . . *We want to burn out all the recent immoral developments in literature, in the theater, and in the press—in short, we want to burn out the poison of immorality which has entered into our whole life and culture as a result of liberal excess during the past . . . [few] years.*" (my italics) Sound familiar? Let me repeat, this is NOT Ann Coulter or Pat Robertson speaking. We needn't expend much more thought to conclude that something grossly mad is transpiring here.

Consider the purported religion of the right, a so-called fundamental Christianity that seems to despise the poor and love the rich, that is vengeful rather than forgiving, that supports international crime in the form of illegal wars rather than seeking world peace by addressing the underlying cause of war, a religion of the right that, in sum, hates rather than loves.

And compare the expressed promises of Hitler toward Christianity, above, with the same sentiments of the non-Christian Christian right we've encountered—what Hitler calls and the Christian fundamentalists call and the born-again leadership of this country calls and the corporate King calls, and all of their blonde handmaidens and the pimps of power call the *"liberal excess during the past."* Those were Hitler's words!—*"the liberal excess during the past."*

I return to Theodore Dreiser, who in 1931 wrote as if he were writing today. His prophetic thoughts preceded the rise of Hitler:

The unlimited use of propaganda! The millions spent on foolish campaigns designed to shape or change public opinion in regard to this or that: divorce, birth control, the falseness of the Darwinian theory, or almost anything in connection with science and history! The blather about saints and cures and bringing all to Jesus while taxes are evaded and the scummy politicians whom they endorse, or even nominate and elect to office, proceed to rob the public in favor of the corporations and churches whom they serve!

Dreiser continued in his rant, not unlike my own:

No wonder ignorance, no wonder illusion, when those with power in the religious field knowingly delude and mislead the masses! The things told them! That it is important to vote for this or that crook; uphold religion; it is good for the people to go to war, to put religion in the schools, to give into the hands of these mental bandits the care and education of all children, so that they may be properly enslaved by religion! (A slave, in my opinion, is the man who does not think for himself. A man with knowledge is not powerless.) But always with suave and polished words. For it is not men who are talking, as they assert, but God through them! and so through the mouths of tricksters and social prestidigitators, and no more and no less, comes all this hooey in regard to the hereafter!

Something is happening in America that fills the thoughtful with dread. Unless we are willing to make an offering at the shrine of hate, we will be left behind. It becomes a wasted day if we have not found something, someone to abhor. The fact that millions believe these insanities of the religious right proves that psychosis can be taught and that hate is contagious. We are experiencing a blatant, unapologetic Antichrist, a revision of the teachings of Jesus, whose gospel was one of love and acceptance, not hate and rejection. The question keeps rattling at the door: To what dark destiny is this leading?

10. Kill All the Lawyers

The Rise of the New King

S o you want to be king? You want to control the greatest nation in the world—perhaps control the world? As we've seen, you must first own the people, own their minds. You must be able to command their prejudices like one can toot a boy's horn. And, if you are to be King, you must also destroy their warriors.

The people are always the enemy of the King, "the stupid mob," as Hitler called them. The people can rise up. They always do in the end. It is only a question of when.

But how can the people fight against the King without their warriors, without champions to fight for their causes? Destroy their warriors and the people can holler and foam but they can do no harm, for even they who are aware enough to shake off the King's propaganda like a dog shakes off fleas, even they are helpless against the King if there are none who can enter the fight for them.

The warriors for the people are trial lawyers—those villains who are not to be trusted, not even when they are shackled and held helpless in those straitjackets of hate. And we have learned to hate them because every day through the King's media we are told outrageous stories of how trial lawyers have aborted the fetus of justice, and we hear malicious jokes so that we have come to believe that the cause of every ill that befalls us lies at their feet.

"First kill all the lawyers!"

Our insurance rates go up because of trial lawyers, those tricksters who bamboozle jurors to return those crazy, bloated verdicts. Our taxes overwhelm us—the devils. They sue like ordinary people breathe. They're to blame for the high cost of medicine, for the high cost of merchandise of every description, for the high cost of drugs—they affect the cost of everything because they hoodwink the juries and buy off judges, and pocket piles of money and amass fortunes! Lawsuits are destroying our economy. Manufacturers can't survive against their foreign competition because of lawyers' suits. Lawyers are destroying America. The courts are packed to the ceilings with their frivolous lawsuits. The system is running wild.

Ann Coulter tells us.

FrontPage Magazine: Why do you hate trial lawyers?

Coulter: Everything you do—from driving to earning a living to making a cup of coffee to owning a home to getting medical care—is more expensive and difficult simply because of trial lawyers, who, at the same time, contribute absolutely nothing of any value to society. . . . But other than the fact that trial lawyers have made every single facet of life worse, I can't think of a single good reason to dislike them.

Rush Limbaugh joined in with the same worn rhetoric. Limbaugh and Bush II as well, these soul mates. It was the second presidential campaign for George W. Bush, and John Edwards was the Democratic vice presidential candidate. "After all, Edwards was a trial lawyer." That's what Limbaugh said. That's all he need say. Trust should end there. Interestingly, Limbaugh comes from a prominent family of lawyers. His father, Rush H. Limbaugh Jr., was a judge. His brother, David Scott Limbaugh, graduated cum laude with a B.A. in political science and was on the Law Review at University of Missouri. He is a practicing lawyer who has served as a member of the Missouri Association of Trial Attorneys. It was Roy Black, a fine trial lawyer, who put the constitutional cloaks around Rush Limbaugh and apparently saved him when he faced allegations of illegal drug use.

And O'Reilly. What does O'Reilly say about trial lawyers? Well, they "have a hidden agenda that is antithetical to the improvement of society." The same stale party line. It was a trial lawyer who represented O'Reilly and led him through that troublesome sexual harassment suit. You remember: The shower. The fantasies. Then a trial lawyer made it all disappear.

We remember Nancy Grace. Hello there, Nancy. She says, "Greedy lawyers have had their hands in the cookie jar for so long that Congress may actually enact a law to stop them," and that she had always viewed them as "quick and wily, like a beautiful snake that you keep in a cage but wouldn't dare touch." The snake? What about the apple, Nancy?

Trial lawyers have been so demonized that George II did not hesitate to pile on in his bid for reelection. He was speaking at the Northern Virginia Community College. August 9, 2004. A campaign speech. The press pressing. He looked around the auditorium with that smile, the half sneer. Then he said, "By the way, you can't be prosmall business and protrial lawyer at the same time. (Laughter and applause.)

"You can't be prodoctor and propatient and protrial lawyer at the same time. (Laughter and applause.)

"You have to choose.

"My opponent made his choice, and he put him on the ticket [referring to John Edwards]," he said with the still smiling grimace. (Laughter.)

"I made my choice. I'm going to work with Congress for liability reform and for tort reform." (Applause.) Note the applause.

The man was not speaking bravely. He was speaking to a

lawyer-hating audience, one created by right-wing propaganda. But George II, too, had already forgotten. They were trial lawyers who argued his case to the U.S. Supreme Court, who saved his bacon and put him in the White House.

Thus, according to Team Hate, the King's men and women who mouth the party line, the world would be immensely improved if we could actually kill all the lawyers. Yes. But we are able to kill them in a more subtle way than Mao or Stalin killed their enemies. Again the method is the power of propaganda. We destroy the lawyer in the minds of the people—and it becomes too clear that if the corporate King can destroy the people's warriors in the eyes of the people, all power will be vested in the King. The contest is over.

Think of John Adams, Thomas Jefferson, Alexander Hamilton, and James Madison. All lawyers. Ask, how could such an honorable profession then become such an object of scorn? How did lawyers become those "parasitical blobs of absolutely worthless protoplasm who are responsible for the decline in civilization"?

The method of destroying trial lawyers has been so astonishingly simple. Pick a few cases with apparent ridiculous results that portray the greed and stealth of a few trial lawyers. Show the supposed stupidity of jurors. Then tell and retell those cases until the public comes to believe that what they're hearing represents the character of all trial lawyers, the intelligence of all jurors, and the results in all courts.

Propaganda in its glory. Goebbels would approve. If no one will trust lawyers for the people, nor the jurors, nor the judges, nor the appellate judges, many of whom have been hoisted up to the high courts by the corporate King, our justice system is gone.

Good-bye.

Snakes and worthless protoplasm.

So how does this poisonous propaganda effect the courts. Can't you see it? The courts are open to all. It is our right under the Constitution to petition the courts for justice. See the judges sitting up there on their benches all stern and pompous, shrouded in their black robes ready to play the judicial game. Are they less concerned with justice and more concerned with being reelected? Do not ask such questions. Can't you see the reporters leaning forward in their seats up front, their notebooks readied, their pencils poised to record the first hinted bud of impropriety that could bloom into a story.

Yes, of course, the judges wish to be reelected and assured of their retirement, and they wish to be welcomed at their clubs. And although they will never admit it, most fear the embarrassment of their rulings being reversed by a higher court.

"Don't give a damn what the Court of Appeals holds. I call 'em like I see 'em."

"Yes, Your Honor."

And one thing for sure. I say, *for sure!* Under such scrutiny the judge will not let one of those slimy trial lawyers come slithering into his court and pry open the door to the corporate King's vaults—the public out there, the voting mob, poised to pull him off the bench at the first sign the judge has let one of those "wily snakes" escape its cage.

So like a good trial lawyer, I overstate the case to make my point. Slightly. I have known a few great judges in my day, and the others? They are not all bad. But listen to me: Today the trial lawyer could be as pure and honest as Jesus in a pin-striped suit—and still the jurors will see him through jaundiced spectacles. Or the woman, as trial lawyer, could be Mother Teresa in a conservative business dress—dark worsted wool, a small string of no-nonsense pearls at her throat, a tiny gold cross pinned at her lapel, her face that of a saint—and still the jurors would undress her to her soul to see if, indeed, she had one. Suspicion. Worse. A thin fog of hate surrounds all lawyers for the people, these warriors for the people's justice.

But in a courtroom there are two sides, are there not? What about the corporate King's lawyers—the insurance company lawyers, the lawyers for the corporations and the big money who oppose the people in their search for justice? These are the lawyers, many good, decent men and women, who fight *against*

the people, who make up the huge firms in every large city, some
with hundreds of partners, gangs of lawyers occupying multiple
floors in the towering buildings where wealth and power are con-
centrated. One looks up to them, doesn't one, those who fight so
valiantly against people's justice?

Groups of these silk-stocking barristers, mostly hired by insurance companies to defeat an injured person's lawsuit, may bill
out thousands of dollars for every hour they spend in such en-
deavor and often they spend thousands of hours in the defense
of a single case. To them it is only work, a job disassociated from
justice and from the pain and devastating loss of deserving, living persons. Too often these mammoth law firms win, not because justice is on the side of the corporation they represent, but
because the people's lawyers are overwhelmed by the numbers of
great legal talents thrown against them, graduates from the
grand universities like Harvard and Yale, the alma mater of the
corporate lawyer, the brainy, clever ones. And in the end, it
makes no difference what the corporate King spends to defeat
the people. The King will spend whatever it takes. The King is
afraid of the people. The people must be defeated, one case at a
time, or whole hordes of them will be pounding at the doors for
justice.

You can see the corporate lawyers over cocktails after the trial.
Bill Matilanan, who's been brain injured by a piece of badly designed equipment that broke and fell on him, doesn't know who
he is, or where he is. He faced the jury and heard the foreman read
the verdict. But he does not understand that it was a verdict for the
company that leaves Bill without money to live another day. Bill
will join the crowd of beggars on the streets and sleep on a grate to
catch a little warmth in the winter.

These are the true elitists, Ms. Ingraham, these corporations,
some of whose white-collar criminals you've defended—some of
the few who were finally charged with crimes, enough to make the
system appear just. I am glad, of course, that you defended them.
They are entitled to a defense and to the presumption of inno-

cence. But I wish, instead, a woman of your obvious skills had defended a mother charged with cheating on welfare and trying to support her hungry children.

I have yet to hear the smooth, unctuous corporate voice denouncing corporate lawyers. They go to church regularly. Their children attend the finest schools. They are seen as leading citizens, and by all popular standards they are. Some become judges, and some go into politics. But they are the corporate strong-arms who hide behind the golden shield of power, rake in huge fees, and disappear into the next case in which they ply their skills in defeating the people's justice. We have already met de Tocqueville. He warned against the sort of lawyers I describe here: "It will always be easy for a king to make lawyers the most useful instruments of his power," he observed.

So Coulter and O'Reilly and the rest demonize the people's lawyers. So what? How does such demonization affect the ordinary citizen, who will one day be a juror? First, let me tell you a true story.

A young woman, Mary, lives in a small apartment with her husband and three small children. She suffered from a sinus obstruction and went to one of those specialists, who said she needed an operation. A routine operation, he assured her. When Mary lay anesthetized on the operating table the doctor's probe punctured her brain like an invading bullet. Utter negligence, as any candid expert would testify.

After the operation Mary, once a fine skier and mountain climber, cannot walk. She must be helped in and out of her bed. Someone must feed her and assist her with her bowels. She recognizes her husband and her children, but she cannot speak to them. She has been hurled into the bottom pits of hell and her family seeks justice. But to get justice she must go into court before one of those judges, and she will face jurors who have been taught that the trial process is a vicious charade, and she will be represented by a lawyer— an honest, competent lawyer—who will be distrusted by the jurors.

The insurance company who insures the doctor will make an

offer, yes, of course. Mary desperately needs the money for her care. The offer will *not* provide for her needs for the rest of her life. It will *not* pay anything for her suffering, for her endless torture. And out of her settlement her lawyer must be paid for his services. Without him the company would have made no offer at all. But the company has held out actual money. She can have it. All Mary has to do is give up her suit, take pennies instead of dollars, and release the doctor and the insurance company.

On the other hand she has the right as an American citizen to go into court and face the judge and the jury and the opposing insurance company lawyer, a very smooth, skilled, smiling, nice man whose job is to defeat her claim. Neither Mary nor her lawyer have the money to hire doctors as expert at testifying as those hired by the insurance company, doctors from, say, Harvard Medical School and the like, doctors who will take the stand and convince the jury that Mary's injury was an acceptable risk of her operation.

The insurance company has put money on the table. If her husband takes it for her—he is her guardian—what will the family do in the years to come when the money is gone and she still needs care? But what if she goes into court and the jury finds for the doctor and she gets nothing? *Nothing.* They say the insurance company's lawyer has won many cases worse than hers.

On the courthouse steps Mary's husband takes the money. He is embarrassed to take it. He feels defeated and like a coward. He thinks he should have fought for his wife. But he could not gamble the loss of the little money the company offered. Her present needs. The present bills. The creditors. His taking the settlement surprised no one. Everyone always knew he would. He had no choice. Over the years to come, the settlement was about as helpful as a Hallmark sympathy card, but it was something in hand. And the nightmare of a trial was over. Behind the husband's decision, in part, was his knowledge that the jurors who would try the case had been conditioned to distrust trial lawyers. The deck was stacked.

Thousands of these stories occur every year, honest cases involving death and various horrors of injury and pain due to the negligence of others, people who through the fault of corporations have suffered and will suffer and are entitled to justice. Simple, plain justice. Nothing fancy. Just dollars to represent all the justice that the system allows when a citizen is injured by the carelessness or intentional acts of another. Who can argue with such a noble ideal?

Most people are insured these days. The careless drivers, the negligent doctors, the slipshod, shortcutting manufacturers, the polluting companies, all are insured so that the majority of personal injury cases are, in actuality, suits against the insurance companies who insure the person or corporation being sued.

When Mary or any other injured person comes into court, on the face of the suit papers it appears to be a suit against the person causing the injury—the doctor, in Mary's case. But it's the insurance company that will pay the final judgment in the case. It's the insurance company that will hire and pay for the defending lawyer and pay the defense costs, and it's the insurance company that will decide how much to pay in settlement to Mary if, indeed, a settlement is offered at all. It will decide when to appeal, and it will pay for the lawyers who conduct the appeal and their costs. And if the appellate court reverses a judgment in favor of Mary and sends the case back for a new trial, the insurance company will again hire and pay the lawyers for the new trial. Many such cases go on for years. But the insurance companies live forever, and their money never runs out. Mary needs the money *now*.

Further, a judicial fraud is being committed here. It is this: No one is permitted to tell the jury the truth, that yes, an insurance company is behind the suit and will pay all the costs of the suit as well as the final judgment. All the jury will ever see, as in Mary's case, is the doctor whom she is suing. He sits there appearing afraid, a nice doctor, or in other cases the drunk, now sober, sitting there in his Sunday suit. It looks as if any money the jury awards will come out of the pocket of the person sued. And if Mary's lawyer were to intimate—*even intimate*—that an insurance company is behind the case, the judge will call a mistrial and assess costs against Mary.

This rule of law creates a judicial fraud. The courts lie to juries by withholding the truth because the law says they must withhold the truth. So what we have here is an injured person, usually persons of ordinary means, sometimes the rich but more often the poor, suing the most powerful financial entities in the history of the world—insurance companies—and some jurors may suspect it, but none know it. And such suits require trial lawyers, lawyers for the wrongly killed, the wrongly injured citizens. And they are hated before they walk into the courthouse doors.

The campaign against trial lawyers, launched years ago by the corporate King through the King's media, has finally turned Americans solidly against *their own interests*. What I mean is the people have been taught that trial lawyers—the only profession that fights for people's legal rights—are evil, greedy bastards; and that juries, who, by the way, are also *just people*, are ignorant fools who are taken in by trial lawyers like a carny takes a mark.

So when Betty Abernathy is called for jury service, even before she takes her chair in the jury box she knows that the other eleven people are not to be trusted, that the so-called plaintiff, the injured person, is probably just feigning injury and will lie, and that the greedy lawyer representing her is there to get rich off of that poor defendant sitting over there next to that kind-looking, smiling person, the defense lawyer, who represents him.

In a money society, justice, of course, is defined in money damages—money to compensate for the loss of a husband for his dead wife, money for the pain and misery of the injured, money for the people's loss of life caused by the intentional or negligent acts of others. You can't give back a dead wife or replace a once pain-free, healthy body. All the justice the law can give is money for the loss. Well, you can see where I'm going with this: if the people do not get justice, which is money, then the corporate King's insurance companies can keep the money and buy more banks with their profit, banks that will take even more of the people's money.

It is so absurdly simple.

Mark this place in this book: There will soon come a time when there are no true, skilled warriors for the people—none of those great trial lawyers of the past. The people's once proud warriors will be reduced to taking petty cases, fender benders, rear-enders, those "nuisance cases," the insurance companies call them, because in the big damage cases like Mary's, the injured persons dare not go to trial for, among other reasons, there will be no skilled trial lawyers to fight for them.

Trial lawyers get their training in the courtroom in actual cases. There will be few who ever go to trial to learn the art. The courts are so crowded and dysfunctional that it sometimes takes years to get even the first hearing. In the meantime lawyers do what they can do best—threaten how much they'll take the insurance company for if it doesn't pay up, and the insurance-company-claims persons laugh and run the case through their computers and offer half what the computer says the case is worth. Along the way somewhere the case gets settled—usually for peanuts, often for a sum less than what it would have cost the insurance company to defend it. If some brave lawyer takes an equally brave client to the jury the odds of collecting a nickel are worse than in Las Vegas, and the immediate, the pressing needs of the injured persons are often overwhelming, even critical to life.

Today, the seriously injured mostly settle their cases. Most must—the man paralyzed for life from faulty equipment, the widows and children with husbands and fathers rotting in the grave from the negligence of drivers, the children hobbling on twisted legs from prenatal dangerous drugs furnished their mothers before adequate testing by the drug companies—all most often go without full justice because the people have been taught to despise their warriors and to distrust juries, always forgetting that *they*, the people, *are* the juries. And when the injured person is you, well, I am sorry. Can you find a lawyer who can overcome decades of this demonization of trial lawyers and juries and the justice system, which, according to the propaganda, is running crazy like a locoed horse?

The fraud and the brainwashing do not stop there.

The insurance companies' latest and cruelest war has been to attack the right of the injured to collect "noneconomic damages." Let me explain: If, for example, you are a housewife not working outside the home and you suffer a slow death from the negligence of a doctor, your unrelenting pain during your last years is a noneconomic damage. If, for further easy example, a doctor cuts off the wrong leg but you can still work, the loss of the good leg, which leaves you a crippled globule of flesh, is a noneconomic damage. Indeed, such damages are often the most severe that the victim suffers. A person who suffers chronic pain, that is, never-ending pain, has been provided a first-class ticket to hell from which there is no return. Pain and suffering are noneconomic damages, as are disfigurement and the loss of the enjoyment of one's life.

If noneconomic damages are barred, a sixty-year-old woman who loses her retired husband from the negligence of a doctor will receive nothing for the loss of her husband since he was not earning money at the time of his death. He was retired. The insurance companies want to totally eliminate or limit (cap) an injured person's recovery for any noneconomic damages because there is where the real damages lie.

Let's say the defendant sitting over there in the courtroom killed my child. But the child earned nothing. Contributed nothing. The jury would not be permitted to return a verdict for anything except the amount of the cap (the amount limited by law). Thus, if the cap is $250,000, which many caps are, that is the most the parents can recover no matter how negligent the defendant, and most cases cost more than the cap to bring to trial so many just cases never see the lights of a courtroom. And the money saved swells the insurance company's profit.

The argument for capping damages is that because the insurance company's profits go down the cost of insurance goes up until doctors, for example, cannot afford insurance and may leave the practice. After a massive campaign in Texas, financed by big Texas money, voters were persuaded to eviscerate their own constitution so that noneconomic damages were capped—those greedy lawyers, you know, and those untrustworthy juries. After the insurance companies' victory, one of the nation's largest medical malpractice insurance company executives told Texas insurance regulators, I suspect with sinister glee, that the newly imposed caps would save the company little, if any, money—maybe 1 percent—while the company at the same time was requesting a 19 percent rate increase from the Texas Department of Insurance. So who lost? Once more the people lost and the profit was pocketed by the insurance companies.

"Tort *reform*" advocates use the words "tort *reform*" as part of their *oppospeak.* These are words that mean exactly the opposite of what the words say. Tort reformers want to cap noneconomic damages as well as to shackle the justice system in other ominous ways. At least they're candid about this: "Insurers never promised that tort reform would achieve specific savings [to the policy holder]," said the American Insurance Association. "We wouldn't tell you or anyone that the reason to pass tort reform would be to reduce insurance rates," said Sherman Joyce, president of the American Tort Reform Association. "Many tort reform advocates do not contend that restricting litigation will lower insurance rates, and I've never said that in 30 years," claimed Victor Schwartz, general counsel to the American Tort Reform Association. The issue always remains the same: *The insurance companies insure one thing: their profit.*

Remember: Under tort reform the citizen's damages are capped. The insurance company's profits are not. And who do we remember made "tort reform" one of the priorities of his campaign for the presidency, a gift to his business buddies and campaign contributors? Do we remember George II?

One of the greatest frauds ever foisted on the American public at large has been the so-called medical malpractice crisis. Here the insurance companies have done a masterful job of terrorizing the already frightened American public. Millions of Americans do not have medical insurance. Millions more struggle each month to pay their health insurance premiums. The national insurance gouge has been going on for a long time. State by state people have been told that the cost that doctors pay for medical malpractice insurance is so high that this crisis is "driving doctors out of our state and threatens your access to care. You won't have a doctor there to deliver your babies. Old people will be ill without doctors."

In my state of Wyoming, the insurance-driven propaganda even claimed that "economic development efforts" in Wyoming, sorely sought, depended on capping people's jury awards. "Attracting new business and keeping our young people in the state depend on it. Making sure your doctor is there when you and your family need care depends on it." In other words, if you don't limit the amount *you*, the ordinary citizen, can recover when *you* are injured by your doctors' negligence, or your loved ones are killed by their wrongs, well, your doctors will leave, your state will remain economically stagnant, and your kids will have to find employment elsewhere. Again, those greedy lawyers, you know. Those runaway juries. Those crazy verdicts that are destroying the medical profession.

This truckload of lies was dumped on the people in Wyoming as well as in dozens of other states. Full-color brochures were sent to the homes of every Wyoming household announcing these lies. The conspiracy hit the television, radios, and newspapers in the state, and shamelessly blasted away with that set of utter falsehoods. The people began to panic—we have to change our State Constitution. We have to protect our doctors from the lawyers or we won't have doctors when we need them.

Caps? Yes, cap noneconomic damages. Even *The Wall Street Journal* pointed out that the losers from such legislation would be, ". . . most notably retired people, children and housewives." Here is the *Journal* quoting Kim Gandy, NOW (National Organization for Women) president: "'When you put a cap on noneconomic damages, quite literally women's lives are valued lower.'"

The doctors' first ethical interests must always be the well-being of their patients. But they have their personal agenda. They not only wanted lower insurance rates, which they mistakenly thought they'd get if caps were imposed on damages their patients suffered from the doctors' own malpractice, *they wanted total immunity* from lawsuits. They championed the insurance sham. *The New York Times,* in its sometimes opaque editorial page, said, "The recent spikes in insurance premiums . . . says more about the insurance business than it does about the judicial system."

Some states that have considered laws capping damages in doctors' malpractice suits have held such laws unconstitutional. They violate victims' protected rights to a jury trial, equal protection, and due process. But this hasn't stopped the insurance companies and their conspirators. Through their influence over the legislatures of the various states, including Wyoming, they sought to *change the states' constitutions.* If caps are unconstitutional, well, so what? Change the Constitution. Frighten the people enough, and they'll throw in their rights. Anger them enough at the scapegoat, the trial lawyers, and they'll chuck their constitutional protections once and for all.

The fraud has done its dirty work in many states. In Colorado, for example, I had to turn down a case for a woman who was blinded by the gross negligence of a doctor simply because the woman didn't work and had no economic losses—a housewife. Under Colorado law, which had capped damages, her life was substantially worthless. She could recover $250,000, the cap, but the cost of bringing a malpractice suit against the doctor would exceed $250,000 after paying experts and the other expenses associated with discovery and preparation. Even if we won, nothing would be left for her. And we would be in litigation at least for two years or more. The insurance company no doubt laughed as it pocketed the profit taken from a blind woman, and perhaps the doctor went blithely on committing other horrors.

In Wyoming the truth was clear. Our state was not losing doctors as the doctors endlessly cried. Figures from the Wyoming Board of Medicine showed that Wyoming had a *net gain* of doctors year after year. Doctors, like many others, love Wyoming's great outdoors, its expanse of untouched landscape, and, of course, that Wyoming has no state income tax. But the doctors' false campaign backed by big business and the insurance industry had to be exposed. Remember, the people have no voice, no people's radio stations, televisions, or newspapers. I took it as a personal crusade to become "the voice." I spoke in person to the townsfolk of nearly every town in our state. I was on the road for several months.

Night after night I spoke to the people at town meetings that I called to expose the lies of this conspiracy. I asked, "Do you think, as the doctors claim, that if you give up your rights to full justice that industry will come to your town?" Given three seconds of thought, the people laughed. "Do you think, as the doctors claim, that if you give up your rights to full justice your kids will stay in Wyoming?" Again the people laughed. The premise was silly. Then I asked, "If you give up your rights to full justice, as the doctors ask, do you think your doctor will lower his fees to you?" That brought on the biggest laugh of all.

I asked my audiences how much they were making a year. Some were not ashamed to admit they were working, both Mom and Dad, and often making less than the poverty level (as are nearly 36 million other Americans). Yet they were paying as much as seven hundred or eight hundred dollars a month for insurance. Often more. I then asked a simple question: "Who do you think pays more for insurance, per dollar earned—you for your health insurance or your doctor for his malpractice insurance?" Again the laughter.

The U.S. General Accounting Office investigated the medical profession's propaganda and found that the supposed crisis of malpractice insurance alleged by the American Medical Association, the insurance industry, and some politicians was unsubstantiated and that the American public was misled. As in any argument, the issues became complicated, and the howling high. But in the end, the truth, of course, was that insurance company *profits* were what the so-called crisis was about. Truth again: According to Weiss Ratings, Inc., an industry-rating organization, HMOs were nearly doubling their profits, and health and life insurers had posted their best profits in a decade.

One study in my own state showed that three officers of one of the principal insurers of Wyoming doctors received more in salaries in one year ($4.78 million) than the same company took in as premiums paid by Wyoming physicians ($3.83 million). And in Wyoming, as well as many other states, the insurance commissioner can do little more than cast a pleasant smile at the insurance companies as the companies gouge our people, including the doctors. Our people-loving legislature had earlier taken away the power of the insurance commissioner to effectively regulate the carriers who were skinning, and continue to skin, the doctors and the citizens alive.

Death by medicine is now the leading killer and cause of injury in this country, ahead of the prior champion killers, heart attacks and cancer. The latest composite figures show death by improper medical conduct of hospitals and doctors ("iatrogenic deaths" they are called) at 783,936 dead each year, while deaths from heart disease is 699,697 and deaths from cancer, 553,251. The authors of this study report that "as few as 5 percent and only up to 20 percent of iatrogenic acts are ever reported." This implies that if medical errors were completely and accurately reported, we would have a much higher annual iatrogenic death rate. Dr. Leape, one of the first investigators of this issue, said his figure of 180,000 medical errors annually was equivalent to three jumbo jet crashes every two days. That was in 1994. The latest report shows that six jumbo jets are falling out of the sky each and every day, killing all aboard.

This same report says the number of unnecessary medical and surgical procedures performed annually is 7.5 million. The number of people exposed to unnecessary hospitalization annually is 8.9 million. Little wonder the medical profession seeks protection.

But what does the profession do about this critical crisis in health care? It wants protection from its own wrongs more than it wants to reform itself. No doctor, no lawyer, and no one else wants to be sued. But wouldn't we think that given the gravity of this crisis, which is obviously *a medical malpractice crisis,* the medical profession would be taking powerful steps to protect the people from negligent doctors and hospitals?

Here is a set of stunning facts published in *The New York Times:* "From 1990 to 2002, just 5 percent of doctors were involved in 54 percent of the payouts—including jury awards and out-of-court settlements—according to the National Practitioner Data Bank of the Department of Health and Human Services. . . . Of the 35,000 doctors with two or more payouts during that period, only 8 percent were disciplined by state medical boards. Among the 2,774 doctors who had made payments in five or more cases, only 463—one out of six—had been disciplined."

This means that the incompetent doctor, that drunk surgeon, that careless, spaced-out doctor, that poorly trained hacksaw, is still out there injuring patients day after day, year after year, and the medical profession does little to protect the people from this scourge.

So, Doctors, is the best way to take care of your patients to prevent the ones you've injured or killed from recovering a just amount in damages for your negligence? Cap damages instead of capping your own negligence? Take away your patients' rights rather than becoming better, more careful doctors and weeding out the really bad ones from your profession?

In the end, in Wyoming, we defeated the attempt of the doctors, the insurance companies, and their moneyed supporters to castrate our Constitution. Wyoming voters voted down the proposed constitutional amendment to allow the capping of damages in medical malpractice cases. For other states to save their own constitutions from the surgeon's knife, trial lawyers themselves must take their message, *face-to-face,* to the people. Trial lawyers should be proud of what they do and have done in making America safer and in bringing justice to ordinary citizens. No longer can trial lawyers silently cower as they're slandered on the corporate King's media. Since the people and the people's warriors have no public voice, trial lawyers must make a grassroots stand—*in person*—where the truth will finally win out and the rights of the people will be preserved from the endless profit raids of the corporate King.

I think of a wonderfully intelligent lawyer, Catherine Crier, who, like our other blondes, makes her living as a television host. I've been with her on her shows several times. This woman sees it right on nearly every issue, from corporate crime, the influence of corporate money on our government, to her despisement of the death penalty—she could be a saint, a pretty one, arising from the depths and gloom of the profession. But even she, dependent as she is on the corporate media for her daily bread—at least for her daily presence on TV—has been co-opted. In short, this woman is so incredibly right and so tragically wrong.

She advocates that we adopt the English system, where there are no contingency fees, and the loser pays the costs. This would end our justice system for the average citizen, what little remains of it.

Let me show you: Suppose you are a single mother who is habitually, daily, sexually harassed at work. No matter where you go in the company compound there are the pinches, the filthy comments, the offensive laughter, the vulgar jokes, the verbal rapes. You have complained, and the complaints have only exacerbated the misery. Finally you're afraid to walk in the company door in the morning. Your life there has become unbearable. But you must continue to endure it to keep your job and to support your family.

You are in a state where the loser pays, as is suggested by Ms. Crier. And, as she further suggests, where there are no contingency fees. (If you are under a contingency-fee arrangement with your lawyer, you pay him and the costs of your case *only* if he wins for you. Otherwise your lawyer gets nothing. Don't we wish we could put our doctors on a contingency fee—they get paid only if we get well?)

First off, you can't hire a lawyer and pay him his hourly rate because the cost in fees and expenses in any important case would amount to hundreds of thousands of dollars and the ordinary person can't find that kind of money to hire a lawyer. That luxury is reserved for the insurance companies. So you'd never get to court in the first place. But even if you could put a second mortgage on the house and get the money to cover the lawyer's fees and the costs of the case, do you dare take the gamble? You'll be faced with company lawyers, who have all the money they need to fight your case and who are the best lawyers money can buy. Your own lawyer is one of modest means and ability. Besides, your lawyer, even the finest, is a trial lawyer, one of those whom juries don't trust.

You ask your lawyer what your chances of winning are. He can't say, of course. And if you lose, you pay the costs the company spent in defending your lawsuit—hundreds of thousands, maybe even millions. You will lose your house, your job, and you and your children will be applying for welfare and become one of those pests of society that Ann Coulter loves to hate.

Suppose you are an ordinary working person. You've been injured by a medicine or a doctor's negligence, a trucking company's negligent driver, or a libel by a local newspaper. Perhaps you've been run over by a drunk driver. Any of these injuries severely affects your life—perhaps has destroyed it. But when you take on one of these big-money miscreants—even if you have a solid case—still, if your lawyer fails, if the jury sees it differently than you, if the appeals court populated by the King's men—former insurance company lawyers—reverses the jury's verdict, if any of these legal misfortunes occurs, you lose not only your case but your life's savings and whatever you had to borrow to finance your case.

This is that wonderful English system that Catherine Crier says was instituted in that country "with great success." No ordinary person in his right mind would ever enter the courts under such a system. No citizen can throw it all down on the crap table of justice for such a small chance at winning.

Ms. Crier says, "Think of all those ridiculous suits that may seem entertaining but are actually clogging the courts and costing money to pursue. If plaintiffs had to pay the other side's fees upon losing, a large number of these cases would disappear—and rightfully so—from the docket."

Well, Catherine, in your business you see mostly the "entertaining cases," a few aberrations of the justice system, the "ridiculous suits" that come to your attention as a host on TV. But we do not see on your show, or any TV show, representative cases of those countless lawsuits brought each year by truly injured citizens, cases that don't grab the attention of the TV producers because there's nothing extravagantly exciting about a run-of-the-mill dead husband in a car accident or one of thousands of other injured, mutilated, or killed citizens. And if your English system were in force, no injured person would have the first chance at justice.

But let's get real. I cannot take a case for someone who claims to be injured unless he *is* injured and a solid case exists against the wrongdoer, one I can honestly prove in a court of law. Even if I were one of those lawyer-crooks Ms. Crier complains of, I could not take on a case that had no merit, spend thousands of my own dollars to get it to trial, sometimes hundreds of thousands paid to experts for their time and testimony, and compensate myself for my own work of months, sometimes years. It is hard enough to win the most meritorious of cases. I cannot win a frivolous case. Every trial lawyer knows that. Although a few fools out there might bring an occasional frivolous lawsuit, the contingency-fee system eliminates nearly all of them. And judges throw them out without a jury trial under their authority to do so—a method of eliminating such suits called "summary judgment." And, Catherine, had you labored very long as a lawyer for the people, you would know that.

What kinds of suits are "clogging the courts" as Ms. Crier claims? Take, for instance, the federal courts where suits between citizens of different states are filed: The Administrative Office of the U.S. Courts finds that only 18 percent of the civil cases filed in the nation were for personal injury, and the numbers of such cases filed each year have been steadily declining, as they have in the state courts as well.

And if the courts are clogged, and too many judges have calendars that are months, even years in arrears, what clogs them? We've seen that nearly all personal injury suits are defended by insurance companies, and that the courts, in short, have simply become clearing houses for the insurance industry, a service paid for at the expense of taxpayers. From over fifty-four years of experience in our courts, I can tell you that insurance companies do not pay a just sum until they are forced to.

Almost without exception companies will not settle an obviously just claim unless they are hauled into court. Only after the injured person has endured months, maybe years, of waiting and his attorney has spent thousands of dollars and more thousands of hours to get the case finally ready for trial can the insurance company be brought to the settlement table. If there is any clogging of the courts it is clearly caused by the insurance companies, which use the courts to avoid payment of honest claims to truly injured people, and also by insurance company defense lawyers, many of whom suck out the last drop of fee-honey from a case before agreeing to settle a just claim.

When Ms. Crier talks about "all those ridiculous lawsuits that clog the courts," she fails to tell you that most of such suits are actually disputes brought by corporations fighting each other over money. Speaking of "ridiculous lawsuits," check out just a few of thousands:

GlaxoSmithKline

Drug manufacturer GlaxoSmithKline sued two generic drug companies after learning that they were seeking approval from the U.S. Food and Drug Administration to manufacture and market a less expensive, generic version of SmithKline's antidepressant drug Paxil. Despite the fact that after a certain period of time all companies have a legal right to create generic versions of prescription drugs and make them available to more consumers who could not afford the brand name, the litigation allowed SmithKline to delay a generic version of Paxil from entering the market by almost three years.

Enterprise Rent-A-Car

In 1998 Enterprise Rent-A-Car filed lawsuits against Rent-A-Wreck of America (a tiny rental company) and Hertz Corporation and threatened to file lawsuits against several other car-rental companies who use the phrase "pick you up," claiming that "We'll pick you up" is Enterprise's slogan. While those suits were pending, Advantage Rent-A-Car countersued Enterprise, claiming that Advantage had used the phrase "we'll pick you up" long before Enterprise did. Enterprise argued in its lawsuits that the phrase means more than "we'll give you a ride"; it means "we'll pick up your spirits"; Competitors said that there was no other way to say "we'll give you a ride." Enterprise attorney Rudolph Telscher said that "we'll decide in the courtroom who is correct here."

Victoria's Secret

Victoria's Secret went all the way to the Supreme Court in an effort to sue Victor's Little Secret, a gift and novelty shop selling sex toys and "Everything for Romantic Encounters" from a strip-mall storefront in Elizabethtown, Kentucky. Victor Moseley, who opened the shop in 1998, named it Victor's Secret after himself, but changed the name to Victor's Little Secret a few months later in a futile effort to satisfy a sharply worded complaint from Victoria's Secret. In 2003 Victor was the ninety-fifth most popular baby name for a boy and Victoria was the twenty-second most popular baby name for a girl.

Mattel, Inc.

Toy maker Mattel spent five years litigating until the Supreme Court turned down their request to reopen a trademark suit against MCA Records Inc. Mattel had claimed that the pre-teen girls who buy Barbie dolls were duped into thinking the song "Barbie Girl" was an advertisement for the doll or part of Mattel's official line of Barbie products. The song, by a Danish group called Aqua, includes the lyrics, "I'm a blonde bimbo in a fantasy world/Dress me up, make it tight, I'm your dolly."

Mattel, Inc., the maker of Barbie, is waging an aggressive trademark war against unsanctioned use of the Barbie name, at-tacking the founders of the "Barbie Makes a Wish" weekend that raises money for critically ill children; artist Paul Hansen was sued for $1.2 billion for making $2,000 from the sale of his Exorcist Barbie, Tonya Harding Barbie, and Drag Queen Barbie. . . . Mattel made almost $4 billion in annual sales in 1996, but has filed copyright and trademark infringement suits against these toy enthusiasts.

Kellogg Co.

In 1998 Kellogg Co. sued Exxon Corp., claiming that Exxon's "whimsical tiger" logo, which had been in existence for over thirty years, would confuse consumers who associate the tiger logo with Kellogg's Frosted Flakes mascot, "Tony the Tiger." A federal judge in Memphis threw out the suit, saying that Kel-logg was "grossly remiss in failing to assert its rights" sooner. This didn't stop Kellogg, which further clogged the courts by appealing the verdict to the Sixth U.S. Circuit Court of Ap-peals in Cincinnati. In its brief Kellogg argued that the Exxon tiger, like Tony, "walks or runs on his two hind legs and acts in a friendly manner."

Do you want to read some more? Well take a look at these:

Wal-Mart Stores, Inc.

Wal-Mart Stores, Inc., the world's largest retailer, is going to court to prevent wares bought at rival Kmart Corp. from going for a spin at the register. Bentonville-based Wal-Mart has a patent on its carousel, which holds its blue plastic shopping bags. The cashier drops items into bags as merchandise is rung up, and spins the rack to make the effort easier for both the cashier and the customer lifting out the bags. Wal-Mart is suing in a Delaware court to keep the Kmart based in Troy, Michigan, from using a similar device.

Hormel Foods

Hormel Foods, the maker of the luncheon meat SPAM, sued Jim Henson Productions to stop the creator of the Muppets from calling a character in a new movie SPA'AM, claiming that the character was unclean and grotesque and would call into question the purity and quality of its meats. A federal court rejected Hormel's claims, and Hormel also lost on appeal.

Walt Disney Company

Walt Disney Company used a lawsuit to force a public apology from the Academy of Motion Picture Arts and Sciences for an "unflattering" representation of Snow White in the opening sequence of the 1989 Academy Awards ceremony.

And I cannot overlook Fox's suit against Al Franken: *FOX News* sued the man for using the term "Fair and Balanced" on his book cover, which called Bill O'Reilly and others liars. Calling the matter "wholly without merit, both factually and legally," the judge, Denny Chin of United States District Court, threw out Fox's case. Judge Chin said the case was an easy one, and chided Fox for bringing its complaint to court. The judge said, "Of course, it is ironic that a media company that should be fighting for the First Amendment is trying to undermine it."

Consider also that Caterpillar sued the Walt Disney Company for portraying bulldozers in a bad light. Caterpillar tried unsuccessfully to block the release of *George of the Jungle 2*, claiming that the film gave the company a bad name because its machines are used to attack the jungle.

Let me return to one of Catherine Crier's "ridiculous suits" that are actually clogging the courts, the most famous one, the McDonald's hot coffee burn case.

Nearly everyone, at one time or another, has heard of this case. It purportedly proves how trial lawyers are greedy charlatans and juries mindless fops. The corporate media so propagandized the case that Americans were led to believe that a woman put a cup of hot coffee between her legs, got burned by it, and collected millions. This, corporate America tells us, is why we cannot trust trial lawyers or juries.

Talk-show hosts frothed endlessly over this supposed example of lawsuit abuse and they knowingly or ignorantly misled their flocks while screaming rhetorical questions like Rush Limbaugh's "Folks, isn't hot coffee supposed to be hot?" or "The lady doesn't know better than to put it between her legs?" Things like that. I was recently in New Zealand. A local there and I were comparing our respective judicial systems. He said, "Under our system no woman could get millions for spilled coffee between her legs." Half-truths travel fast. Finally here's the whole truth on the McDonald's coffee-spilling case. The lawyer who represented the injured woman, Stella Liebeck of Albuquerque, New Mexico, was a student of mine. His name is Reed Morgan, and he attended my not-for-profit Trial Lawyer's College. He is a fine lawyer and a decent man.

McDonald's coffee was not just hot, it was scalding hot—capable of almost instantaneously destroying skin, flesh, and muscle. Stella was in the passenger seat of her grandson's car. She was seventy-nine at the time. She ordered coffee that was served in a styrofoam cup, one designed to maintain the heat of the coffee. She was served at the drive-through window of a local McDonald's.

Her grandson pulled his car forward and stopped momentarily so that Stella could add cream and sugar to her coffee. The media concocted most of the salient facts and then repeated them ad infinitum—that Stella was driving the car or that the vehicle was in motion when she spilled the coffee. Neither is true. Stella placed the cup between her knees in her attempt to remove the plastic lid from the cup. As she removed the lid, the entire contents of the cup spilled into her lap. The sweatpants Stella was wearing absorbed the coffee and held the scalding heat firmly next to her skin.

A vascular surgeon determined that Stella suffered full-thickness burns—third-degree burns—over 6 percent of her body, including her inner thighs, the region surrounding the urogenital and anal openings, her buttocks, groin, and let's just say it, the lips of her vagina. She was hospitalized for eight days, during which time she underwent skin grafting. Perhaps Rush would be more understanding had he suffered third-degree burns on the head of his penis.

Stella, who underwent a series of horribly painful debridement treatments, sought to settle her claim for $20,000. But McDonald's said, "Take it to court, Honey. Yes, isn't coffee supposed to be hot?"

During the discovery procedures in the case McDonald's was forced to produce documents showing more than seven hundred claims made by people burned by its coffee between 1982 and 1992. Some claims were as serious as Stella's. Such a history established that the temperature of the coffee was a hazard to which McDonald's was intentionally subjecting its customers.

Yes, coffee is supposed to be hot, Rush. But McDonald's kept its coffee between 180 and 190 degrees Fahrenheit. Coffee served at home is generally at 135 to 140 degrees. McDonald's quality-assurance manager testified that the company requires its stores to keep its coffee at 185 degrees, plus or minus five degrees. He also testified that a severe burn occurs with any food substance served at 140 degrees or above, and that McDonald's coffee at 180 to 190 degrees would burn the mouth and throat. But he testified that McDonald's had no intention of reducing the "holding temperature" of its coffee.

Stella's expert, a scholar in thermodynamics as applied to human skin, testified that liquids at 180 degrees will cause a full-thickness burn (third-degree) to human skin in two to seven seconds—something few of us knew, but McDonald's knew, seven hundred times over.

The jury awarded Stella $200,000. This amount was reduced to $160,000 by the judge because the jury found Stella was 20 percent at fault in the spill. The jury also awarded Stella $2.7 million in punitive damages, which equaled about *two days of McDonald's coffee sales.* The trial court reduced the punitive award to $480,000—we never heard that. We only heard that she recovered millions. The judge called McDonald's conduct reckless, callous, and willful. We never heard that either.

Later Stella settled the case with McDonald's and was required to sign one of those confidential settlement agreements that keeps the exact amount of the settlement secret. We never heard this. But one thing we can pretty well be assured of: the amount of the settlement was many thousands less than what the judge finally awarded after reducing the jury's verdict. How about something less than $480,000 in exchange for third-degree burns on the *male* sex organ with consequent debridement? How about the jury trying to tell McDonald's by their verdict, "Please stop this. Please be careful of unsuspecting people who will get burned. Give Stella two days' coffee sales. Maybe that will cause you to care."

I doubt that the sum McDonald's likely ended up paying in the case changed anything. Probably the jury's attempt to make McDonald's coffee safe for people in the future went for naught. I know of no investigation that has been made to determine if McDonald's changed its ways. But one thing we do know. The case gave the corporate King a story it could deform and distort and use to further turn the people against trial lawyers and jurors.

Today the hatred of trial lawyers seems endemic in our culture. I think of Honest Abe, who was a lawyer, as were Franklin Delano Roosevelt, Mahatma Gandhi, and most of our Founding Fathers. The profession has changed little. But the voice of the corporate

King has sucked the truth from our brains and replaced the vacancy with hatred.

After over half a century in the profession, I have memories. I have watched once proud warriors wither and shrink in the endless heat, not because they lack bravery or a devotion to their clients' causes, but because they have finally become exhausted in a deluding, broken system controlled by the corporate King.

Some have given up because they can no longer honestly tell their clients that there is "justice for all" in this country, because they've had to admit that the system they are sworn to uphold has, in too many ways, become a mockery, that the cost of justice is beyond the reach of most, that the judges, many the minions of the moneyed interests, will take from their clients what the juries have given, that the legislatures of many states have wrested from the people their right to full justice by interfering with what juries can award, and because lawyers have at last had to admit to themselves, and finally their clients, that justice for all in America has become mostly a myth.

I grew up in small Wyoming towns and have practiced from these small Wyoming towns all of my life. Although I eventually fell into a national practice with my first well-publicized case, the Karen Silkwood case, nevertheless, I have always seen myself as a country lawyer. People say, "Come on, Spence, that country lawyer stuff tells us we ought to watch our pockets." But we are what we are—you know the old saw, "You can take the boy out of the country, but you can't take the country out of the boy."

I have met some bad trial lawyers in my day. But I know infinitely more good ones, decent men and women who care deeply about people. I'm not here as an apologist for the profession, for there's much about which to apologize. But I have memories.

I remember when there were only the belly-buster seat belts in cars, and people were ripped in two by those death traps that served mostly to help the medics find the dead bodies after a head-on. I remember those cases with victims still strapped into their seats, some with their backbones severed and their guts hanging out. And I remember the bodies strewn over the landscape in automobile wrecks before the advent of any seat belts. The cases trial lawyers championed for the dead and injured demanded that the automobile manufacturers provide safe seat belts. And they finally did, and after that, air bags that have saved untold thousands of lives.

I have memories. I remember when we used to find heads cut off bouncing around on the pavement after they were severed in a collision by unsafe windshield glass. The automobile companies knew of the hazard all along. But it was cheaper to defend suits brought by some small-time lawyer for the dead and pay the occasional verdict than to correct the danger by installing shatterproof glass in their cars. And the companies, and the insurance corporations who insured them, hired those defense attorneys from the big firms, those sweet-talkers with the kind eyes who could hire the eloquent experts they needed to convince unsuspecting juries that their products were safe. But finally, the cost of defending the cases exceeded the cost to the companies to change over to safety glass.

I have memories. Many thousands of cases came to the forefront in America, say, of SUVs that were roll-over traps, tires that were defective, steering wheels that failed to collapse in collisions, door handles that gouged and killed the occupants in wrecks, and endless other unsafe designs—to mention only the automotive industry. And because of lawsuits brought by trial lawyers for the injured and dead, these hazards were finally eliminated and automobiles made safer.

I have memories. I remember a certain car whose doors jammed shut and whose gas tank often exploded when the car was involved in a frontal collision. The car was aflame in the case I took for an orphaned child. After the crash the mother couldn't get the door open and knew she and her husband were going to burn to death. Somehow she broke a window and threw her child to safety. He survived but was severely burned. The company's own crash tests showed this tragedy could be expected. Nevertheless the company made no changes in the design of its car. Worse, it knew there were many other horrors out there like this one—cases that would be brought if my case ever saw the light of day. The company paid a large sum for the child's injuries and for the death of his parents, but the company, as usual, demanded a secret settlement that his guardian was obligated to sign because the boy needed immediate care and couldn't afford years more of litigation. But eventually the dangerous design was abandoned by that car company.

I have memories. I remember a time when Ford conducted actual studies to determine which was more profitable—to continue manufacturing a vehicle with an unsafe gas tank and to pay for the deaths and injuries caused by it, or to correct the defect at a cost of a few dollars per unit. As usual it was a question of profit versus human lives. Ford's studies showed that it was more profitable to keep on manufacturing the dangerous fuel tank and to pay for any of the dead or injured whose few cases might get through the legal system than it was to make the product safe. The people died. So? But the exposure of the company by Ralph Nader, a lawyer, brought this nightmare to a close.

I have memories. I remember how trial lawyers for people got just verdicts for dead children who choked on a dangerous toy— one the manufacturer knew was dangerous—and the toy was eventually taken from the market. I remember how millions were awarded against pharmaceutical companies for feeding pregnant mothers a drug that deformed their babies—babies born without legs or arms or tongues to speak with but with brains to suffer the misery eternally. And the drugs were finally banned. So the system began to work.

Asbestos cases were filed, thousands of them. The companies knew their product caused cancer of the lung. They knew of the unspeakable torture that is the long, painful prelude to such a lingering, choking death. But the companies hid the truth about their knowledge and lied about it. When trial lawyers discovered the truth and the piteous victims were paid for their misery and their lives, it was then that the companies began screaming about the lawyers and innocents like Catherine Crier complained about the wealth of the asbestos lawyers. Yes, some plaintiffs' lawyers grew immensely wealthy. But what of the staggering wealth enjoyed over the years by the corporations that killed and poisoned and reaped their profits over the dead and cancerous bodies of their workers?

I have memories. The tobacco companies set out to addict our kids, drew up those ads that lured youngsters to the addiction that would eventually kill many of them as adults. And the companies laced their tobacco with even more drugs than the natural plant provided, then hid the fact, lied about it, lied under oath about it, and when they were exposed and were ordered to pay many millions in damages they began the chorus—those greedy lawyers! But again we hear little about the billions of profit the tobacco companies have taken from their treachery. And continue to do so.

Yes, a handful of lawyers made fortunes. And the American public was soon propagandized by the advertising experts of Madison Avenue to the conclusion that lawyers for the people were bad human beings—those hoggish, snouts-in-the-trough crooks with a license to steal. So where am I going with this? I'm saying that big business, manufacturers, insurance companies, the pharmaceuticals, the stockbrokers, and CEOs of those companies who cook the books, and yes, the banks have only one thing to be afraid of out there—the lawyers who represent ordinary people. And so, predictably, they have been demonized.

We know the best way to slow down the murderous pillage of the people and the earth is by clipping a feather or two from the wings of the high-flying vultures. The scissors are punitive damage verdicts, damages in an amount commensurate with the crimes the corporations commit. You can't put a corporate criminal in jail. It has no physical presence. Punitive damages are the only punishment that can be leveled against the corporation in cases in which the wrongdoer has been grossly, intentionally, or criminally negligent. But no matter how vile the corporate crime, the people, yes, the judges, and even those towering judges on high in the appellate courts have been taught that it is un-American to stop the injuring, the poisoning, and killing of the people and the earth with large punitive damage awards. And the U.S. Supreme Court has stepped in to limit punitive damages against corporations, in effect capping punitive-damage awards and thereby protecting corporations against the living persons they injure and kill.

We are never plainly told by our leaders that people have become merely parts of the profit machinery, that they can and will be replaced as they are worn out. Congress is sold out to profit and will not protect the people. William Greider in his fine work *Who Will Tell the People?* says that the Democratic Party has lost its function as a power base for citizens and has become merely a "mail drop for political money."

The only segment of the system that faithfully fights for the rights of people are trial lawyers. Yet they have been so besmirched that in California the trial lawyers, hoping to avoid the infamy heaped upon them, have changed their name to Consumer Attorneys of California. A pity. It's like honorable, careful surgeons having suffered such defamation that they are seen as butchers, so they now call themselves "physiological reconstructionists." In passing I wonder: What if we trusted doctors as we have been taught to trust trial lawyers? What if we thought that doctors might steal one of our organs and sell it while we're under the anesthesia? Many operating rooms of the nation would soon be closed.

Still, even today, I know lawyers who have borrowed money and mortgaged their homes to finance just causes for their poor clients—and lost it all. They have fought for our freedoms and our justice against the tyranny of power, and they continue the fight for justice in thousands of nearly anonymous courts across the land. They do so against great odds, the worst of which is their slaughter by slander.

We have been taught to hate the forgotten and abandoned members of our society, our mentally ill, whom we've thrown out on to the streets. There are laws against throwing empty bottles on the streets, but none to keep us from throwing the lost and help-less there. We have been taught by the dupes of power to turn our backs on whole segments of our society that are left without jobs, without pride, without hope and to consider them lazy welfare hogs. Someone said that we judge the civility of a society by the manner in which that society protects its least fortunate. We do not stand high by this test.

But trial lawyers have fought endless battles for the poor and mentally ill—for those charged with heinous crimes and for those the King's men portray as society's scum. Nancy Grace mocks and scorns trial lawyers as soulless prostitutes of the pro-fession who are "just doing their job." But many are the true he-roes of the profession. They are men and women who are usually understaffed, underfinanced, and underrespected, trial lawyers who believe that the bottom is entitled to the same protections as the top—as, say, the CEO at Enron—and that the worst of us are entitled to the same rights as the white-collar criminals (those true elitists) that Laura Ingraham, as an elitist, once defended. These heroes of the profession understand that when the rights of the most hated are protected, the rights of the most exalted are protected as well.

With saddened ears I have heard many of those cruel lawyer jokes. Example:

Q. Why are scientists now using lawyers in laboratory experi-ments instead of rats?

A. Three reasons: (1) lawyers are more plentiful than rats, (2) there is no danger the scientists will become attached to the lawyers, and (3) there are some things rats just won't do.

Or how about this one:
"All lawyers are assholes!" declared a man in a bar.
"I resent that!" someone replied.
"Why, are you a lawyer?"

"No, I'm an asshole!"

Or still another:

A man was on vacation when he ran into an old acquaintance. "Hello, Joe," he said. "I haven't seen you in years. What are you doing these days?"

"I'm practicing law," whispered Joe. "But don't tell my mother. She thinks I'm still a pimp."

Ha. Ha.

Every "I hate lawyers" joke I hear is no longer a laughing matter to me. These jokes hurt me. It's not that I have no sense of humor or that I'm blind to the infirmities of my profession. It's not that I can't take a joke or that the jokes mock me or trial lawyers. It's that they are *against the people* who need lawyers. The jokes are not against lawyers but *against a country* in which the people's freedom will be lost because their lawyers are held in such disgrace. And the jokes are but another form of a carefully crafted propaganda that is part of the corporate King's agenda we've been examining.

Lawyers have disappointed many, and sometimes their failure is inexcusable. Every profession has within its membership those curs, those scoundrels who disgrace themselves and their colleagues. Certainly the legal profession is not without its crooks and shysters. But the profession at its best labors in a system that is not geared to deliver justice to people. Too often it will not. And despite the fact that its function is to deliver justice, the justice system often ends up providing little more than a closing door to those who seek to enter.

Many of our young people have sought a legal education because they want to help, to take part in an honorable process by which people in need of justice might receive it. I have seen them, the young, their starry eyes set on the great battles they intend to fight. I have also seen them finally trudge away from today's dysfunctional system disillusioned and disappointed.

As we've seen, our bloodthirsty blasters, all lawyers, seem to hate their own profession. Nancy Grace hates those who defend our rights under the Constitution. Of defense attorneys she goes on to say: "Still, it's so disheartening that juries are hoodwinked every day by defense lawyers just 'doing their jobs.'" How is it then, Nancy, that you have been able to win a hundred prosecutions in a row against these hoodwinking charlatans?

O'Reilly, Limbaugh, Robertson, the bloodthirsty brigade, and the others are all picking at the same one-stringed guitar. These conservatives love to curse trial lawyers—until they need one. Then they want the best money can buy. As Melville wrote: "All that most maddens and torments; all that stirs up the lees of things; all truth with malice in it; all that cracks the sinews and cakes the brain; all the subtle demonism of life and thought; all evil, to crazy Ahab were visibly personified and made practically assailable in Moby Dick." As with Ahab and the whale, so with the corporate King and trial lawyers.

Without effective lawyers and a functional justice system the profit of the corporate King will continue to swell, and its power over the people will become utterly invincible. And the people?— the people will grow poorer, more desperate, more indebted, weaker, and, at last, exist beyond the myths of freedom, they can become the new masses of American slaves, slaves not with shackles on their legs, but with eternal debt over their heads; slaves not with the whip at their backs, but citizens beaten by the injustices of an unfettered power core.

Lawyers are to our sacred rights as doctors are to our valued health. In the long run I would rather be an unhealthy free person than a healthy slave. I have observed throughout a life of representing ordinary people that a person can do without adequate food, even without a decent shelter over his head. A person can live with little to cover his nakedness and be broke to the bone. But that person cannot live without justice. Patrick Henry said it in a different time, "Give me Liberty or give me death."

Justice is the first necessity of life. The justice system must respond, or people will take justice into their own hands. The injured, the damned, the slandered, the lost, the forgotten, and the voiceless all demand justice and, failing its delivery, the system as we know it will finally collapse.

We look upon those who are cheated of justice and somehow we are consoled that it has happened to them not to us. But we *are* they. If not today, tomorrow. Without respected warriors for justice we will be like the sick and injured without competent doctors.

Without trial lawyers and fair courts and unbiased juries to hear our cases, we will be rewarded with the same justice that people across the world experience—no justice at all, not even the empty promise of it. At last we will not be able to differentiate our system from China's or those of third world governments where people have never heard of justice. We are on that road, for without justice, and without a respected profession that can fight for it, the fate of the nation is to join the rest of the earth's enslaved.

11. Hate and the
New American Slavery

I speak often of the corporate King. That corporate conglomeration has been the King of America for a long time.

I have also spoken of slaves. Variously I have referred to those in servitude as the people, the masses, indentured servants, the great American citizenry. These are, of course, symbiotic relationships. Without a king there can be no serfs, no slaves, no indentured servants; and without those in servitude, there can be no king.

I have meant no disrespect for the slaves for I am of them and am them. Indeed, I hold no respect for the King. As we have seen, this king is not human. The apologists for the corporate state point to the obvious, that the corporation is run by people. But they, too, are slaves to the corporation—the CEO, the board of directors, all are slaves in a hierarchy at the bottom of which labors the cleaning woman, who may be the most noble of them all. She is real, she cares, she feels and suffers and plods on every day to put food on the table for her children. Without her, and those who labor above her in that human hierarchy, the corporation could not open its doors, much less rake up its profits. The irony runs deep.

I have already considered a variety of the causes of hatred—in sum it arises from a sense of finding one's self inexorably trapped, enslaved to one degree or another in a state or system from which there is no escape. And debt is the most enslaving factor of all.

Studies show the average consumer can potentially be exposed to more than three thousand marketing messages every day. In the last decade, it's been estimated that solicitations by marketers have jumped from 1.52 billion annually to 4.29 billion—*and debt lurks at the end of every potential solicitation.*

The average per household debt in the United States, not counting mortgage debt, is about $14,500—especially noteworthy because before the 1930s, most middle- and working-class people had no major debts. Banks would not lend to them; folks rented their homes; and if they did own a house, it was paid for as it was being built. As a child I remember our neighbors digging a basement by hand and living in it, the roof of which would someday be the floor above.

The easy-payment plans—no payments due until next year, interest free until a distant date down the line—are traps set for Americans, the endless, seductive drill that has transformed us into a nation not of free citizens but of indentured consumers.

A $1,000 charge on an average credit card will take almost twenty-two years to pay, and will cost more than $2,300 in interest ($3,300 total)—if only the 2 percent minimum payments are made. A startling statistic: Some 40 percent of American families annually spend *more than they earn.* The average card debt among people who have at least one card is $9,205—triple what it was in 1990.

The average personal wealth of a fifty-year-old American, including home equity, is less than $40,000; and 23 percent of Americans admit to maxing out a credit card. Typical health care debt is $25,000.

Angry? Filled with hate? We are a nation of debtor slaves and one is pressed to find many happy slaves. But why have we transformed ourselves from free persons to enslaved debtors?

Since we cannot begin to see our future, the bomb, the burning up of the planet, the takeover by third world countries that will reduce us to a third world country—since our leadership provides little trustworthy insight as to where we are going—we tend to live for today. To hell with the kids, and the grandkids, and theirs. The debt we have encountered is their problem. It is as if to say, "To hell with everybody and everything. We have to get what there is to get *now*. I don't mean now. I mean *right* now. *This instant!*"

And I do not want just a few things—like a good roof over my head and a pot of beans. I want the new cars I see on TV. Everyone else obviously has them, all except me. I want the new house in the gated, planned neighborhood. I want the great body or at least the body machines to create one, as promised. I want all of the newest appliances, the vacation to Tahiti, the pants that women look at, the new cool shoes that are manufactured by little slave girls for a few cents and sold with that cool emblem for a couple hundred dollars a pair, and the sunglasses of the stars—I want them and the membership in the country club and season tickets to the ball games and the newest computer, the best deal on a cell phone and a digital camera. I want my hair restored . . . and one of those four-wheelers. There's no end to my wants because my worth is expressed in the things I have. If I have nothing or little, or at least not as much as Joe Average Hard-Working American, I do not amount to much. We live in a society of things, and I want everything. *Everything!*

We've become a commodity-driven nation. I call it *thingism*. Relentlessly we're subjected to a propaganda of things called, euphemistically, "advertising." Out there lies that awful malaise, people who feel numb and dead. To many, life has become a sort of walking death. Albert Camus wrote: "Without work, all life goes rotten, but when work is soulless, life stifles and dies."

As we've seen, many feel trapped, trapped in their jobs, their marriages, their lives. The most painful of human experiences is the sense of being trapped within the self—an inescapable trap that brings on self-hatred. I think of the coyote whose leg is caught in the hunter's trap. The coyote will chew off its leg to escape. The beaver caught in a trap will drown itself. The person who is trapped has few alternatives. He can become morose, listless, depressed, and join the "walking dead," or he can become angry and strike out.

Almost a thousand workers are murdered on the job each year, and nearly one in twenty is physically assaulted annually. One in six workers report being sexually harassed, and a third report being verbally harassed. In one study of more than a thousand workers, "desk rage," a phenomenon that is akin to "road rage," resulted in nearly a third of the workers admitting that they yelled at someone at the office. Sixty-five percent said workplace stress was at least a problem, 23 percent said the stress had driven them to tears, and 34 percent blamed their boss for causing them loss of sleep. The masterminds on Madison Avenue recognize this field for harvest. The wearied, trapped worker can escape momentarily into a different, sometimes magical realm by replenishing himself with something new. Things promise to fill the miserable void and ease the pain of one's anger.

Women suffer profoundly as victims of *thingism*. They've been lured out of the home by Madison Avenue. They've given up their children to day care so they can work and buy more *things*—more gadgets and appliances, perhaps a face-lift and breast implants, without which they may not be competitive in the markets of romance or work. Self-esteem is no longer based on what one does with one's life as much as how one looks. Are you beautiful? Well, at least, have you gotten rid of the "unders," bulges under the eyes and the saggy skin under the chin? Are you working out at the gym so that your belly is flat enough to play a game of pool on? And how can a woman bearing her ordinary bust, one intended to efficiently provide milk for her infant, make it in today's world, where the bosom's function has been altered—to lure men and to intimidate other women?

What about a *new car* for the man of the house? We see it on the screen, the long, sleek, shiny thing—the suggestion of the longed-for monster phallus; the laughing, happy people around it, the beautiful women looking invitingly at the driver, or the macho conversion of the guy who now drives a Ford pickup. Brawn! And when we buy the new sports car, the SUV, the convertible, well, we immediately feel something we have not felt for a long time—something approaching joy. The enslaving debt to come, like the hangover, is forgotten in the thrill of the moment.

But soon we're overtaken by the same malaise that is now exacerbated by the monthly demand of the bank for its ransom. We realize we feel worse than before. But something new out there promises to fill the nagging void. This time it's high-definition TV. By its magic we're surrounded in the living room with beautiful women who seem as real as if you could touch them, yes, those lovelies, those humongous bouncing breasts and long, luscious limbs; and everyone is drinking Bud or having a mud-wrestling orgy with Miller's; and life on the screen is bounteous, heavenlike, for surely heaven provides sex, beer, and widescreen TV.

But we have those payments, nothing due, of course, until after the first of the year. Then the payments descend upon us and we're left feeling worse than before. No one else seems to be getting default notices in the mail. No one else on that wide screen with its high-definition picture seems in the least anxious. They just laugh and pop a Coors. It's the same dynamic suffered by the heroin addict. We need a fix—a salvation from the horrors of boredom, of failure, of being cheated out of our just dues. And the witches and warlocks on Madison Avenue know how to provide it for us.

The television screen educates us on three critical subjects:

First, what we must buy. *Must.* Otherwise we're left behind.

We're not even normal. Imagine what the neighbors would say if we had one old car in the garage and no TV and the kids had a swing made of an old tire and a rope hanging down from a limb of the tree in the front yard instead of one of those nifty play sets with swings, a covered slide, and maybe a trampoline.

Second, of course, we must learn how to pay for what we've bought. Remember those easy payments and the delayed interest. Any fool could afford the thing. *Thingism* at full throttle now. We bet on the come. The boss said something a little complimentary the other day. Maybe a raise.

We are saved momentarily by those magical plastic widgets called credit cards and those gentle and friendly understanding mortgage companies, the smiling women on TV who say their company will take seconds on our houses, maybe thirds, so we can still get our thing-fix. Do not ask me about tomorrow. That, too, is un-American. Corporate business runs from quarter to quarter. American people run mouth-to-mouth, month-to-month. Long-term planning is unacceptable because we have to have whatever we seek, things and happiness *now.*

But the pressure of mounting debt enslaves us, and the changing of the laws of bankruptcy by a corporate-controlled Congress makes it nearly impossible for the drowning debtor to ever get his head above water—the new indentured servant is born. Yes, boss. But the slave is an angry slave.

When at last we can no longer get another fix by buying something new and exciting because our credit will no longer allow it and there has been no raise and none promised, along comes the next lesson.

Third: Call that nonprofit corporation, also advertised on the screen, that will help us get out of debt—like going to Betty Ford or something. We can become a member of "Debtors Anonymous," twelve easy steps to get our creditors off our backs. All we have to do is sign our paychecks over to this corporation that will parcel them out to those we owe, in general, the corporate King. And with what's left we can buy that pot of beans.

The deadly killer, *interest,* destroys our lives by enslaving us further to the corporate King, which is, of course, the bankers, the credit-card companies, the manufacturers touted by the advertising industry, the propagandists of *thingism.* It has come to pass as Karl Menninger, the psychiatrist and philosopher, observed over sixty years ago in his masterwork, *Love Against Hate:* "It is as if an indigent couple should borrow money from a loan shark in order to buy a washing machine and thus save some manual labor for the wife, only to find that in the end both have to do ten times as much manual labor as before in order to pay the accumulating and increasing burdens of the loan for the 'labor saving' machine."

Yes, we've had it. But if, like good slaves, we're honest and do as we're told and do not waver, not once, we can get out of debt (no big nights out at McDonald's) in something like 9.67 years. By then we'll need a new car and a new TV, not to mention that junior wants to go to college and the boss is telling us that our jobs have been taken over by computers and some kid fresh out of school toting a B.S. in computer science or maybe by some hungry Indian in Bombay who'll work for ten cents on our dollar.

But why should we be angry about this? *Thingism* is a way of life. *Thingism* is American. Spend so the economy can stay healthy. As Ann Coulter argues, God loves spenders, especially those who drive those big gas-guzzling SUVs. God says it is OK, remember?

Those who own the nation own the company store. A nation of consumers has become a nation of debtors. Consider the sanctity of Christmas, which has been reduced to a national obligation to buy, to buy when we cannot afford to buy, to incur debt to buy, to buy to show love—the sickening sentimental TV ad showing the man's proof of love by giving his wife a diamond ring in a black velvet case—"every kiss begins with Kay"—or a new car with a red ribbon around it and the wife's eyes radiating love with heart-throbbing ecstasy, all without mention that the family has to pay for the gift in monthly installments for years that soon convert the entire experience to hate. Even love has now been turned into a commodity to buy on time.

Santa Claus—that loving, giving elf—has been transposed into the pimp of the corporate marketer. I saw an ad on TV where even this bounteous old spirit gives Mrs. Claus a diamond for Christmas and she gives him back that look that says, "Well, things will be pretty good for you tonight in bed, Honey" (even though he may need Cialus to get it up and a doctor to help get it down if it lasts more than four hours).

Can't we put an end to this endless madness? Can't we engage in at least a nonviolent revolt against this servitude? But if one is consumed in consumption, in paying off debt, in devoting one's life to the acquisition and payment of things, then there is no time or energy left to rebel, to consider, to think; to contemplate intelligently one's condition, much less the condition of the community, the country, or the world. *Thingism* leads us to apathy. Fatigue sets in. Pop a beer. Turn on the TV for Nancy Grace. There's no energy left to intelligently consider anything. Yet there's a sense of futility, of frustration, of hopelessness, and a growing anger. But in the end, all that is left is consumption, its addiction and its misery.

That we should be so diverted from our lives by *things,* by our search for immediate pleasure, that we're unable to attend to the business of democracy, was predicted years ago by that young French upstart we have already met, Alexis de Tocqueville, who roamed around the new nation during Jefferson's administration making his prescient observations.

De Tocqueville saw these alienated people "incessantly endeavoring to procure the petty and paltry pleasures with which they glut their lives." Sound chillingly familiar? We want our good times, the beer we deserve, the thousand songs we can play out of something no larger than the sole of a baby's shoe, the movies, the romance, yes, the XXX stuff, the . . . on and endlessly on.

In George Orwell's *1984* the protagonist, Winston, longs for

some kind of a revolution that would free the proles from Big
Brother, a revolution that seemed so at hand but yet so impossible.
"If there is hope," wrote Winston in his diary, *"it lies in the proles.*
[his italics] . . . But the proles [the masses], if only they could
somehow become conscious of their own strength, would have no
need to conspire. They needed only to rise up and shake themselves like a horse shaking off flies. If they chose they could blow
the Party to pieces tomorrow morning. Surely sooner or later it
must occur to them to do it? And yet—"

For a moment Winston thought the revolution had started.
His heart jumped. It had finally come! But, alas, the proles were
fighting over hard-to come-by saucepans. "Why was it that they
could never shout like that about anything that mattered?" Winston asked.

So CNN shoots us Nancy Grace to keep us fighting over
saucepans—the Peterson and Jackson cases, and all the others.
And our hate is popped like an infected pimple. Here is Orwell
describing how "Two Minutes Hate" on the screen took over:

"In its second minute the Hate rose to a frenzy. People were
leaping up and down in their places and shouting at the tops of
their voices in an effort to drown the maddening bleating voice
that came from the screen. The little sandy-haired woman had
turned bright pink, and her mouth was opening and shutting like
that of a landed fish. . . .

"In a lucid moment Winston found that he was shouting with
the others and kicking his heel violently against the rung of his
chair. The horrible thing about the Two Minutes Hate was not
that one was obliged to act a part, but that it was impossible to
avoid joining in. . . . A hideous ecstasy of fear and vindictiveness,
a desire to kill, to torture, to smash faces in with a sledge-hammer,
seemed to flow through the whole group of people like an electric
current, turning one even against one's will into a grimacing,
screaming lunatic."

Later, "Winston succeeded in transferring his hatred from the
face on the screen to the dark-haired girl behind him. . . . He

would flog her to death with a rubber truncheon. He would tie her naked to a stake and shoot her full of arrows like Saint Sebastian. He would ravish her and cut her throat at the moment of climax."

So, hello again, Mr. O'Reilly, and Ms. Grace! Yours is not "Two Minutes Hate," but an hour, a *whole* hour (less fifteen or twenty commercials) daily, prime time!

And on the way to work, fighting the traffic, fighting the dread ahead, fighting the "Jesus I wish it was Friday" thing, well we can turn on Ms. Ingraham, or any of the other hatemongers whom the corporate King airs during drive time, and there we can get our daily fix of hate. And, also, we can learn about the new and wonderful things out there, the Nirvana of things, things out there that we *must have now;* things that stand in the stead of mind, body, and heart—even love, all the things we can have with no down payments and no interest until who knows when.

But let us use a kinder word than "slavery." None of us wishes to be seen or thought of as a slave, or to see ourself as such. Let us recognize that we are *free* to incur enslaving debt, and be grateful for a freedom that far exceeds that of many other nations in the world. But let us also consider the human condition of slavery. What are its most common elements?

First, a slave is bound to a master. In America most citizens work for either the government or a corporation. Certainly if we don't like our job we can quit and take our chances on finding a better one at another corporation or government entity. But the risks are great. No more gripping fear takes over a family than when the principal wage earner loses a job.

I remember so vividly when my father was without work for the first time in his life. The family did not panic. My father was a good worker and an honest man. But an air of impending danger hung over the house. What if Daddy couldn't find a job? What would become of us? Would we have to go on relief and suffer the humiliation? Would we lose our house? My mother's lower lip quivered when my father's joblessness was mentioned, and she tried to smile and pass it over. I could see the worry on my own brave father's face. I could hear the hushed discussions in my parents' bedroom, words I could not make out. But the sound of their whispered talk was ominous.

If the worker leaves his job to find another it's likely he'll be working for another corporation that sees workers in the same light as did his former employer. The change will likely prove to be little more than a change in location, a different roof over the head where he works. In the end, the worker has merely moved from one cotton field to another.

Second, a slave can be replaced by his master at will. The master no longer sells the slave but dumps him into the labor pool, where the worker now bears the responsibility of finding himself another job. The AFL-CIO reports that U.S. companies will send some 406,000 American jobs overseas this year, compared to 204,000 jobs three years ago. Of those jobs, 140,000 will be moved to Mexico and 99,000 will go to China. Since January 2001, Americans have lost more than 2.7 million manufacturing jobs and 850,000 professional service and information sector jobs. Many companies continue to slash jobs. To pound the streets for work, any work, when your company has sent yours to Mexico or China or to India creates a sense of anger and resulting hate.

Third, a slave is not permitted to contest his master. The master's word, his whim, is law. Ever try to bring a complaint against *any,* I mean, *any* corporation for its wrongful conduct? There is no one to speak to, no one who will take responsibility. Yes, there are forepersons (field bosses in the slave world) who get their orders from a division head, who gets his orders from, say, the vice president of marketing, who gets her orders from a committee that was formed by the CEO and who, in turn, sends the matter, as rote, to the Board of Directors, which rubber-stamps it. In turn, the board represents millions of shareholders who don't have the first idea about what is going on and who don't give a damn so long as the stock price accelerates as promised. The organization is mechanical.

Machines do not discuss problems. They only endure them and wear them out.

Fourth, a slave's children can be sold by the master and thereby separated from the family. Our own children are educated at our expense. In educating our children we incur indebtedness from which we may never fully recover. Our children are then separated from the family as workers for one corporation in the East and another one in the West. *We* prepare our children as workers for the master.

Fifth, when the slave is old and no longer able to work, the slave is retired and replaced. In the past the master provided at least meagerly for his worn-out slave until he died. When today's worker has been used up, he will receive a pittance for his retirement, or his retirement may be stolen from him by his former employer. He will get Social Security, perhaps enough to fight off starvation. Such parallels offer grist for thought.

Sixth, slaves suffer an underlying, repressed anger. Slaves were preached to and told that a good slave received his reward in heaven. Slaves composed songs and sang away their blues. Propaganda to the slaves held that the slave owed his allegiance to the master, that he must be faithful and loyal and fight for the master's welfare, a sort of patriotism to the slave system. And finally, out of sheer helplessness, the slave became apathetic. Today many citizens ask, "What difference does it make who I vote for? Why bother? It will always be the same."

Propaganda, not the bullwhip, is the ultimate tool of oppression in America—one that teaches the people the easy road to slavery, one that also teaches the people to distrust those who fight for their rights and to view their own freedoms as antithetical to their security. The people are angry, but their anger has been wrongly placed.

Nothing changes. No point in deodorizing the past. In all of history there have been the kings, the tyrants, the rich, the slave owners, the lords, and the systems of government that protect the oppressors, and there have been the masses, those who are enslaved.

I am not a Marxist, but it is clear to me that as long as one class has oppressed another, a condition that has extended across the entire history of civilization, hatred has been the principal dynamic at play and has provided the energy for both enslavement and revolution. In modern times, the manipulative brilliance of the corporate King is measured by its ability to convince the slaves they are free and to redirect their hatred against "the enemy," which proves to be the slaves themselves.

The ravages of hate in America are as painful and deadly as a cancer in the belly. Husbands are abusing wives. Parents are beating children. Workers are assaulting fellow workers. People drink too much and turn to drugs. Those who have fallen over the edge grab a gun and randomly kill innocent bystanders. Road rage and desk rage are now everyday occurrences. Anger clinics have sprung up across the land. Some people slog along in a sullen stupor. Other repudiate themselves with suicide. Masses are despondent and depressed. As we've seen, one of the ways we sublimate anger is to tune in to one of our hatemongers and pound the walls. But, as we have also seen, such hate, in the hands of ambitious leaders, portends no good ends. Team Hate is important only because its members are symbolic of the Judas goats who lead the lambs to slaughter. For those who seem perfectly normal with all those smiles and good manners, underneath there remains the secluded seething.

I've never heard of a happy slave except the Uncle Toms of every color and national origin who give their lives to their masters under whatever illusion justifies their slavery. Yet the growing dominance of the corporate King has, as in the old slavery of the South, created an environment of servitude as immoveable and unchangeable as the mountains that surround me. We are strangled by the ligaments of the law. We are born into the system and accept it like the panda born in the zoo. But the first step toward change is to recognize the truth, to sweep away the myths, and to move on toward new, real frontiers of freedom. The trek is long, hard, and frightening.

12. The Rise of the Fourth Reich

Entrance to Hell

I f we have not already fully arrived, the road we travel is one inevitably leading to a corporate-government oligarchy we may politely call electoral fascism. The difference between the fascism of Hitler and Mussolini is that in the former the Fascist nation controlled both corporate power as well as the people. In the new electoral fascism the corporation is King and controls the government and the people.

It's plain to see we have fallen into the bog of fascism when the two political parties are nourished from the same corporate feedbag; when a single party dominated by corporations and devoted to their interests controls the executive, both houses, and the judiciary; when corporations and government have become merged to the end that often no clear distinctions can be made between them; and finally when war and the threats of war rule our nation's agenda. The evidence is nearly irrefutable that the democracy envisioned by our founders has, in major ways, failed.

We have yet to face it. Frank Zappa, the American musician,

composer, and satirist, nailed it. "The illusion of freedom will continue as long as it's profitable to continue the illusion. At the point where the illusion becomes too expensive to maintain, they will just take down the scenery, pull back the curtains, and you will see the brick wall at the back of the theater."

It is true that differences exist in the loudly mouthed constructs of the two parties. One claims to be neoconservative, just plain-old conservative, or moderately conservative, or whatever level of conservatism a given group or spokesperson wishes to admit to, while the other claims to be liberal, or if not liberal, progressive, or if not progressive, well, at least moderate, and, again, whatever portion of liberalism the group or spokesperson on that side wishes to confess to. And, indeed, there are sometimes vital differences that show up in the choice of judges for the various federal courts. But from the standpoint of power in force, the nation has taken the road toward fascism with the advice and consent of both parties.

One can hardly argue that the Democrats present an opposing philosophy when their anemic leadership approaches no leadership at all, when we hear only their pipsqueak protests, when that party struggles to find ways to distinguish itself from the dominant party, and, in the end, their piteous attempts present little more than a poor imitation of the opposing party's platform. The difference that we hear is mostly the yapping of puppies.

The long-cherished notion that a two-party system can correct itself from time to time by means of vigorous debate and honest dissent has proven to be the most disheartening and dangerous myth of all. The nation, like an automobile drunkenly steered to the right and nearing the brink, cannot regain control of its course when the passenger reaches over for the wheel and applies *further* pressure to the right. A crash of democracy is inevitable. The impending crash, frightening as it is, is the course the nation is taking. Shall we call it the rise of the *Fourth Reich?*

Franklin D. Roosevelt warned us: "But I venture the challenging statement that if American democracy ceases to move forward as a living force, seeking day and night by peaceful means to better the lot of our citizens, then Fascism and Communism, aided, unconsciously perhaps, by old-line Tory Republicanism, will grow in strength in our land."

I am about to direct our attention to the startling similarities between the state of the nation and the rise of Hitler's National Socialism, the Third Reich. *Reich* is German for "empire." Adolph Hitler claimed he was creating a third German empire, a successor to the Holy Roman Empire and the German empire formed by Chancellor Bismarck in the nineteenth century—hence the *Third Reich*.

The parallels of America today under the domination of the far right with the rise of Hitler are not in all ways precise, and that, of course, provides both hope and room for opposing argument. But history is never exact, and, contrary to the old maxim, never precisely repeats itself. It only provides lessons. The most we can expect is that something can be learned from holding these two scraps of history up side by side in the sunlight. And, admittedly, one must be careful of the polemics that grow out of these exercises. They can lead to wrong conclusions. Mark Twain said, "History doesn't repeat itself, but sometimes it rhymes."

We have already seen how Christian doctrine has been manipulated as the Christian right finds such perversions useful. And we've observed how the democratic doctrines of our founders have been mangled beyond recognition as authority for propositions that would have brought on acute apoplexy to the likes of Jefferson and Madison. But much of what went on in the Nazi movement and that which is occurring in America today are similar both in substance and methodology, and the risk to America can't be ignored. It calls for careful consideration in the present rather than someday reviewing it remorsefully as history.

To begin with, these are different economic times than those experienced by the Germans during the Great Depression when Hitler took power. Moreover, America suffers no humiliation such as did the Germans with the signing of the Treaty of Versailles, an event that many Germans felt was a stab in the back and that brought great shame to the German people. As Hitler rose to power, Germany sought a return of national community and pride. But our defeat in Vietnam, and yes, perhaps in Iraq, is not ancient history, and a shaky economy from the standpoint of working people also plays a part in forming a national apprehension about our future.

Pundits and fools have forever taken history into hand and have selectively drawn from it those facts that support their apocalyptic warnings. The end is near. Perhaps not. But something new and disturbing, something portending danger for a people who claim they cherish freedom blows is in a worried wind.

Some easy parallels at first:

The Reichstag fire: Hitler had been sworn in on January 30, 1933. A month later, at 9:14 p.m., the Reichstag, the location of the German Parliament, was ablaze. The police quickly found Marinus van der Lubbe, half naked, hiding behind the building. Van der Lubbe was a Dutch Communist and an unemployed bricklayer who had recently arrived in Germany.

William L. Shirer writes in *The Rise and Fall of the Third Reich:* "The coincidence that the Nazis had found a demented Communist arsonist who was out to do exactly what they themselves had determined to do seems incredible but is nevertheless supported by the evidence. The idea for the fire almost certainly originated at the top with Goebbels and Goering. Hans Gisevius, an official in the Prussian Ministry of the Interior at the time, testified at Nuremberg that 'it was Goebbels who first thought of setting the Reichstag on fire,' and Rudolph Diels, the Gestapo chief, added in an affidavit that 'Goering knew exactly how the fire was to be started' and had ordered him 'to prepare, prior to the fire, a list of people who were to be arrested immediately after it.'"

Goering declared that the fire was set by the Communists, and Hitler ordered a state of emergency, the result of which was abolishing most of the human rights provisions of the 1919 Weimar Republic Constitution.

I make no suggestion that the administration's explanation of who was to blame for 9/11 was similarly invented. I only observe that the people immediately accepted Bush's explanation without an in-depth investigation and watched our president declare unilaterally that we were at war. At the same time we witnessed little effort on the part of the president to calm a nation or to act through the United Nations. While the parallel with Hitler's grab for power is not exact, the underlying dynamic is disquieting.

The infamy and horror of the criminal, barbarian 9/11 assault on America can never be diminished. But one thing we can all admit: the assault was the product of *hate*. That attack engendered, in turn, our own, unremitting hate.

Hate grows.

Hate echoes itself.

I hate and you hate back.

Your hate back makes me hate more.

And the more I hate, the more you hate back, *ad infinitum*.

Some things seem as obvious as pie on the tie. If we are a peace-seeking nation, the cure for hate, can never be more expressions of hate. The doctor does not prescribe strychnine as an antidote for strychnine poisoning. Although it is now universally admitted that Saddam was not connected to the bin Laden gang, nevertheless fear arising out of 9/11 soon was converted to hatred and took us into war, both in Afghanistan and Iraq. Obviously we did not seek to save ourselves from bin Laden by attacking Iraq. Nor was our attack vindicated by any real threat that Saddam represented to America. The underlying motive of the administration has never been confessed. It never will be.

Consider Hitler's "preemptive attack" on Poland. The announced purpose to the world was to protect both Germany and Germans within Poland against the aggression of the Polish government. Hitler wrote that an appropriate propaganda for invading Poland would be published, the truth or falsehood of which was unimportant, since "the Right lies in Victory." But the bottom line of Hitler's motivation for the invasion was territorial conquest, pure and simple.

No individual was more adept at harnessing hatred to produce the energy for his evil agenda than Hitler. In the early days of his regime, Hitler drummed up the hatred of the German people for Jews as to build his Third Reich and to obtain widespread support for his solution, the death camps.

Because Germans felt they had been mistreated by the international community, when property belonging to Jews was confiscated, when their furniture and personal belongings were auctioned off, when thousands of Jewish apartments were taken over and Jews excluded from good jobs, many Germans felt a sense of retribution. Such criminal conduct by the state could never have been possible without a deep-seated preexisting hatred that fueled it.

As a result of the so-called national emergency of 9/11 we blindly, thoughtlessly abdicated many of our sacred rights under our panic-driven acceptance of the Patriot Act. Under that "emergency legislation," the constitutional guarantee of the Fourth Amendment against unreasonable searches and seizures was waylaid. The language of the Constitution is clear: *The right of the people to be secure in their persons, houses, papers, and effects, against unreasonable searches and seizures, shall not be violated, and no Warrants shall issue, but upon probable cause, supported by Oath or affirmation, and particularly describing the place to be searched, and the persons or things to be seized.*

Now, under the Patriot Act, its provisions a cruel oxymoron and a mockery of American democracy—you are a Patriot if you insist on surrendering your rights preserved in that great document—as we've seen, a secret federal officer can go to a secret court and file secret papers and obtain a secret warrant to secretly search your home or office. The basis of the warrant is little more than suspicion that you are an enemy agent. No probable cause is required. The warrant is not served as in the ordinary case. It is secret.

One's house and office, as in the case of our client, Brandon Mayfield, a modest attorney, can be secretly broken into and evidence secretly gathered, from DNA taken from his toothbrush to many other personal items. Microphones can be hidden under the table in the family kitchen, under the bed in the couple's bedroom, their phones tapped, their computers copied, and his clients' files gone through. All the while the FBI had every reason to know of his innocence, and later admitted his innocence, only after he'd been incarcerated and faced the possibility of charges that could have included the death penalty.

Today nothing personal or sacred is beyond the eyes of the government. The justification for the loss of our rights, as in Germany with its Reichstag fire, has been the "security of the nation." Both had agencies referred to as Homeland Security. Perhaps George II could have been a bit more original in his choice of agency names.

As in the Mayfield case (and how many other cases we shall never know), in Hitler's Germany, the term *Schutzhaft,* meaning "protective custody," permitted the regime to take possession of the person and put him behind barbed wire, his civil liberties suspended with no protection from possible harm. Under National Socialism, Germany ceased to be a nation of law. "Hitler is the law," the legal lights in Germany declared, and Goering is said to have emphasized it to Prussian prosecutors with his summary, "The law and the will of the Führer one."

Dachau was the earliest internment camp in Germany, and at its inception it had not yet been converted into a "death camp." But it housed the "enemies of the state." Take a look at Guantánamo, our indefinite "detention camp," new cells of which were built by the vice president's former company, Halliburton. As we have already seen, inmates have died in Guantánamo, and to the interns there it *is* a death camp, one where humans selected as enemies of the United States are tortured, some to death, and none with a trial to determine whether they are guilty of anything other than breathing in the wrong place at the wrong time.

This is American democracy at work?

In Hitler's Germany, Hitler himself had the right to quash criminal prosecutions. A case was brought before Hitler in which the minister of justice strongly recommended the prosecution of a high Gestapo official and a group of S.A. The evidence was said to establish the most "shocking torture" of inmates in a concentration camp. Hitler promptly ordered the prosecutions dismissed. Where torture has been alleged, our own cover-ups and failure to prosecute any but lower-level offenders, and often not even them, are more than suggestive.

In Germany, a brilliant feat of propaganda was the perfected weapon of the Third Reich used to accomplish the Nazi takeover of a country and the people, from the laboring class to the elite. Shirer reports in *The Rise and Fall of the Third Reich* that at first the elite were suspicious. But Hitler appealed to their vulnerabilities, their sense of national tradition, and assured them he was a German nationalist and their redeemer, one that the nation sorely sought after the breakdown of the former Weimar Republic. Hitler made promises to nationalize trusts, to institute profit sharing in the wholesale trade, to communalize department stores, and to provide cheap leases to small traders. Land reform was promised as well as the abolition of interest on mortgages. What worker wouldn't rejoice at such visions?

But the elite and the men of industry soon realized that Hitler did not intend to honor a single plank in the party platform that would threaten them. Some few party radicals attempted to take over certain department stores, but they were soon dispossessed and replaced by conservative business types. Promises were made to every class, to every interest, but the only ones kept were those to the industrialists—whose cartels Hitler saw as indispensable to the production of weapons of war. Shirer observed that the one tragic error that consumed all German classes was their failure to comprehend the ruthless violence of the government they embraced.

Today in America the administration, as with all political entities, makes its promises. It promises jobs for all. It promises lowering taxes. It promises morality, care, and compassion. But behind the promises are its acts, which, in fine, constitute the further redistribution of wealth, more wealth to the wealthy—in short—the bequeathing of final economic power to the corporate King, which includes the mammoth, profit-rich, world-dominating weapons makers that have become ensconced in the American economy.

The so-called military-industrial complex has long been identified in America and was the subject of a farewell warning by Eisenhower in 1961. In his departing speech he said, "We annually spend on military security more than the net income of *all* United States corporations. [my emphasis]

"This conjunction of an immense military establishment and a large arms industry is new in the American experience. The total influence—economic, political, even spiritual—is felt in every city, every state house, every office of the federal government. We recognize the imperative need for this development. Yet we must not fail to comprehend its grave implications. Our toil, resources, and livelihood are all involved; so is the very structure of our society.

"In the councils of government, we must guard against the acquisition of unwarranted influence, whether sought or unsought, by the military-industrial complex. *The potential for the disastrous rise of misplaced power exists and will persist.* [my emphasis]

"We must never let the weight of this combination endanger our liberties or democratic processes. We should take nothing for granted. Only an alert and knowledgeable citizenry can compel the proper meshing of the huge industrial and military machinery of defense with our peaceful methods and goals, so that security and liberty may prosper together."

We have not heeded that Republican military president, nor did the German people reflect upon their own history. In America the danger Eisenhower foresaw has never been more clearly at hand.

We have already seen how the power of the corporate King has confiscated control of all radio, television, and the nation's newspapers. *FOX News,* MSMBC, CNBC, and lately CNN, in its tragic struggle to stay alive, along with the wildly popular, far-right talkers in the persons of Rush Limbaugh, Ann Coulter, the reactionary radio diva Laura Ingraham, the closeted conservative Bill O'Reilly, the Hannity fellow (the seer of all evil), the far, far religious right that infects millions of minds with hate, along with CBS, NBC, and ABC, all totally dominated by their corporate advertisers—all have joined to take over the means of mass communication and provide the principal news and political insight available to the America citizen.

The Nazis foresaw the same simple proposition: With the help of the father of propaganda, Joseph Goebbels, Hitler became heir to the German mind. Similarly, vast masses of the American public have come to accept the leadership of those whose ambitions are antithetical to the welfare of the people. Blinded by the mindless mantras of patriotism and fear, mostly created by the administration itself with its terror alerts of various hues, the people have abdicated their rights and embraced this new Fascist state under the illusion that their freedoms are a hindrance to their security.

Propaganda was as powerful a tool in Germany as its war machine. Propaganda was the heart of the movement, the meat in its hamburger. Like seven tools in the toolbox, seven messages consistently appear in the propaganda of hate, and our star players on Team Hate have, from time to time, used all of the tools.

First: The enemy is different than us. With muscular prose the hate propagandist points out the differences. The enemies of Team Hate are liberals, seculars, trial lawyers, and those who stand in the way of the neoconservative plan to dominate the world. The differences are not only in values but in religion and race.

So it was in Nazi Germany—the differences between Christians and Jews, and the assertion—and finally the belief—that all of Germany's suffering lay at the feet of the Jews, a people of a different ethnic origin and religion.

Second: The enemy stands for unspeakable evil. We remember the abhorrence that Team Hate expressed against liberals. They are traitors. They comfort and aid the enemy. The Democrats have been held up as "friends of faggots" and "baby killers." In Hitler's Germany the historical evil was again the Jews, who, as Nazi rhetoric held, were responsible throughout history for the fall of many empires, including Rome and Egypt; and if their influence were allowed to persist, the Jews would destroy the Third Reich.

Third: The enemy has harmed us in the past. Successful hate propaganda holds that the enemy has an evil, hurtful history. Team Hate charges that liberals have willfully wounded America in the past. Coulter resurrects Joseph McCarthy as her hero, who she claims attempted to save America from the choking clutches of communism. Liberals caused our defeat in Vietnam. And liberals under Clinton failed to destroy bin Laden when they had the opportunity. Liberals have undermined our war effort in Iraq and have given the nation over to the indolent, the criminal, and welfare mothers.

Hitler made the same allegations against the Jews in Nazi hate propaganda. It was the Jews, not the Germans' attempt to take over Europe in the First World War, that led to Germany's downfall. And his hatred of the unions and social democratic movements was pathological.

Fourth: The enemy will hurt us in the future. We are told by Team Hate that liberals, the Democrats, and the antiwar demonstrators are not to be trusted. They are anti-American. They are treasonous and plan to deliver the nation to the enemy, to criminals, of course, to trial lawyers, and to a policy of appeasement that weakens and destroys the country.

Still again, the Nazi propagandist held up the Jews as an evil community of plotting, dangerous conspirators along with the Communists. "Know, dear Christian," one Nazi propagandist proclaimed, "and have no doubts about it, that next to the Devil you have no more bitter, poisonous and determined enemy than a genuine Jew. . . . If they do something good for you, it is not because they love you, but because they need room to live with us, so they have to do something. But their heart remains as I have said!"

Fifth: The enemy is not favored by God. But we are. We are the great and the noble—so says the hate propagandist—while the enemy supports the Antichrist. Hate propaganda holds that patriotic Americans must recoil against those who dissent. We are told by Team Hate that America and the conservative leadership are engaged in a great cause to free the world, to install democracy in totalitarian nations, and to see to human rights in certain nations, while liberals at every step of the way attempt to abort those goals.

Hitler, of course, laid out the goal of the Third Reich as the great Godly calling of the fatherland, which included conquering its neighbors to the glory of Germany and the superior Aryan race.

Sixth: The enemy is united against us. Look at the Muslim world and the Axis of Evil. We must unite against the enemy. From the beginning this has been the clarion call of the neoconservatives. The propagandists tell us that we must unify behind true American leadership that manifests true Christian objectives. Team Hate maintains that America is the most powerful nation in the world and that we must bring democracy and moral salvation across the earth, which goals, of course, provide America the rhetorical foundation to dominate the world.

Hitler enflamed an entire nation to unite in order that an Aryan nation of superhumans should at last rule the world. All Germans were to be utterly, uncritically unified behind the Nazi Party's proposed solution to the "Jewish problem." As one writer put it, "One must either affirm or reject anti-Semitism. He who defends the Jews harms his own people. One can only be a Jewish lackey or a Jewish opponent. Opposing the Jews is a matter of personal hygiene."

Seventh: The enemy has brought the end of the world upon us. The hate propagandist tells us that in this age of a nuclear holocaust the final struggle for good against evil is at hand. We face the "Axis of Evil" and their invidious, relentless attempts to obtain nuclear weapons that will end the world. That tune lends a sense of urgency to our lives but provides us with worthy human goals.

Hitler's hate propaganda sang the same tune. The following example was lifted from an anti-Semitic magazine: "Now there is war! The Jews forced us into a struggle for life and death. . . . The devilish hatred of the Jews plunged the world into war, need and misery. Our holy hate will bring us victory and save all of mankind."

Propaganda is the tool of rabid patriotism. Every nation in time of war, on either side of a conflict, employs it to the demonization of the other and to establish the irrefutable righteousness of its own cause. Hitler himself said, "As soon as by one's own propaganda even a glimpse of right on the other side is admitted, the cause for doubting one's own right is laid." In other words, never admit you are wrong—in any way. Remind us of anyone?

I do not foresee the extreme cruelty of the Third Reich descending upon American citizens, not immediately. But I say *not immediately* because the steps to perdition are just that—steps, one at a time, downward. I would never have dreamed that in my lifetime I would hear U.S. senators, much less the vice president, indeed the president himself, excusing torture under any circumstance, particularly in a foreign war in which the purported goal is to establish a democracy.

In America we would never dream of defending our torture of even the most heinous criminal because torture converts the torturer into a criminal as well. Torture and democracy are obviously incompatible. A true democracy can only be the product of enlightened minds. Torture is derived from the most base, despicable dregs of a diseased, inhuman soul.

To sermonize that America's plan for the world is freedom and democracy, and at the first confrontation with the enemy to resort to torture, are in perfect alignment with the hypocrisy we so frequently encounter with the neocon pontificators who are so practiced in identifying evil in others. When we point to the monstrous conduct of others as an excuse for our own, that is to say, when we claim we have the right to torture because others torture, we deliver to our enemies the power to convert us into terrorist thugs as well. One is immediately put in mind of the Third Reich, where torture became the standard weapon against the regime's enemies, that and the furnaces.

Without regard to one's skin color, one's country of origin, one's religion, without regard even to the evil intent or acts of a purported terrorist, every human being, by virtue of his birth, is endowed with certain "inalienable rights," the most important of which is the right to be treated humanely. To do otherwise is to transform ourselves into the beasts we oppose. One of Jefferson's absolutes to which there is no exception: "Nothing then is unchangeable but the inherent and inalienable rights of man." He was not speaking of Americans. He was speaking of mankind.

In Germany scapegoats were identified and demonized. As we have already seen, in this country we've been provided a smorgasbord of hatred, scapegoats that include liberals, trial lawyers, Muslims, immigrants, homosexuals, the poor, and people of color. We are warned against the "Axis of Evil" and told that we must see the thousands of innocent Iraqis killed, including helpless women and children, and other thousands maimed, as mere "collateral damage." And loyal citizens who chose Islam as their religion now fill the files of the FBI. In America the abdication of the people's rights to the corporate state has become progressively more alarming. The courts are packed with judges whose minds click in harmony with the interests of the corporate King. Lawyers and juries are hated so that more and more the only operational law is the law dictated by corporate interests.

Dr. Hans Frank, Commissioner of Justice and Reich Law Leader, told the jurists in 1936—note, he is talking to the judges who will decide the people's cases—"There is no independence of law against National Socialism. Say to yourselves at every decision you make: How would the Führer decide in my place?" Do we see our leaders checking out the way judges think and selecting only those who are in harmony with the interests of power? Sadly, many judges of America no longer conduct an independent judiciary. And more often the law is not the law of the people. It has become the law of the nonpeople.

Under National Socialism there was no effective organization of lawyers that fought for the people's rights. The people's rights, if any, were dictated by the Nazi Party. The Nazi method of destroying the effectiveness of lawyers was, of course, different but dazzlingly effective. Trial lawyers for the people were simply abolished.

Those who have been indoctrinated by the corporate King to hate their warriors might consider what a nation without trial lawyers would be like. Some henchman in a brown shirt would determine our guilt or innocence in accordance with the whim of power. There would be no lawyers to test the state's case against us. We would be simply hauled off to the camps or executed. It can happen.

In the end, perhaps the "justice" of the Third Reich has become the model of the neoconservative. Why worry about human rights? Ask Nancy Grace and Ann Coulter. When trial lawyers are emasculated in the system by the continuous slander of their profession, how does that differ from a simple decree of the Führer that disenfranchises the legal profession's authority? Blacklisting trial lawyers from the species takes only a little longer than an order from the Führer that outlaws the profession outright.

As we have seen, hate is a valuable crop to grow. Its products which are money and power, are stored in the granaries of the government. As O'Reilly has said, and correctly, you have to get them (the people) very "annoyed, aroused, banging at the walls." The Third Reich grew out of the same hate premise.

Jefferson, the slave owner—living in a time of national hypocrisy—was, nevertheless, often perceptive. One of his quotes most relevant today: "When the government fears the people there is liberty. When the people fear the government there is tyranny."

War and Hitler were symbiotic bedfellows, one necessary for the life and power of the other. The rise of the Third Reich was dependent upon its ability to wage war. Today we say we are fighting terror. But who or what is Terror? bin Laden, yes. Perhaps a few lesser known radicals, but at last, *who?*

We *experience* terror. But when we are challenged to personify it, we cannot point our fingers, our guns, or direct our bombers to an identifiable person called Terror. We are then left with the awesome power to hate and attack whomever we wish under the rubric of fighting terror. Without the ability to put better names on our enemies, we identify them by labeling them as "the Axis of Evil." And we rattle our swords at them and conduct ourselves like ignorant primitives without the benefit of history's repeated lessons that teach that the hatred of whole nations, religions, and races gains us only a similar gift of their hatred in return.

William Shakespeare saw it clearly, as he set out in the character Julius Caesar of Rome, who lived during the years 100–44 BC. Here are Ceasar's apocalyptic words: "Beware of the leader who bangs the drums of war in order to whip the citizenry into patriotic fervor, for patriotism is indeed a double-edged sword. It both emboldens the blood, just as it narrows the mind.

"And when the drums of war have reached a fever pitch and

the blood boils with hate and the mind has closed, the leader will have no need in seizing the rights of the citizenry. Rather, the citizenry, infused with fear and blinded by patriotism, will offer up all of their rights unto the leader and gladly so.

"How do I know? For this I have done. And I am Julius Caesar."

So, indeed, was the fervor Hitler fashioned with hate that sired the Third Reich.

Must we learn these lessons over and over, ceaselessly like the blind finding their way through the forest and falling forever over the same precipice? Edward R. Murrow warned that we must not equate "dissent with disloyalty." Already we've heard O'Reilly's take on dissent as unpatriotic. Patriotism was the lifeblood of National Socialism, a belief in a crowning role for Germany in the world. And remember: Throughout the rise of the Third Reich, Hitler maligned liberalism as a Marxist-Jewish conspiracy. Team Hate sees it simply as treason.

Reverend King saw the arrogance of the nation and would have been appalled had he seen George II strutting on the deck of the USS *Abraham Lincoln* proclaiming, "Mission accomplished!" What would Dr. King have said? Here's his quote: "God has a way of standing before the nations with judgment and it seems I can hear God saying to America, 'You are too arrogant! If you don't change your ways I will rise up and break the backbone of your power. And I'll place it in the hands of a nation that doesn't even know my name. Be still and know I'm God.'"

In the beginning Hitler dressed up all of his proclamations in the clothing of the Christian church. In a speech on April 12, 1922, Hitler said, "My feelings as a Christian point me to my Lord and Savior as a fighter. It points me to the man who once in loneliness, surrounded only by a few followers, recognized these Jews for what they were and summoned men to fight against them and who, God's truth! was greatest not as a sufferer but as a fighter. In boundless love as a Christian and as a man I read through the passage which tells us how the Lord at last rose in

His might and seized the scourge to drive out of the Temple the brood of vipers and adders. How terrific was His fight for the world against the Jewish poison."

Hitler was as far right as the wall of insanity and opportunism would permit. In a speech on May Day, 1933, he prayed, "Lord, Thou seest that we have transformed ourselves, the German people is no longer the people of dishonor, of shame, of war within itself, of faintheartedness and little faith: no, Lord, the German people has become strong again in spirit, strong in will, strong in endurance, strong to bear all sacrifices. . . . Lord, we will not let Thee go: bless now our fight for our freedom; the fight we wage for our German people and Fatherland."

In a speech at Würzburg on June 27, 1937, Hitler said, "I am convinced that men who are created by God should live in accordance with the will of the Almighty. . . . If Providence had not guided us I could often never have found these dizzy paths. . . . Thus it is that we National Socialists, too, have in the depths of our hearts our faith. We cannot do otherwise: no man can fashion world-history or the history of peoples unless upon his purpose and his powers there rests the blessings of this Providence."

Again, there are lessons to be learned as we see the leaders of vast masses of Americans endorsing war in the name of Jesus and preaching against the very principles of brotherly love that form the foundation of Christianity. It is clear, both from our observation of such rubbish as is spewed by the likes of Pat Robertson and the demagoguery of Hitler, that the words of Christ can be twisted to support a world vision antithetical to Christ. One ought not pass judgment on the religious experience of George II, but his "born-again" confessions contrast with the actions he condones under the acclaimed cloak of Christianity.

Seymour Hersh, writing in *The New Yorker* magazine, insists that "Bush's [George W.] closest advisers have long been aware of the religious nature of his policy commitments." A former senior official said that after 9/11 "he [the official] was told that Bush felt that 'God put me here' to deal with the war on terror," and after his reelection "Bush saw the victory as a purposeful message from God that 'he's the man.'"

Is the man aware of what is happening in the world under his command? Hersh, quoting the former senior official, advises, "He [Bush] doesn't feel any pain. Bush is a believer in the adage, 'People may suffer and die, but the Church advances.'"

I shudder.

It is a fact that in the rise of the Third Reich many of its leading personalities, especially among the clergy, sympathized with Hitler or openly worked for his party. In Germany National Socialism became a disguised religion. Fritz Stern, a refugee from Hitler's Germany and a leading scholar of European history, described the religion as a "rebellion of the German mind against the West, the hatred for Modernism—in economics, politics, art—and for anything that could be described as *liberal*." Stern said that the Nazi movement fed on the simple fact that "our liberal and industrial society leaves many people dissatisfied—spiritually and materially. The spiritually alienated have often turned to the ideology of the *conservative revolution*." (my italics)

Stern summarized the movement in his acceptance speech upon receiving the prestigious Leo Baeck Medal. "In the late 1920s a group of intellectuals known as conservative revolutionaries demanded a new volkish authoritarianism, a Third Reich." One is immediately put in mind of the conservative power gang in America, some of whom claim to be intellectuals, who endorsed the "Project for a New American Century." We have heard little of the Project for a New American Century (PNAC). It is a Washington-based, neoconservative think tank founded in 1997 to "rally support for American global *leadership*" (a euphemism for world dominance). PNAC's agenda thinks well beyond a regime change in Iraq. Its mission statement begins with the claim that "American foreign and defense policy is adrift" and calls for "a Reaganite policy of military strength and moral clarity."

PNAC's proposal is unilateral military intervention (preemptive strikes—think of Iraq) to protect against threats to America's status as the lone global superpower. In other words, the signers are saying, "We have the power, and we are going to use it to control the world." The statement is signed by such notables in the neoconservative camp as Dick Cheney, Jeb Bush, Lewis "Scooter" Libby, Donald Rumsfeld, Paul Wolfowitz, and others.

Most of the founding members of PNAC held positions in the Reagan or Daddy Bush administrations or in neoconservative think tanks, publications, and right-wing advocacy groups—the "gang of seven" or something like it.

An important step in PNAC's developing power was its major publication, "Rebuilding America's Defenses: Strategy, Forces and Resources for a New Century" (RAD), released in September 2000. RAD argued against defense cuts and urged that "preserving the desirable strategic situation in which the United States now finds itself requires a globally preeminent military capability both today and in the future." The United States must have the ability to "fight and decisively win multiple, simultaneous major theater wars" and to reposition permanent forces in Southeast Europe and Southeast Asia.

Taking on the "Axis of Evil" has become a reality. We have the power to beat up on half the world at once. As stated in RAD, "At present the United States faces no global rival. America's grand strategy should aim to preserve and *extend* this advantageous position as far into the future as possible." (my emphasis) These are simply long words to say in short, "We should conquer the world. We have the power. Use it."

Now read this from RAD: "[N]ew methods of attack—electronic, 'non-lethal,' biological—will be more widely available . . . 'combat' likely will take place in new dimensions: in space, 'cyber-space,' and perhaps the world of microbes . . . advanced forms of biological warfare that can 'target' specific genotypes may transform biological warfare from the realm of terror to a politically useful tool."

God Bless America.

This agenda of PNAC lay substantially dormant, and PNAC

admitted that their project would likely take a long time to see fruition "absent some catastrophic and catalyzing event—like a new Pearl Harbor." Then fortuitously along came 9/11. Just what PNAC had hoped for. Some suggest, I think without any convincing evidence, that they or their fellow conspirators had a hand in bringing about this "catalyzing event," something, say, like Germany's Reichstag fire.

Shortly after September 11, PNAC sent a letter to President Bush II welcoming his call for "a broad and sustained campaign" and encouraging the removal of Saddam. We remember Cheney's futile attempt to link Iraq with bin Laden. Thereafter weapons of mass destruction became the theme. Imperialists always need a theme, the message, the propaganda, the call to arms, the patriotism—you know the drill.

In recounting the Third Reich's conservative movement in Germany, Stern said, "Richly financed by corporate interests, they denounced liberalism as the greatest, most invidious threat, and attacked it for its tolerance, rationality and cosmopolitan culture." Stern went on to observe, "These conservative revolutionaries were proud of being prophets of the Third Reich—at least until some of them were exiled or murdered by the Nazis when the latter came to power. Throughout, the Nazis vilified liberalism. . . ." No one denies that it was a conservative revolution that led Germany's elite into National Socialism.

But why would a nation of decent people succumb to a movement as patently evil as Nazism? Nietzsche's dictum is informative: "Weariness that wants to reach the ultimate with one leap, with one fatal leap, a poor, ignorant weariness that does not want to want anymore: This created all gods and other worlds." It's Nietzsche's weariness I've been writing about—the sense of futility, of being trapped, of never being able to get ahead, of being helplessly ensconced in routine from which there is no escape and where one is cheated of his just dues. A weariness does evolve, and an anger.

Eric Fromm in *Escape from Freedom* wrote: "Psychologically, this readiness to submit to the Nazi regime seems to be due mainly to a state of inner tiredness and resignation which is characteristic of the individual in the present era even in democratic countries." Fromm was writing as early as 1941. He saw in Nazi Germany a people who believed that Hitler's government *became* Germany, and that fighting Hitler was the same as cutting oneself off from one's homeland.

The longing for tribe, the need of people to belong to a larger group, is as endemic in the species as birds that flock and fish that school. Fromm said, "It seems that nothing is more difficult for the average man to bear than the feeling of not being identified with a larger group." We see its power to attract countless thousands on any given Sunday afternoon to our national corporate sports.

The inner tiredness recognized by both Nietzsche and Fromm leaves the working American, indeed, most Americans who are caught in the corporate trap, feeling irrelevant and powerless. The most common statement we hear from people in all levels of society today is: "What can I do? I am nothing." Fromm said of the rising Nazi power, "The vast majority of the population was seized with the feeling of individual insignificance and powerlessness which we have described as typical for monopolistic capitalism in general."

In America today there is little chance for advancement at the workplace, and, in such economic times as we have encountered, a job is worth the near total subservience required to keep it. The employee enjoys a paucity of rights in the workplace, and if he endeavors to enforce the few he has he will likely receive the dreaded pink slip for whatever reasons management may concoct. The worker is exhausted.

It is against a similar background that Fromm observed, "Although foreign and internal threats of Fascism must be taken seriously, there is no greater mistake and no graver danger than not to see that in our own society we are faced with the same phenomenon that is fertile soil for the rise of Fascism anywhere: the insignificance and powerlessness of the individual."

The fear of being alone, of being left out, can lead to dangerous places. In Germany even those who might have opposed
Nazism preferred defending it than be alone. In the American Indian tribes, the horror of being ejected from the tribe was the fear
that kept the tribe together. The greatest punishment was not the
death penalty. It was expulsion from the tribe. This power over the
people presents itself in every society.

In America today, the fear that one might be seen as un-
American if one does not support the war effort in Iraq motivates
people to blindly, often irrationally, defend it. In Germany, Goering attacked the peacemakers as unpatriotic, which also left them
exposed to the death camps if their opposition was much more
than impotent grumbling.

Every American knows that so-called preemptive strikes
against any nation are, except in the most extreme circumstance
where our annihilation is plainly imminent, not the act of a democratic nation, but the campaign of an aggressor undertaken in the
name of whatever rationalization is touted by the propaganda of
the time. Most of America rallied behind the attack of Iraq. So,
too, in Nazi Germany were the Nazi invasions of peaceful European countries celebrated in the cause of a free and expanding
German Empire.

There can be no question that the war in Iraq was launched to
forward the interests of the people in power. What were those interests? Those interests were both economic and ideological. We
are running out of oil. People in power have economic interests,
laid aside like a cask of gold waiting to be dug up. The people in
power have political interests, namely, the retention of power. But
the average American doesn't give a damn about the Israel-Arab
issue—not enough to lay down the lives of thousands of American youths whose caskets we are not allowed to see.

Still, Americans do care if they think some insane leader across
the world is about to launch a nuclear bomb on our country.
Hence, the cry of weapons of mass destruction; the anthrax scare,

which, incidentally, has never been solved; the rallying of the troops behind a "great wartime leader," who can't figure out how to get from Washington, D.C., to New Orleans; and the invasion of Iraq, which has bankrupted a nation morally, spiritually, and economically.

Power has tickled and seduced military leaders from Alexander the Great to Caesar. Napoleon had his excuses; the Crusaders theirs. Hitler and his gang sent out their rationalizations for invading their neighbors. And George II claims he and God are in this hand in hand. But the bottom line on all such territorial conquests is power, the testosterone-laden male who follows his perniciously powered penis to conquer like a pack of marauding rodents led by an alpha rat.

As I have noted, the mainstay of the individual's security is the family, and in America the family has been shattered. We have seen that the new family is television, and the collective voice of that family is one that purveys extraordinary quantities of hatred and violence. That danger—as manipulated in the hands of a movement, a party, or some future charismatic leader—is incalculable and has never posed a greater threat to America.

However, we need not be alone when we oppose that which is simply wrong. To be thrown out of the community for our ethical beliefs is to be joined in a world community where that which is right still remains audible. *We* choose the club, locally, nationally, or worldwide, in which we seek membership.

I have asked, Who can we trust today? We no longer trust the church, the priest, the preachers, the politicians, the professions, the power corporations, or the people. Who do we trust? A powerful, charismatic leader can emerge; and when and if that happens, the longing for someone to trust can suck up our trust hunger like a descending tornado. So it was in Nazi Germany. However, the most compelling danger is not the corporate oligarchy under which we are enslaved, but the people themselves, who feel lost, powerless, and trapped, who have given up, and who are unable to free themselves.

The gross hypocrisy of Hitler is fairly well matched in our own times by the blatant, unapologetic hypocrisy of Team Hate, the likes of them, and the Christian right, as well as by the current administration, which seeks to spread democracy through killing, freedom by torture, and Christianity by violence.

Kill for Jesus!

Hitler spoke of freedom and grabbed absolute, dictatorial power. He condemned the Jews for stealth and lying, while being a master at it himself. One must realize, lest one be caught in one's own hypocritical trap, that hypocrisy is not reserved for only Team Hate or the Nazi regime. In the end it belongs to all of us in various degrees and, as we have seen, usually reveals that which we hate most in ourselves.

Hitler's rise to power, as that of any demagogue, was the product of the leader's appeal to the emotions and prejudices of the people. Propaganda and hate were his weapons. War sealed his power, since war demands patriotism, and patriotism denounces critical debate. In the end, as has been the case in every civilization, the power of the people is delivered to the tyrant or stolen from the people by fraud or force. Democracy remains safe so long as the people have not been converted into a citizenry of hate. But when hate, as in Nazi Germany, is cultivated, and when skillful spokespersons of the corporate King foment hate continuously in the kitchens, the living rooms, and the bedrooms of a nation through the electronic media, our freedoms—indeed, the fate of a nation—are at serious risk.

13. The End of Hate

Return to the Garden

John Lennon once said, "Our society is run by insane people for insane objectives. . . . I think we're being run by maniacs for maniacal ends . . . and I think I'm liable to be put away as insane for expressing that. That's what's insane about it."

Must all who criticize offer solutions for the insanity we have encountered here? Team Hate is remarkable for its silence on suggested remedies, except their assurance that we must rid ourselves of liberals and conquer both the nation and the world as God's chosen. They do, however, want to take care of Halliburton, make corporations even more powerful, and save the world for their brand of democracy.

Conservative thought has not changed in my lifetime. No new ideas, no growth. When I was a young conservative still wet and dripping behind the ears (we have all sinned) I ran in the Republican primary against a do-nothing, many-termed congressman named William Henry Harrison—named after his president-grandfather. The grandson, before he came to Wyoming to get into politics, was a native of Indiana. I learned that Wyoming Republicans, which was every rancher and a few oil dudes, wanted their lone congressman to do nothing.

Nothing!

Stay out of our hair. Change nothing. Keep government locked in some political closet back there in Washington, wherever that was. Leave us alone. Go back to Washington and shut up. Your name, William Henry Harrison, is pretty and that's enough. (His president-grandfather died before he could do anything, and the family tenaciously held on to that tradition—turned it into a sacred tenet.)

After a door-to-door state-wide campaign, I remember how a few of us were huddled around the radio listening to the returns on election night. Bill, Wyoming, proud that it had always been the first to report, reported first. It was Gerry Spence, two votes, and William Henry Harrison, one. Two to one! I was practically in!

But you can't beat a name like that, and my campaign premise was dead wrong. I kept telling the people, "Let's be heard in Washington." The people didn't want to be heard in Washington. They wanted good old William Henry to stay where he was on a bunch of do-nothing committees and if he could disappear in Washington—maybe buy some Girl Scout cookies, but nothing much more—and if Wyoming could disappear from national consideration, that is exactly what the people of this great state yearned for.

Nearly all successful Wyoming congresspersons and senators have abided faithfully to that tradition. When was the last time you heard anything from or about our congressional delegation? People mostly think Wyoming is a town up there someplace in Montana.

Anyway, I had launched my vigorous door-to-door campaign in most of the little towns—a couple dozen of them. Only about three hundred thousand people in the state. Lotta open space, lotta jackrabbits, antelope, prairie dogs, rattlesnakes, mountains, and desolation. Not many people. After I'd knocked on every door in the town of Kemmerer, about two thousand souls (JCPenney's first store was in Kemmerer, and I have no doubt that his success was totally attributable to the fact that he couldn't stand the isolation, few could, so he started stores elsewhere and just kept moving on)—in any event, after I'd knocked on every door in Kemmerer and told the householders that we should be heard in Washington, and gave them my big Wyoming howdy, my big Wyoming smile, and my little card telling why we should be heard in Washington, I decided to do a little polling. Those were the days when polling was done only by a bunch of rich Washington know-it-alls. No one polled in Wyoming.

So I got holed up in my motel room, one of those motels that has a hand-painted sign out front that reads "Modern," which means they had running water, maybe, a toilet, with luck, and in this case, a phone inside. I began calling randomly from the names in the phonebook. It was about suppertime.

"I am calling to see what you think about the race for Congress between William Henry Harrison and Gerry Spence," I'd say.

"Gerry Who?"

"You know, Gerry Spence, that young prosecutor, that native son from Riverton, Wyoming, who is running for Congress against William Henry Harrison in the Republican primary. If you were to vote today, who would you vote for?"

"It's none of yer fuckin' business."

Some just plain hung up. But most claimed they'd never heard of Gerry Spence, whoever he was, and they were likely to stick with the old horse. "Ya gotta stick with the old horse." The plug. Harrison's margin of victory over that thirty-two-year-old Spence, who wanted Wyoming to be heard in Washington, was embarrassing. I did carry my own county, which is more than Dick Cheney's party did (Cheney claims Teton County, Wyoming, as his). Today it's my county as well. It was the only county in Wyoming that went blue in the last election.

I've observed conservatives during a lifetime, and they've not changed one little bit, except to add *super*hate and *mega*war to their agenda. They offer few other creative ideas about anything. But that is the definition of conservatism. What was good enough for Grandpa is good enough for me. As someone quipped, "A conservative is someone who thinks nothing should be done for the first time."

Of course, during those days to which I refer with some ambivalence, homosexuals were still locked in the closet, doctors who performed abortions were criminals, gasoline was about fifty cents a gallon, we were loved in the world because we'd fought Hitler, Tojo, and Mussolini, and won. We'd actually brought democracy to a few parts of the world. Halliburton, if it existed, was minding its own business cleaning up oil wells in Wyoming; and Jesus lovers still loved everyone, especially us sinners. African-Americans were unheard of in Wyoming, and Martin Luther King Jr., who was exactly one week younger than I, would start his march about a year after I ran for Congress. He had a better vision for America than I, but even his visions were, as he confessed, dreams.

Television was still in its infancy. We had those antennas on the rooftops and got ABC, CBS, and NBC—sometimes. In Wyoming static and snow attacked us from both inside and outside on both the TV and from the sky. Porn, whatever it was, was outlawed. The First Amendment had not yet been stretched to shield it, and Justice Potter Stewart on the Supreme Court couldn't define it but said, as one might say about beauty, "I know it when I see it." Having seen it, I'm not confident the good judge ever recovered from it.

But in the end Wyoming conservatives saw things about the way they do today. The poor should work harder. Minorities are really not Americans, and women know their place, which is in the home and on the bed when beckoned. Abortion and homosexuality are against God, and we are on his side and he's on ours.

We all know that the only effective weapon against hate and its hateful produce is love. In writing this book I'd not realized how hard it is to love when those we hate don't love us back. The love feeling has not often overwhelmed me as I've laid out the foregoing chapters. Perhaps truth must precede love. It is hard to love a high pile of lies. Even Jesus didn't have to deal with that. He only had to run money changers out of the temple and face the Romans who wanted to kill him. They were at least honest about it.

Today we're divided into two camps of spiraling hate. It is a two-party system of hate. To be sure all the hate is not lodged on the right. A division in the philosophies of the two parties is what America has become. The division is often hazy, often contradictory, and what one party holds close today the other party may hail as its own tomorrow. But the differences at any given time have been necessary in theory because if there isn't a difference, then what's the point of a two-party system?

In most ways differences between the parties have not been differences in measuring truth or honesty or what is good for America, but what is good for the party or the politician seeking power. The political game is one that is carried on above the people—like a couple of thieves who've decided to steal all the chickens locked up in the chicken house. Their fight over the chickens has little to do with the well-being of the captured poultry. The politician's war is a power game that uses people for the politician's purposes rather than a process to uplift and better a people. As we've seen, hate has become the principal fuel that drives this game.

Today hate rages in America at its highest levels since, perhaps, the Civil War and has become intractable, as evidenced by the rash and irresponsible diatribes of Team Hate. Ann Coulter is still calling liberals traitors. Nancy Grace still insists that lawyers who defend our constitutional rights in a trial are snakes. Laura Ingraham still thinks those with brains are elitists, and Bill O'Reilly still suggests we starve the hell out of civilians because they are responsible for the leaders they've chosen.

As for the religious right, I'm for their freedom to rake in fortunes by prostituting the teachings of Christ. This is still America. I think the nation and the people would be better off, however, if the conservatives, yes, the Republicans, would follow their own advice and keep government out of things. If you don't like abortion, well, don't get one. If you don't think same-sex marriage is any fun, or is quirky, even immoral, then don't marry someone of the same sex. Forget it.

The noble calling of a democracy is the willingness of people of different views to follow their beliefs in peace, and to let everyone else freely follow theirs. To dip religious issues into the political vat so that they come out dripping with intolerance and hate does not help the country or set an example for the world about how a democracy honors the rights and lives of a minority. To kill people who run abortion clinics, and to condemn people to hell for being as God or a set of random genes made them, do not assist us in getting along with each other.

We ought never elect a leader who, as Caesar in Shakespeare warned, "beats the drums for war." We must seek a leader who, by his own conduct, encourages people to care about each other and who lays it all down for their right to worship and live together in peace.

We need to return to a tribal view, to convert America into one large, truly democratic community of tolerance and trust. We need an army, but an army to first fight critical battles against poverty and the natural disasters we suffer at home. Whole communities at risk, their workers unemployed, their homes being foreclosed by the banks, can be greatly assisted for the cost of a single rocket of death that is launched in these criminal wars. The air force brags that its $2.2 billion batwing bombers are nearly invisible to radar and are capable of dropping sixteen bombs on as many as sixteen different targets. These bombers are also invisible to the objectives of world peace. I can't calculate how many millions of kids could be educated for the cost of the twenty-one stealth bombers that this country has already acquired for something in excess of $40 billion.

Where do we begin to bring about the change that is necessary for peace—for peace at home and in the world, without which we will surely perish? We can no longer look to our neighbors to change, our leaders to change, or other countries to change. We, ourselves, each of us, must change. It all begins with us. Personally. Individually.

The task, as simple as it seems, is for each of us to become a *person*. This was not intended to be a book of sermons, but sometimes I fail. What do I mean by "becoming a *person?*" It is a life's work that recognizes that all others are persons as well. It is the acceptance of our own uniqueness and beauty that grows out of a respect and acceptance of the uniqueness and beauty of all others. It is a goal at which I too often fall short. But when the goal is expressed and thereby recognized, the first step toward its achievement has been taken. If the world were filled with *persons,* hate would be a useless force.

Peace and democracy are not compatible with war and hate. We must change America's view of itself from a monstrous power of killing and destruction and world domination to a worldwide spirit of caring, peace, and compassion. A new generation of children should be taught peace games, not war games. We must convert ourselves from an incomparable world power that—at the whim of stupid men—can release our ungodly force of destruction on innocent populations, to a nation of *persons* who can release a godly power to assist our world neighbors in the problems that are critical to their survival.

We must condemn statements like Ann Coulter's when she says, "We should invade their countries, kill their leaders, and convert them to Christianity." What would Jesus say about that, Ann? My book is mostly a polemic, an argument for human dignity and human rights. But someone needs to *say* those words clearly, for such words as "peace" and "love" and "understanding" and "caring" contain more power than all the rhetoric of hate that the ignorant and malevolent can devise.

The church, once the fountainhead of peace and love, too often fails to exercise its power to create peace and love. Too often it has become but another instrument of hate and leaves a fearsome void that cries to be filled by a new, genuine Christian leadership, one that can lift us up from this downward plunge toward our own destruction. Hate kills. Wars destroy. Every war leader in the history of the world has led his troops to final destruction. Such will be our fate and the fate of our children if we fail to stem the flooding flow of hate that escapes from many of our Christian churches.

We are called to fight a war against terror. Those who have sought to terrorize us by their criminal acts of 9/11 have already won the battle of terror. We *are* terrorized. But we have delivered to our enemy a greater power—the power to transform us into terrorists ourselves as, in turn, we terrorize whole populations across the world whose innocent citizens had nothing to do with the attacks made on us.

Let's reverse roles here for a moment. Suppose we are an ordinary family in Iraq. Father runs a small neighborhood grocery store, has for many years, like his father before him. He is a Muslim of the Sunni tribe. Mother is occupied with the family of three small children. The family has lived under the pressures imposed by a dictator, as have the family's parents and grandparents. Like an average American family, the concerns of democracy have little to do with their day-to-day lives.

One day bombs are dropped on the city and the people are, indeed, terrorized. The earth shakes. There is no electricity. There is no water. The sewers are plugged. No telephone. The air is filled with poisonous smoke. The mother's parents were killed the first day when a bomb landed in their neighborhood. There was no way to conduct a religious burial. Unleashed terror and pandemonium. *Shock and awe.* When the father finally arrives at his store, he finds that it has been looted by the roaming lawless.

The next day the earth continues to shake. The roof in the house caves in and the smallest girl's back is broken, but there is no way to get her to a hospital. The streets are blocked with rubble

and soldiers. The father's car is turned back. Then someone speaks
to him about democracy and freedom.

We cannot mock the teaching of Jesus or Mother Teresa or
Gandhi or Martin Luther King Jr. by waging war. The war we
must wage is one to understand our world neighbors and to become a *part* of a world community as opposed to becoming its op-
pressor. We must begin anew to create a nation that exports love as
opposed to a nation that revels in its ability to bully its neighbors.
Martin Luther King Jr. called for "an overriding loyalty to
mankind as a whole" and "unconditional love for all men." That
idea, as simple as it is, befuddles heads brimming with hatred and
greed—those lusty bedfellows. In the end a war against terrorism
such as we've seen is an oxymoron undertaken by morons.

I do not attach myself to any church. If one is required to accept all of the dogma of the fundamental Christian religion, I am
not a Christian. But the teachings of Christ, stripped of all of the
myth surrounding them, are the only ideals that can save this nation and the world. I am speaking again of love, not hate, of turning the other cheek, not turning on the threat of nuclear war or
launching a war of "shock and awe." I am speaking of a national
conscience that puts people first and pulls greed down from the
top of our list of virtues, that puts peace first and sees war as ar-
chaic and uncivilized. Here is a part of Mohamed ElBaradei's Nobel lecture. He asks us to use our imaginations:

> Imagine what would happen if the nations of the world
> spent as much on development as on building the machines
> of war.
>
> Imagine a world where every human being would live in
> freedom and dignity.
>
> Imagine a world in which we would shed the same tears
> when a child dies in Darfur or Vancouver.
>
> Imagine a world where we would settle our differences
> through diplomacy and dialogue and not through bombs or
> bullets. Imagine if the only nuclear weapons remaining were

the relics in our museums. Imagine the legacy we could leave to our children.

Unless we use our imaginations wisely and with love, ours will be a legacy of hate and debt and, eventually, death.

We must drive corporations out of politics and return the control of the nation to Americans. Corporations are nourished and flourish in war. They consume people as fodder. I have pointed out that our founders did not anticipate the existence of a corporate state. They had been dominated by the East India Company, the queen's corporation, chartered in 1600 to carry on the business of the throne. That corporation maintained its own standing army and fought its private wars, which ultimately opened up the opium trade with China. The Hudson's Bay Company, another corporation, exploited the Indians and stripped large portions of the continent of its fur-bearing animals.

It was the East India Company that forced cheap government-subsidized tea on the colonists, leading to the Boston Tea Party, a prelude to the American Revolution. Our founders saw corporations as entities of their enslavement.

But a judiciary of their own creation would soon betray the founders. Jefferson saw it coming. He said,

> . . . The germ of dissolution of our federal government is in the constitution of the federal judiciary, an irresponsible body working like gravity by night and by day, gaining a little today and a little tomorrow, and advancing its noiseless step like a thief over the fields of jurisdiction, until all shall be usurped from the states, and the government of all consolidated into one.

The court that Jefferson warned of, in fact, gave birth to the American corporation we know today. At that moment the doom of a democracy was sealed. When the idea of a corporation once reared its ugly head, Jefferson said, "I hope we shall crush in its birth the aristocracy of our moneyed corporations which dare already challenge our government to a trial of strength, and bid defiance to the laws of our country."

The founders had never foreseen that corporations would be given the rights of people. But in 1886, Justice Harlan delivered the opinion of the United States Supreme Court in the now infamous *Santa Clara County v. Southern Pacific Railroad Company* case, which granted corporations *the same rights as living persons* under the Fourteenth Amendment to the Constitution.

The constitution makes no mention of a corporation. Even more disturbing is the fact that the doctrine of corporate personhood found its way into the decision in *Santa Clara* without argument, the presiding judge stating that the court did not wish to hear argument on that proposition because all of the judges had agreed in advance that a corporation had such rights.

The Constitution, at least the one envisioned by Jefferson, contemplated that our nation would be run by people for people, not by money for money. Lincoln left us his lasting entreaty, that "government of the people, by the people, for the people, shall not perish from the earth." I join him in that prayer. Although Lincoln led us through the Civil War, which freed black slaves, still, ironically, he could never have foreseen the more subtle slavery we suffer today that began with the massive expansion of the corporate industrial state following that war.

How do we extricate government from corporations? The question can be expanded to ask how can we drive big money out of government. Legislative efforts to limit campaign contributions and to fence corporations out of the political process have been blithely tossed out by the Supreme Court on the grounds of the First Amendment and other such specious notions. Because the Supreme Court of the United States will always stand guardian over the rights of the illegitimate offspring it produced, namely the corporate person, and since its history is to favor money over people, it will require a constitutional amendment to return America to Americans—a difficult way out, something like escaping from Alcatraz.

Here's why: As required by the Constitution, how do we go about convincing two-thirds of both houses in Congress or the legislatures of two-thirds of the states to bring the amendment forward for consideration by the states, which then requires approval by three-fourths of the states, when, indeed, the legislatures, national and state, are controlled by the corporations we are attempting to disenfranchise? This is as ridiculous as asking the king to open his vault for the poor. Reform always requires a revolution. As Rosa Parks opined, "People, not government, bring change."

A revolution begins not with guns but with a revolution of thought. A revolution of thought begins with a revolution of knowledge. A revolution of knowledge requires that people be fully informed. But here again we face a nearly impossible obstacle: the media that informs the people is also owned by the corporate King. Can you see IBM sponsoring a television program that calls for the ousting of corporations from the elective process? How about Toyota sponsoring some sitcom in which the theme is to rid America of corporations. The Simpsons suddenly see the light. They realize they are slaves of the corporate overlord and start a movement. What corporation will sponsor such programs? *The entertainment cuisine that is fed Americans is to distract us from the servitude we suffer, not to assist us in overthrowing it.*

Can you even imagine the Academy Awards being sponsored by some interest other than new cars and credit cards? What would happen in America if such a program were sponsored by, say, an organization called Tell the Truth (TTT) that, in fact, tells Americans how our government is bought and sold by huge corporations, and that before we can change our Constitution to protect us from corporate servitude we must understand that truth? Even if we could finance it, do we think that such an advertising campaign would be tolerated by our corporate-controlled networks?

What about National Public Radio or Public Television? These so-called people's networks are also controlled by the same corporate glob. Public radio and television, in most part, look to our corporate-controlled Congress and to corporate sponsors for their existence. They can pretend independence, but even their pretenses are as transparent as window glass. The day a campaign against corporate America is commenced on public radio or television is the day these "independent networks" disappear.

So what am I saying here? To change our Constitution requires that the people be informed, that they be told the truth (TTT). To tell the truth to the people we must obtain a free media. A people such as ours, who are already steaming with anger, who know something is wrong but cannot quite understand what it is, a people who are being distracted from the issues that face them while being fed a diet of hate by the corporate King—such a people cannot free themselves and take back their government. It is all very simple. No voice, no revolution of thought, no power to amend the Constitution, no taking back the government—indeed, a continued servitude to the corporate King.

What we see is something akin to the piteous power held over pre–Civil War black slaves. The slaves outnumbered their masters manyfold, but they could not communicate with each other and had no collective voice. They were mostly born into slavery and did not know of a life beyond their slavery. That model has been dutifully followed by our corporate masters. Yes, I speak out here freely, but if the voice gets too loud and is heard by too many, well, there will perhaps be that knock at my door.

I have already said that it is likely fewer people than attend a Sunday afternoon football game in any given stadium across the land will read this book, and I hold great sympathy for those fewer still who have braved the preceding chapters to bring themselves to this, the last chapter. The distractions are too many. It takes energy to read. People are weary. And it takes courage to consider ideas different from the ones we've been taught. It is easier to let others think for us. But I have hope, else I would not have bothered you or myself with all this in the first place.

I have often not been kind when kindness would have been a better course. The ideas here are not radical, but they will be attacked as radical. What is radical about returning America to Americans? The language may, at times, be seen as excessive. But William Lloyd Garrison, the great abolitionist, said of his own excessiveness, "I will be as harsh as truth, and as uncompromising as justice. On this subject [slavery], I do not wish to think or speak or write with moderation. No! No!"

We can accomplish some reform without a constitutional convention. When corporations are caught in crimes, they most often pay a fine that is less than the amount of profit they enjoyed from their crime. Since corporations enjoy the same rights as we humans, corporations should be subject to the same punishment. They should be subject to the same "Three strikes and you're out" rule as are human felons. Three felony convictions and you and I go to the pen for life as an habitual criminal. Three felony convictions of the corporation, and it is dissolved and put out of business permanently.

Corporations that commit crimes or negligently cause injury should be required to advertise their conviction or the adverse finding against them as a part of every ad they put on television—something like the warning we hear from a siren's voice on television that sweetly, lovingly tells us that this drug may have bad side effects. Can you hear some voice for a given company saying after its commercial, "And you should be advised that we have been previously found guilty of defrauding our shareholders," or, "You are advised that our product has been found unsafe in the case of *Jones v. Get Well Drug Company*"?

By law we can and should make every employee a whistleblower. If the employee becomes aware of a corporate violation, it becomes his responsibility, subject to penalty, to advise his superiors in writing of the same. No longer can the people "upstairs" claim they didn't know of it. Moreover, it will be the responsibility of the supervisors to advise the CEO and the CEO the board of directors. If appropriate action is not taken forthwith by the people on top, the immunity that has traditionally protected workers and officers along the hierarchy would be lost, and each individual who had a duty to act and failed to do so would be subject to direct criminal prosecution.

Other corporate reforms are possible and available to the creative mind. In the end, the ability to rein in the corporate overlord can bring some sense of the restoration of power to the people and reduce the quantum of hate from which Americans suffer.

We suffer from a form of government that favors the self-interested and power hungry over the pure and the selfless. No politician that I know of ever told the people the truth—that his first goal was not to help the people but to benefit himself—that his narcissistic needs demand attention—that his troubled, ambitious psyche is hollering at him to obtain power. He cannot obtain the power he hungers for by telling the truth, even if he knows the truth, which, if he said the truth, would sound like this:

"Folks, I want to be your senator because I crave power. I want recognition. I want to be called 'Senator' and 'sir.' I want to feel the headiness that is associated with being a big shot. I want to associate with the big shots. You know, I want to go to those Senate prayer breakfasts."

And if one were to ask, "What about the people's wants?"

If he knew the truth and answered truthfully he would say, "The people? Oh, well, I will take care of them, of course. But the real reason I want the job is for myself. Don't you understand? *For myself.* If it ever comes between me and the people, the people can go to hell."

This is not to disparage all politicians, some of whom may harbor noble ideals about standing in as the savior of the people despite their personal ambition. Don't forget, even the founders of our constitution were men of wealth who wanted to enhance their wealth, and Washington held ambitions that extended into the frontier West, where he owned large tracts of raw land.

The ancient Chinese understood the dilemma in politics. They saw that those who sought power ought not be trusted with it, that the very seeking of power disqualified the seeker, for personal ambition is nearly always in conflict with the best interests of the governed.

To travel to another galaxy is impossible. But Einstein provided us a theory by which to reduce our fictional dreams of space travel to *possible* dreams, a dream resting at the most distant edge of reality. Accordingly Buck Rogers might zoom around in outer space by reason of the ideas contained in Einstein's famous equation, $E=mc^2$. It is axiomatic that we cannot accomplish that which we cannot imagine.

Let us dream together. Dreams are road maps to reality. I will share some of mine with you. And although I hold no realistic ambition for them, nevertheless they offer a place for idle thought, something perhaps marginally more productive than working the day's crossword puzzle.

I dream of *pancake government*. A simple idea about a simple idea. You can make pancakes from scratch, or you can buy ready-made pancake mix. Democracy is the same. It has few ingredients beyond the flour of freedom, the eggs and milk of knowledge, and the baking powder of opportunity. But most of us have our democracy handed to us in a box, the pancake mix sold on the grocer's shelf, a democracy that is premade for us. Our knowledge is limited—what's in the box is what we are told. Often we are given false knowledge to ensure a result the corporate King seeks. The best way to obtain a pure, functioning democracy is to get out of the box. And, yes, to *eliminate elections and political parties.*

But how do we enjoy a free government without elections?

By eliminating elections, we eliminate the politician. By eliminating the politician, we eliminate the grasp for personal power in government. By eliminating the grasp for power, we deliver the government back to the people. We simply *choose our representatives by lot,* by random selection. Every eligible voter's name is contained in the computer. When we seek a representative we simply let the computer pick our representative by random selection. No campaigns. No false promises. No money spent buying the office. No vile propaganda. Hate for the other side is eliminated.

Yes, to be sure, the computer can pick a fool, but the person selected has not sought the job. He or she has been drafted and *must serve.* Already we've eliminated the frauds and charlatans who overrun the system. And surely we don't contend that those who represent us today are especially qualified. Some are proven idiots. All have personal agendas. Many have already sold out. Fools and fakes abound in Congress. At least by this method we are not dealing with those who have sold their souls for a smidgen of power.

Just compensation commensurate with the needs of the person drafted would be paid by the state—a lot less expense than the cost of government-financed election campaigns and the millions spent by corporations to elect their toadies. Yes, remember, elections are abolished. Campaigns are over with. The opportunity to buy candidates with campaign contributions (a euphemism for the "bought" candidate) is history.

We ask, "How do we know what the person selected stands for?"

How do we know what any candidate really stands for? All candidates lie or fail to tell us the whole truth, else they couldn't be elected. That is the simple essence of politics. The office seeker tells us what we want to hear in order that he or she may steal our votes. In establishing *pancake democracy* there is no opportunity to lie. And what we come up with is a reasonable cross selection of representatives from the population. By that I mean there would be more persons randomly selected from the working class than from the moneyed class—that is how a true democracy should function. And those who have been chosen from humble beginnings are more likely to know what is good for our country than those who have never worked a day in their lives and seek office because they have the money to buy it.

I believe it can be scientifically demonstrated that people with names as plain as Jones and Smith are as likely to be as human, as caring, as understanding, as intelligent and qualified to represent their fellow humans as those with names like Rockefeller or Kennedy or Bush.

True, we have had some good, decent, dedicated men and women in office in this country, but the most common complaint we hear today is that those especially qualified do not run for office. They will not subject themselves to the slanders and infamy that candidates must today endure in order to be elected.

This scheme would result in a true representative democracy. Putting control of the country in the hands of workers and minorities and women might be a little frightening to some. Yet those who would be most frightened would be our corporate overlords. I trust people to know what is good for a nation. They would protect their environment, their health, indeed their rights. But there is an underlying wisdom in the people. They would not so burden their former corporate masters that they can no longer compete and thereby place the workers' jobs in jeopardy. On the other hand, the greed of corporate managers would be, at last, controllable.

The person whose name automatically goes into the computer must be a citizen free of a felony conviction, at least thirty-five years of age, and must have a high school or equivalent education. The computer gives those who have a higher degree of education a better chance at being selected than those with a lesser education—that is to say the computer, like a slot machine, will slightly favor education. The person would be drawn from the community in which the person lives so that a farming community is more likely to send a farmer to Congress than an accountant. In the cities, a great variety of representatives would obviously be selected.

In this People's New House of Representatives, the person so selected would serve a term of, say, six years. If our youth can be drafted to fight wars, to lay down their lives for their country, it follows that citizens can and must be drafted to serve their government as well.

I would choose membership to the U.S. Senate in an egalitarian way as well—yes, *pancake democracy*. I dream of a Senate composed of the best minds, the most experienced, the proven qualified persons in the nation. They would be chosen by the House of Representatives we have just created. Each state would caucus and select, say, seven representatives from the total representatives of the state. In the case of a state such as Wyoming with only one representative, six others would be randomly chosen from the state by the computer to make up the state's Senate Selection Committee. This committee would then conduct a search for the best qualified persons in their state to represent them in the People's New Senate.

The person selected might be a scholar, a university president, a poet, an outstanding mother. The person might be a professor, a manufacturer, a small business person, an author, a proven civic leader—yes, even a lawyer. The persons chosen would be exceptional in their fields and would be persons of whom the state is most proud. Each state would send only its best and its brightest, and once and for all those old devils who, election after election, return to the same worn-out seats in the Senate would be sent off to play shuffleboard. Yes, we would miss their knowledge of how government works. But we would not miss the corruption, stagnation, political alliances, and the unholy games that eternal life in the Senate promotes.

In the first selection in both houses, those chosen would be selected for two-, four-, and six-year terms so that in any given selection year thereafter experienced representatives would remain.

Limiting terms of our representatives is automatic. Political parties are ancient history. The evilness of political manipulations that stacks the House with representatives who are *not* representative of the people would be over. The destruction of the good names of good people will no longer keep good people from serving.

How do we select the president? Let the New Senate under fair rules, nominate two candidates from its members or perhaps from the nation at large. Campaigning for nominations in any form would be outlawed. Then let the New House of Representatives, also under fair rules that reflect the ideals of this new methodology of government, select the president by majority vote, again without campaigning.

I would choose judges in the same way—every practicing lawyer's name would be in the computer. Citizens are drafted to serve as jurors. Why shouldn't lawyers be drafted to serve as judges? Their time in office would be limited to a court term or two. In both the state and federal courts, appellate judges would be chosen at random from those who had previously served as trial judges. As many lawyers as might be required to keep the docket current would be drafted. No more waiting years and years for judges appointed by politicians to decide our cases. Politics would finally be chased out of the judiciary.

What about the United States Supreme Court? The president, elected as above, would nominate the judges with staggered terms, with the approval of the Senate.

Such ideas, oversimple, perhaps in ways seemingly silly for their naïveté, at the same time stand as examples of how minds that permit themselves to think out of the box can challenge the old and the sick and offer a new start, for such dreams nourish hope where once only apathy and hate prevailed. What I'm trying to do here is suggest ways to take campaigning out of politics, to eliminate political parties, to install term limits, and at the same time to enjoy a government of the people rather than a government of the corporate King.

Likely better ways to accomplish these goals can be fashioned by a collection of minds that can think out of the box. Such were the minds of our founders. Give us a constitutional convention attended by caring, creative citizens whose objectives are to correct the political diseases and their side effects that are destroying us, and we can yet survive and become the great caring world power that can save ourselves, the earth, and its inhabitants.

But a national epiphany that causes a people to rise up and act must occur soon before the people's anger has completely consumed us; before a charismatic leader—crazed with ambition, one that history has always provided—makes his appearance; before an angry national mob joins him, waving flags and hollering slogans, and the end of America as we have known it and dreamed of it, and perhaps an end to the world, is then at hand.

When our government is returned to the people, much of the anger that results from an overriding sense of helplessness and apathy will have been quelled. The revolution to take back our country must and will begin at the grassroots. It will begin when the preachers' tents are filled with citizens who hear the Evangelists tell the truth, TTT, when they begin to teach the actual gospel of Jesus, of love, forgiveness, and tolerance. TTT must become our national slogan. The revolution will begin, not only in the tents, but in the city halls where caring people will gather to inform themselves, to debate public issues, and to resolve public controversies.

Our democracy was put to bed many years ago. It has lain in bed like a sick old man and has become weaker with every generation. To recover, the sick must arise. It must, little at a time, take its first feeble steps down the hallway to freedom. Day by day, year by year, it must gather its strength until at last the sick is again healthy and robust with the strength to resume its duties—to rescue the nation from its corporate master.

The Internet will provide information. It, too, is under attack, but more and more it will become the source of knowledge, as it has been the source of a good deal of the information forwarded on to you in this book.

Franklin Roosevelt, in his State of the Union address to Congress delivered on January 6, 1941, spoke to the nation about a bargain between the people and its government. Europe was fighting World War II and America was preparing for its likely entry into the war. I was just a boy, but I remember how the nation joined with him.

In exchange for the war effort and the sacrifice it entailed, he made an implied promise on behalf of the nation for a betterment of its people. He said:

> For there is nothing mysterious about the foundations of a healthy and strong democracy. The basic things expected by our people of their political and economic systems are simple. They are:
>
> Equality of opportunity for youth and for others.
>
> Jobs for those who can work.
>
> Security for those who need it.
>
> The ending of special privilege for the few.
>
> The preservation of civil liberties for all.
>
> The enjoyment of the fruits of scientific progress in a wider and constantly rising standard of living.
>
> These are the simple, the basic things that must never be lost sight of in the turmoil and unbelievable complexity of our modern world. The inner and abiding strength of our economic and political systems is dependent upon the degree to which they fulfill these expectations.
>
> Many subjects connected with our social economy call for immediate improvement. As examples:
>
> We should bring more citizens under the coverage of old-age pensions and unemployment insurance.

We should widen the opportunities for adequate medical care.

We should plan a better system by which persons deserving or needing gainful employment may obtain it.

He went on to say that the sacrifice meant the payment of more taxes, but that "no person should try, or be allowed to get rich out of the program, and the principle of tax payments in accordance with ability to pay should be constantly before our eyes to guide our legislation."

Then he made the following pledge to America:

In the future days which we seek to make secure, we look forward to a world founded upon four essential human freedoms.

The first is freedom of speech and expression—everywhere in the world.

The second is freedom of every person to worship God in his own way—everywhere in the world.

The third is freedom from want, which, translated into world terms, means economic understandings which will secure to every nation a healthy peacetime life for its inhabitants—everywhere in the world.

The fourth is freedom from fear, which, translated into world terms, means a *world-wide* reduction of armaments to such a point and in such a thorough fashion that no nation will be in a position to commit an act of physical aggression against any neighbor—anywhere in the world. (my italics)

Roosevelt did not speak of world domination but of world community.

He said:

A good society is able to face schemes of world domination and foreign revolutions alike without fear. Since the beginning of our American history we have been engaged in change, in a perpetual, peaceful revolution, a revolution which goes on steadily, quietly, adjusting itself to changing conditions without the concentration camp or the quicklime in the ditch. The world order which we seek is the cooperation of free countries, working together in a friendly, civilized society.

The nation embraced FDR's call for sacrifice. Later both Roosevelt and Churchill proclaimed his Four Freedoms as a pledge to the world. In his speech Roosevelt revealed the fundamentals of a true democracy.

It is time that this pledge be honored by us, his successors. It was a pledge of love, not hate, and only when its noble tenets are pursued can we alter the dangerous course we follow.

We live in the most dangerous of times. The earth has borne a species, *Homo sapiens,* who live in the twenty-first century and whose brain still skulks in the Stone Age. The question is, how can man save himself when technologically he has acquired the ability to destroy the world and all that is in it, and mentally he is still guided by his savage, testosterone-fueled emotional immaturity? I see no way out except to acquire a constant blazing awareness, one displayed in bright, flashing lights that remind us incessantly of the danger we face in foraging on hate and that recognizes that the only permanent power in the world is love. As Ben Franklin once cautioned: "We must all hang together or surely we will each hang separately."

The struggle to take back America will be daunting and relentless. It must start now, as the seed of a great tree was once planted in good soil. Tender and vulnerable, but endowed with the indomitable will to grow, it was attacked by the many forces of nature, but despite the tromp of hoofs and the heaps of snow it grew into a magnificent tree. The will of the people to become fully free will, as the growth of the great tree, encompass generations.

It will be nourished and protected as new leaders are born, men and women who understand that nothing is more essential to the human condition than freedom, and nothing more elusive and fragile.

Afterthought

I've come to believe that the members of Team Hate are what and who they are because of what and who *we* are. The mirror is always at work. None of our bloodthirsty women and none of our pious pontificators could survive one segment on the tube but for the fact that they are speaking to us, the *real* us, that is, that part of us that resonates to their rantings of hate as when two pianos sit in the same room and someone strikes a note on one. The exact note reverberates on the piano across the room as well.

I think of the consummate talent of these celebrities, these proficient talkers, and the sad perversion they make of it. We are to blame as much as they. Yes, as much. They speak to us. But we listen. They pluck the string of hate, and that string resounds in our own angry psyches. As we, they are angry because they, too, must have been forgotten, misled, and lied to; because they are disappointed and have felt pain; and because their expectations have not been met. They are as trapped as we. They are thinly wise. But they have learned to profit from it.

We and they were born in the same culture, one that was not of their choosing, nor ours. They, as we, are like children who have grown up in a slaughterhouse and have forgotten the soft touch of a lamb. Might there one day be remembrance.

Notes

A Beginning Thought

Bitch magazine, see, www.bitchmagazine.com
www.heartless-bitches.com/collected_quotes.shtml

1. Hate Sells

Grace's interview with Jackson jury foreman, Rodriguez, transcripts.cnn
.com/TRANSCRIPTS, August 8, 2005.

The *Malleus Maleficarum*, Introduction to the 1948 edition (N.Y.: Dover
Publications, 1971), p. viii.

That the witch could not be condemned to death without a confession, see
the *Malleus Maleficarum*, ibid., pp. 222, 223.

Grace's comment that our system is not one where both sides seek the truth,
see Nancy Grace, *Objection*, Hyperion Books, 2005, p. 16.

Grace's interview with King—her wish for the use of truth serum, beatings,
and torture against suspected criminals, transcripts.cnn.com/TRAN-
SCRIPTS, July 11, 2002.

Grace's reference to the Salem witch trials, see the *New Republic Online*,
"Presumed guilty. Trial by Fury" by Jason Zengerle, March 14, 2005,
www.tnr.com/doc.mhtml?i=20050314&s=zengerle031405.

How the witch should be stripped, etc., see the *Malleus Maleficarum*, ibid., p. 225.

Grace's boost of CNN's ratings, and her statement re her impartiality, *Washington Post*, "CBS News's Unstuffed Shirt," Howard Kurtz, *Washington Post* staff writer, Monday, March 28, 2005, p. C01.

"We are very pleased," statement of Jautz of CNN, that she gathers half a million viewers nightly, and the comments of David Allen and Jason Zengerle, *Atlantic Journal-Constitution*, April 4, 2005.

Larry King's interview of Grace concerning the death of her betrothed: http://transcripts.cnn.com/TRANSCRIPTS/0304/26/lklw.00html.

For an interesting and apparently in-depth review of the facts surrounding the murder of Keith Griffin, the discrepancies between Grace's story and the facts the investigator uncovered (which appear in italics) see the investigation of Mike Scanlon reported in "Media Drop," March 13, 2005, http://www.themediadrop.com/archives/003505.php. See also, "Did Nancy Grace, TV Crimebuster, Muddy her Myth?" by Rebecca Dana, *New York Observer*, www.observer.com/20060306/20060306_Rebecca_Dana_page one_nytv.asp.

That "Every good story is entitled to some embellishment" is the famous quote of John Zelbst, Lawton, Oklahoma, one of America's great trial lawyers.

Matt Zoller Seitz's comments about Grace's use of her boyfriend's murder: "TV Talk Host Makes a Career Out of Righteous Rage." Matt Zoller Seitz Newhouse News Service as reported in the *Las Vegas Tribune*, July 15, 2005.

That Grace doesn't need a jury to tell her who is guilty, "Nancy Grace, Ruling for The Viewer, A Television Legal Analyst Holds Court in Washington," by Libby Copeland, *Washington Post* staff writer, Monday, June 27, 2005, p. C01.

That the witch's deeds are often done in secret and definite proof is therefore difficult, see *Malleus Maleficarum*, supra, p. 211.

Steven Brill's regrets concerning Grace on *Court TV*. See "As Court TV Gets Ever Bolder, So Does Its Star," Lola Ogunnaike, *New York Times*, December 2, 2004.

The Georgia Supreme Court's comments about Grace's conduct as illegal and inexcusable and the duty of the prosecutor to see that justice is done, *Carr v. State*, 267 Ga. 701 (1997).

In 1994 the Georgia high court voted six to one to reverse a heroin trafficking conviction won by Grace because she "exceeded the wide latitude of closing argument" by referring to drug-related murders and serial rape, which were not at issue. *Bell v. State,* 263 Ga. 776 (1994).

Grace was chastised by the Eleventh Circuit Court of Appeals as having "played fast and loose" with her ethical duties as a Fulton County, Georgia, prosecutor in 1990. See *Stephens v. Hall,* no. 03-15251 (11th Cir., May 2, 2005).

The advice that the names of the accusers ought not be given the witch, see *Malleus Maleficarum,* p. 216, supra, and the suggestion that the inquisitor tell the accused that she can guess who the witnesses might be, p. 219.

Grace's support of the idea of eugenics, and the comments of Peter Hartlaub, see *San Francisco Chronicle* VIEW "Guilty or not, here she comes—Nancy Grace brings mob justice to CNN" by Peter Hartlaub, Friday, May 20, 2005.

References to the *Malleus Maleficarum* (N.Y.: Dover Publications, 1971), p. 211 et seq.

That she claims she is cured by trying to cure injustices, see Nancy Grace, *Objection,* supra, p. 2.

Joy Press's comments from the *Village Voice,* "Full of Grace, Court TV's secret weapon brings her flaring nostrils and female rage to CNN Headline News," by Joy Press, April 11, 2005.

As for Ms. Grace's statement, "I am proud to say that I get more hate mail than anyone at Court TV," see "As Court TV Gets Ever Bolder, So Does Its Star," by Lola Ogunnaike, *New York Times,* December 2, 2004.

2. Why We Love to Hate

Coulter's claim that we have a constitutional right to hate, see David Brock *Blinded by the Right,* Three Rivers Press, originally published by Crown Publishing Group, a division of Random House, N.Y., 2002, p. 198.

Her statement on the death penalty, www.jewishworldreview.com/cols/coulter062700.asp.

Coulter's statement, "We should invade their countries, kill their leaders and convert them to Christianity," appeared in her piece in the *National Review Online* (September 13, 2001).

Her remark about nuking North Korea from an interview with George Gurley, a columnist for the *New York Observer,* January 10, 2005.

Women should be armed but not allowed to vote . . . etc. Her remark on Bill Maher's *Politically Incorrect,* February 26, 2001.

"There are 22 million Americans on food stamps . . ." See: Ann Coulter, December 10, 2003, www.uexpress.com/anncoulter/?uc_full_date=20031210.

"Ann is fearless, in person and in her writing. But fearlessness isn't an excuse for crappy writing or crappier behavior." *National Review Online,* www .nationalreview.com/nr_comment/nr_comment100301.shtml.

Coulter was alledgedly fired from MSNBC, see NNDB, nndb.com/people/ 474/000022408/.

Coulter was canceled from *USA Today* (July 26, 2004).

The number of Americans living below the poverty level, etc. *Washington Post,* August 27, 2004.

Coulter's problems at the University of Connecticut, Associated Press (December 8, 2005).

That "there should be a literacy test and a poll tax for people to vote," her comments on "Hannity & Colmes," August 17, 1999.

Her remark about liberals loving America like O.J. loved Nicole, her column, January 6, 2005, www.townhall.com/opinion/columns/anncoulter/2005/ 01/06/14158.html.

That she was allegedly canceled at Harding University, story by Shelley K. Wong, Associated Press (December 7, 2005).

Her disparaging remark about Canada, from the November 30, 2004, edition of *FOX News*'s "Hannity & Colmes."

Coulter's longest relationship of eighteen months, see Jonathan Freeland, *Counterpunch,* www.counterpunch.org/freedland05192003.html.

Her trouble with dating in Washington, D.C., Ann Coulter, *How to Talk to a Liberal (If You Must)* (N.Y.: Crown Forum, 2004), pp. 314–16.

Comments by David Brock, *Washington Post,* Tuesday, February 26, 2002, www.washingtonpost.com/wp-srv/liveonline/02/politics/brock022602 .htm.

Democrats behave like pigs, etc., see Coulter, *How to Talk to a Liberal (If You Must),* supra.

Ms. Coulter's father represented Phelps Dodge Corporation and presided over the largest union decertification ever. *The New York Observer,* August 20, 2002, 8:08 p.m. "Coultergeist" by George Gurley, *AntiCoulter. com,* users.rcn.com/skutsch/anticoulter/observer.html.

Coulter's history working in a mine, etc. *AntiCoulter.com,* ibid.

Her love affair with Joseph McCarthy, see Ann Coulter, *Treason,* supra.

Her defense of Rush Limbaugh and his drug problem, see, theconservative-voice.com/articles/article.html?id=10798.

For Jonathan Swift's essay, *A Modest Proposal,* see, art-bin.com/art/omodest .html.

3. Hate, the Road to Power,
and the Elitists of Laura Ingraham

Laura Ingraham's biography, en.wikipedia.org/wiki/Laura Ingraham.

Her joke about Clarence Thomas's penis size, archive.salon.com/news/1999/
01/23newsa.html.

Definition of elitism, Microsoft Bookshelf, 98.

How Ingraham sees elitists, see chapter 1, *Shut Up and Sing*, Laura Ingraham
(Washington, D.C.: Regency Publishing, 2003).

Jefferson's quote concerning the danger of the clergy, Thomas Jefferson on
Politics and Government "52. Freedom of Religion," etext.virginia.edu/
jefferson/quotations/jeff1650.htm.

The composition of the men who founded the nation, see Howard Zinn,
A People's History of the United States (N.Y.: Harper and Row, 1980),
p. 89 et seq.

David Brock *Blinded By the Right*, First paperback edition, Three Rivers
Press, originally published by Crown Publishing Group, a division of
Random House, published 2002.

Brock's admission concerning the scandals of the era and his confession
that he worked and fought on the wrong side, and that he was sickened
by the statement of Ann Coulter, *Blinded by the Right*, Prologue, p. xx.

Brock's denouncing the hateful scapegoating of Robertson and Falwell,
Blinded by the Right, Prologue, p. xxi.

Sigmund Freud's view of religion, quoted in Karl Menninger, *Love Against
Hate* (N.Y.: Harcourt, Brace and Company, 1942), p. 190.

Walter Cronkite's statement, "We're an ignorant nation . . . ," transcripts.cnn
.com/TRANSCRIPTS/0509/30/lkl.01.html.

The extent of white collar crime, see, today.uci.edu/Features/profile_detail
.asp?key=107.

The FBI's stats on corporate crime, bank robberies, etc., www.newint.org/
issue358/facts.htm.

New York Times report on the Roper poll, "New Surveys Show That Big Business Has a P.R. Problem," by Claudia H. Deutsch, December 9, 2005,
www.nytimes.com/2005/12/09/business/09backlash.html?pagewanted=1.

4. For I Have Sinned

O'Reilly's adoption of the definition of the working class and that they account for 62 percent of the labor force: Bill O'Reilly, *Who's Looking Out
for You?* (N.Y.: Broadway Books, 2003), p. 4.

That parents should have the right to administer corporeal punishment to
their children, O'Reilly, *Who's Looking Out for You?*, p. 2.

He thinks George Bush is honest, but a child of privilege. O'Reilly, *Who's Looking Out for You?*, pp. 50, 51.

O'Reilly's concern about fatherless children, O'Reilly, *Who's Looking Out for You?*, pp. 7, 8.

That Fox is a "flag-waving network . . ." O'Reilly, *Who's Looking Out for You?*, pp. 7, 8.

That the government is not good at helping people and is not designed to do so, O'Reilly, *Who's Looking Out for You?*, pp. 34, 36.

O'Reilly's attack against the media as "coarsening children," see chapter 4, *Who's Looking Out for You?* And his criticism of how the church handles the priests', abuse of children, p. 124.

O'Reilly's criticism of the morality of Jennifer Lopez and Whitney Houston, O'Reilly, *Who's Looking Out for You?*, p. 72 et seq.

O'Reilly's admission that the corporate news organizations do not criticize each other etc. . . . how he veers off at the last moment, O'Reilly, *Who's Looking Out for You?*, p. 80.

O'Reilly's statement that he is one of the angriest journalist around, O'Reilly, *Who's Looking Out for You?*, p. 105.

His criticism of Tim Russert as a stooge when it comes to GE, O'Reilly, *Who's Lookin Out or You?*, pp. 103, 104.

O'Reilly's criticism of the consumer society, its addictive effects. O'Reilly, *Who's Looking Out for You?*, pp. 19, 20.

O'Reilly's criticism of the justice system, O'Reilly, *Who's Looking Out for You?*, p. 159 et seq.

O'Reilly's confessions about sinning and still casting stones, etc., see O'Reilly, *Who's Looking Out for You?*, p. 187 et seq.

O'Reilly's statement that you have to control the sex impulses or they will control you, etc., see, *The O'Reilly Factor* (N.Y.: Broadway Books, 2000), p. 26.

The allegations made by Ms. Mackis in her suit against O'Reilly are from a copy of the complaint in full seen on, www.thesmokinggun.com/archive/1013043mackris1.html.

CNN's report of the O'Reilly harassment suit and his statement that he was "stupid," cnn.com/2004/LAW/10/20/oreilly.suit/.

The article about the settlement of the O'Reilly-Mackris suit, "Bill O'Reilly, Producer Settle Harrassment Suit," by Howard Kurtz, *Washington Post*, October 29, 2004, www.washingtonpost.com/wp-dyn/articles/A7578=2004-Oct28.html.

O'Reilly's preachments about that passionate feeling working out, about infatuation etc. O'Reilly, *Who's Looking Out for You?*, p. 201.

O'Reilly definition of personal success based on respect, see *The O'Reilly Factor,* supra, p. 169.

O'Reilly admonition to forgive oneself, to drop the guilt, see O'Reilly, *Who's Looking Out for You?,* p. 206.

Why are most successful talk shows conservative and the best are those that can get the listener annoyed, O'Reilly, *Who's Looking Out for You?,* pp. 51, 52.

5. Hate, Hypocrisy, and the Pimps of Power

O'Reilly asking, "You want to have two guys making out in front of your four-year-old?," brainyquote.com/quotes/authors/b/bill_oreilly.html.

The definition of "secularism," http://en.wikipedia.org/wiki/Universe.

O'Reilly statement that conservatives see things in black and white and liberals in gray, etc., http://en.thinkexist.com/quotation/conservative-people-tend-to-see-the-world-in/349136.html.

That *FOX TV* led the networks in sexually exploitive programming, the quote about "Temptation Island" etc. and about the nudes in the British paper, *Sun,* see, http://www.beliefnet.com/story/156/story_15614_1 .html.

That the porn business is estimated at $12 billion a year, and its availability in major hotels though Liberty Media and Lodgenet Entertainment et al. See, http://moneycentral.msn.com/content/CNBCTV/Articles/TV Reports/P80813.asp.

The self-stated morality of Limbaugh, "the epitome of morality," "commie libs," etc., Brock, *Blinded by the Right,* Three Rivers Press originally published by Crown Publishing Group, a division of Random House, published 2002, p. 61.

That Limbaugh did not seem in person what he represented himself to be on radio. Twice married, etc., Brock, *Blinded by the Right,* p. 68.

Ann Coulter's claim that "liberals adore pornography" see Ann Coulter, *Treason* (N.Y.: Crown Forum, 2003), p. 292.

Ann Coulter's dating Bob Guccione Jr., her approval of lying to the FBI, and her dating a Jew although she supposedly left her law firm to get away from them, etc., Brock, *Blinded by the Right,* p. 198.

Brock's statement about Laura Ingraham and her fox coat, etc., see Brock, *Blinded by the Right,* p. 254.

That Laura Ingraham didn't believe much of what she said on her show, see Brock, *Blinded by the Right,* p. 255.

That Brock was surrounded by an empty right-wing circle, see Brock, *Blinded by the Right,* p. 257.

About the Coors Twins, see, www.salon.com/sex/feature/2003/05/30/coors/index_np.html.

Pete Coors's run for the Senate, and the Coors Brewing Company's history re homosexuals and the boycott in San Francisco, see "Drinking out of both sides of their mouths," by Susan Jordan, http://ec.gayalliance.org/articles/000394.shtml.

Calls to Murdoch to clean up his empire, see, www.beliefnet.com/story/156/story_15614_1.html.

Statistics about Fox's viewership and increase from its reporting on the Iraq war, see, en.wikipedia.org/wiki/FOX_News#Controversies_and_allegations_of_bias.

The bias of *FOX News* seen by critics and a world audience as a Bush propaganda vehicle, see, en.wikipedia.org/wiki/FOX_News#Controversies_and_allegations_of_bias.

The history of the *FOX News* organization, its members' history, etc., see, FAIR, July/August 2001, "The Most Biased Name in News, *FOX News* channel's extraordinary right-wing tilt," by Seth Ackerman, fair.org/index.php?page=1067.

Ailes assurance that Fox is not programming for conservatives, see "Center for Media & Democracy," *FOX News*, www.sourcewatch.org/index.php?title=Fox_News#Fox.27s_close_relationship_with_Republicans.

Hugh Hewitt's view of journalism set out in the *New Yorker* magazine (August 29, 2005).

Ann Coulter's statement, about Democrats shirking their honor of leading us to war, etc., Coulter, *Treason* (N.Y.: Crown Forum, 2003), p. 1.

Matt Gross's statements about the right-wing tilt at Fox and their motivation, http://www.sourcewatch.org/index.php?title=Fox_News#Fox.27s_close_relationship_with_Republicans.

Reference to Scott Norvells's statement in the European addition of the *Wall Street Journal* came from, http://slate.msn.com/id/2119864/.

The quote from Sean Penn, http:www.hollywood.com/news/detail/id/1099510.

The O'Reilly quotes on how to deal with Afghanistan, Iraq, and Libya, oreilly-sucks.com/specificbias.htm.

The references to hate commodities for sale, their sellers and their effects on children, their goals, etc., see Southern Poverty Law Center, "Hate for Sale," by Bob Moser, http://www.splcenter.org/intel/intelreport/article.jsp?pid=108.

The right-wing Republican T-shirts, etc., that were sold at the college Republican convention, and the quote from the Log Cabin Republicans. "Hate for Sale," http://atheism.about.com/b/a/029962.htm.

Kill Bush and a wish for Tom Delay suicide, Michelle Malkin, "Unhinged Liberal Products for Sale," http://michellemalkin.com/archives/002059 .htm.

6. The Noxious Garden

Coulter's claim that liberals "nearly went stark raving mad at having to mouth patriotic platitudes while burning with a desire to aid the enemy," Ann Coulter, *Treason* (N.Y.: Crown Forum, 2003), p. 9.

The UN ranking of worldwide standards of living, www.2ontario.com/ welcome/coca_801.asp.

Senator Lieberman article in *Policy Review*, no. 77 (May–June 1996).

Coulter: "Liberals choose man. Conservatives chose God." *Treason*, supra, p. 9.

About the "bleating for Saddam Hussein" see the collection of best quotes from Ann Coulter, www.nndb.com/people/474/000022408/.

Her imperative, "We've got to attack France," *How to Talk to a Liberal*, supra, p. 28.

The stats on the comparative salaries of the minimum wage earner and certain CEOS, see *The Nation*, May 1, 2006, "13,700 an Hour," Katrina Vanden Hewvel, p. 6.

Frederick Taylor wanted a man "of the type of an ox," Frederick W. Taylor, *The Principles of Scientific Management* (N.Y.: Harper Bros., 1911).

Coulter's, "Liberals malign the flag, ban the Pledge, and hold cocktail parties for America's enemies," etc. *Treason*, supra, p. 5, and "Whenever the nation is under attack, from within or without, liberals side with the enemy." *Treason*, supra, p. 1.

Coulter's statement, "God said so. Go forth, be fruitful, multiply and rape the planet—it's yours. That's our job . . . ," etc., see, Biography, http:// ann-coulter.biography.ms/.

Boss Tweed's quote: en.wikiquote.org/wiki/William_Marcy_Tweed.

7. Freedom of Speech

For a fine summary of the findings of de Tocqueville, see Tom Hartmann, *Unequal Protection, The Rise of Corporate Dominance and the Theft of Human Rights* (Rodale, 2002), p. 223 et seq.

The revolt of the proles: George Orwell, *1984*, Alfred A. Knopf, a Borzoi Book, first published in 1949, p. 74.

De Tocqueville's, "men are seldom forced to act . . . ," Thom Hartman, *Unequal Protection,* supra, p. 225.

De Tocqueville's, "the press is the chief democratic instrument of freedom" as quoted by Thom Hartman, *Unequal Protection,* p. 225.

James Madison's quote, "A popular government without popular information . . . ," Newspaper Association of America, naa.org/ppolicy/PDFs/freedomofthepress.pdf.

A. J. Liebling's statement about freedom of the press: see Thom Hartman, *Unequal Protection* (2002), p. 225.

George Bush, in a paid speech to roofing contractors, said he hated the press as a group. Thom Hartman, *Unequal Protection.*

George W. Bush didn't want snoopers in his papers, see Thom Hartman, *Unequal Protection* (2002), p. 225.

Only 54 percent of eligible voters cast their votes in the last election, etc., see "Family Education," www.familyeducation.com/article/0,1120,20-4128,00.html.

Who owns what among the media giants, see *Columbia Journalism Review* (October 27, 2005), www.cjr.org/tools/owners/.

Goebbels quote about books, "Dr. Goebbels and his Ministry" by Hans Fritzche, www.calvin.edu/academic/cas/gpa/goeb62.htm.

"We Now Live in a Fascist State," Lewis Lapham, *Harper's Magazine* (October, 2005).

The decline in American literary reading, and statistics, on reading and electric media, "National Endowment of the Arts," www.arts.gov/pub/ReadingAtRisk.pdf,nea.gov/pub/ReadingAtRisk.pdf.

80 percent of all newspapers are owned by corporate chains. Jamie Court, *Corporateering,* Jeremy P. Tarcher, (N.Y.: Putnam 2003), p. 179.

Four corporations have been allowed to buy up radio stations nationwide so they control 90 percent of all radio advertising revenues, see Thom Hartman, *Unequal Protection,* p. 227.

For information concerning corporate welfare go to Google, type in "Corporate welfare," and see for yourself.

For the media ownerships of General Electric, Disney, and Viacom, see *Columbia Journalism Review* (October 27, 2005), www.cjr.org/tools/owners/.

Viacom owned enough TV outlets to reach 39 percent of the nation. See The Center for Public Integrity, www.publicintegrity.org/telecom/report.aspx?aid=407.

Only three corporations control most of the business of eleven thousand magazines, and twenty-three corporations control the twenty-five thousand outlets of books, magazines, television, etc. See Thom Hartman, *Unequal Protection*, pp. 226, 227.

That the web is controlled by a small number of large corporations, and the quote from Thom Hartman, *Unequal Protection*, see *Unequal Protection*, p. 227.

MoveOn.org's ad that was refused by CBS for the Super Bowl, see MSNBC, *Newsweek*, "Censored at the Superbowl," by Jonathan Darman, January 30, 2004, /www.msnbc.msn.com/id/4114703/.

That Americans are not permitted to see on TV the caskets of servicemen shipped home, see, *USA Today* (December 31, 2003), "Return of U.S. war dead kept solemn, secret," by Gregg Zoroya, www.usatoday.com/news/nation/2003-12-31-casket-usat_x.htm.

For a summary of The Pew Research Center Report, see, fair.org/index.php?page=2013. For the detailed report itself see, people-press.org/reports/display.php3? ReportID=39.

O'Reilly's comment about people in network news can tell stories of betrayal and deception, see Bill O'Reilly, *The O'Reilly Factor* (N.Y.: Broadway Books, 2000), p. 46.

The stats on where Americans get their news and concerning the Sinclair Network are from a speech by Robert F. Kennedy Jr., Common Dreams News Center, December 2, 2005, www.commondreams.org/views05/0916-27.htm.

The Robert Kennedy quotation is from his speech, ibid.

That business chiefs can and do dictate to editors about content, see Ben Bagdikian, *Media Monopoly* (Beacon Press, Sixth Edition, 2000), p. xxv et seq.

About video news releases (VNRs) see Jamie Court, *Corporateering*, supra, p. 199.

That corporations focus on the individual's morality, not corporate morality, see Jamie Court, supra.

Ann Coulter's disparaging remark against former president Carter and her endearing remark about McCarthy, see Coulter, *Treason*, supra, pp. 11, 15.

Michael Powell's comments about the public interest standard, see Jamie Court, *Corporateering*, supra, p. 181.

Limbaugh's explanation why he does not have liberals on his show and his statement about liberals surrendering the country at war, see *Media Matters for America*, mediamatters.org/items/200510190010.

Coulter's statement concerning McCarthy and working people, see Coulter, *Treason*, supra, p. 69.

Coulter's belief that people believe stupid statements once they hate, *Slander*, supra, p. 33.

Availability as the first condition of consumption, see Michael Parenti, "Free Speech—at a Price," michaelparenti.org/FreeSpeech.html.

The recent revelation that Bush has authorized eavesdropping without court warrants, see *New York Times*, December 16, 2005.

The quote from *The New York Times* concerning the warrantless searches by NSA, see December 24, 2005, www.nytimes.com/2005/12/24/politics/24 spy.html?hp&ex=1135400400&en=efaa31928aa6c87b&ei=5094&partner= homepage.

George II's statement about wiretaps, and court orders and valuing the Constitution, see www.whitehouse.gov/news/releases/2004/04/20040420-2 .html

The impeachment quotes and the quote of Lewis Lapham are from his essay "The Case for Impeachment," *Harper's Magazine*, March 2006

Ann Coulter's take on such warrantless searches by the NSA, see, hammerof truth.com/2005/12/24/ann-coulter-to-intern-japanese-and-torture-arabs/.

What are "daisy cutters"? See "The US Military Starts Using 'Daisy Cutters' Against Afghanistan," by Andy Buckley, www.globalresearch.ca/articles/ BUC111A.html.

Ann Coulter's hatred of *The New York Times*, and her wish that Timothy McVeigh had attacked the *Times* instead, see Ann Coulter to George Gurley, *New York Observer*, August 21, 2002.

Ann Coulter's statement that whenever the nation is under attack liberals side with the enemy, *Treason*, supra, p. 1.

How the Bill of Rights was first rejected and later inserted as the first Ten Amendments to the Constitution, see Michael Parenti, "Free Speech—at a Price," supra.

To read the whole of Madison's "Federalist No. 10," see, www.constitution .org/fed/federa10.htm.

The expenditure of $50 million to be elected in California, see, feingold.sen- ate.gov/speeches/97/09/2002916A26.html.

To read the *Declaration of Independence* in its entirety see, earlyamerica.com/ earlyamerica/freedom/doi/text.html.

O'Reilly's statement about the Holloway case, "see this is what happens" etc., his calling two security guards "slugs," lamented Aruba didn't have the death penalty, what about Reyna Gabriella Alvarado-Carerra, etc., see, kuro5hin.org/story/2005/7/3/491/18474.

The Bob Costas story on the Holloway case and the skitterings of the CNN people, its plummeting ratings, see *New York Times,* August 24, 2005, p. B1. What the ACLU stands for see, aclu.com.

O'Reilly hateful statement about the ACLU: The Radio Factor, Bill O'Reilly, January 9, 2004, reported, www.rotten.com/library/culture/aclu/.

ACLU's statement concerning Rush Limbaugh's rights, see, http://www.aclu.org/Privacy/Privacy.cfm?ID=14698&c=27.

Limbaugh's gratitude to the ACLU, see, rotten.com/library/culture/aclu/.

8. The Ghost of Goebbels, Propaganda, and the Rock-Hard Right

For Kimel's coments see, *Online Holocaust Magazine,* Alexander Kimel, Holocaust Survivor, kimel.net/hitjew.html.

Goebbels quote, "Propaganda must facilitate the displacement of aggression . . . etc.," see, psywarrior.com/Goebbels.html.

After 911, that innocent Americans were the victims of scapegoating, see Levin and Rabrevovic, *Why We Hate* (N.Y.: Prometheus Books, 2004), p. 15.

For a discussion of scapegoating, see Levin and Rabrevovic, *Why We Hate,* ibid, pp. 25–28.

As for methods of scapegoating in America concerning race, sex, AIDs, etc., see *Public Eye.org,* "Behind the Culture War to Restore Traditional Values," by Chip Berlet and Margaret Quigley, publiceye.org/magazine/culwar.html.

That Ann Coulter admitted that the Paula Jones case was a right-wing conspiracy, Brock, *Blinded by the Right,* supra, p. 196.

Brock's statement about the right's politics being built on hatred of those who were not straight, white, God-fearing men in nuclear families, see Brock, *Blinded by the Right,* supra, p. 68.

Goebbels, Two ways to make a revolution quote, http://www.calvin.edu/academic/cas/gpa/goeb62.htm.

O'Reilly's comments on the treatment of detainees at Guantánamo Bay—dissent, see Media Matters for America, mediamatters.org/items/200506220006.

For prisoner abuse at Guantánamo Bay, see en.wikipedia.org/wiki/Guantanamo_Bay_detainment_comp.

The action of the United Nations in demanding that Guantánamo Bay be closed, see *New York Times,* February 18, 2006, Editorial.

For a discussion and description of torture, its legality, and its adoption by the Bush administration see, "The Memo," by Jane Mayer, *New Yorker* (February 27, 2006).

That U.S. citizens are bound by the Nuremberg Principles, see U.S. Code, TITLE 18 > PART I> CHAPTER 118> § 2441.

O'Reilly on San Francisco's refusal to let military recruiters invade their schools, see "San Francisco voters disrespectful of U.S. Armed Forces," November 26, 2005, his syndicated column.

O'Reilly—incarcerating liberals, see, mediamatters.org/items/2005062 20006.

O'Reilly—his familiarity with Goebbels, *The O'Reilly Factor* (N.Y.: Broadway Books, 2000), p. 184, http://www.fair.org/index.php?page=1070.

For the report prepared during the war by the United States Office of Strategic Services in describing Hitler's psychological profile, one that matched the teaching of Goebbels, see "Big Lie," *Wikipedia,* en.wikipedia.org/wiki/BigLie.

O'Reilly on health care. *The O'Reilly Factor.* September 8, 2004, www.newshounds.us/2004/09/14/oreilly_on_health_care_reform.php.

The *doublespeak* of corporations about the environment, G.E., etc., from *Online Journal,* Goebbels and today's mass mind control: Part One, Carla Binion, April 23, 2001, angelfire.com/hi3/pearly/htmls2/right-goebbels .html.

Mussolini's definition of fascism, "Fascism should more properly be called corporatism, since it is the merger of state and corporate power." Benito Mussolini, cited by Lewis Lapham in *Harper's* (January 2002).

Hitler: "If you wish the sympathy of the masses, you tell them the crudest, most stupid things," see, freedomdomain.com/misquote.htm.

Goebbels's using movie stars, etc., to promote his propoganda instead of out of the mouth of Goebbels, http://www.angelfire.com/hi3/pearly/htmls2/right-goebbels.html.

Goebbels, that "Propaganda is a means to an end . . ." see *Calvin, Minds in the Making,* German Propaganda Archive, Goebbels at Nuremberg—1934 by Joseph Goebbels, www.calvin.edu/academic/cas/gpa/goeb59 .htm.

Goebbels, "The rank and file are usually much more primitive than we imagine. Propaganda must therefore always be essentially simple and repetitious," www.geocities.com/northstarzone/TV.html.

Goebbels, "The most brilliant propagandist techiniques will yield no success unless one fundamental principle is born in mind . . ." etc., en.thinkexist.com/quotation/the_most_brilliant_propagandist_technique_will1/162045.html.

"How fortunate for governments that the people they administer don't think," Adolph Hitler, http://www.geocities.com/northstarzone/TV.html.

"How easily one is taken in by a lying and censored press and radio in a totalitarian state . . . ," William L. Shirer, *The Rise and Fall of the Third Reich* (N.Y.: Simon & Schuster Paperback, 1959) pp. 247, 248.

Goebbels: "Think of the press as a giant keyboard . . . ," see, en.thinkexist .com/quotation/think-of-the-press-as-a-great-keyboard-on-which/ 383183.html.

Goebbels pioneered the use of broadcasting in mass propaganda, promoting the distribution of inexpensive radio receivers to the German public . . . *Wikipedia,* en.wikipedia.org/wiki/Goebbels.

Herbert Krugman's research that concluded that whoever owns TV controls the past, the present, the future, http://www.geocities.com/northstar zone/TV.html.

The federal government's packaging news, see "Under Bush, a New Age of Prepackaged Television News," by David Barstow and Robin Stein, *New York Times,* Sunday 13, March 2005.

That 90 percent of TV newsrooms now rely on video news releases," ibid.

That the Bush administration paid commentator Armstrong Williams to promote its education reform law, "No Child Left Behind," see Greg Toppe, "Education Dept. paid commentator to promote law," *USA TODAY* (January 7, 2005).

The General Accounting Office's finding that the failure of the agency to identify itself as the source of the news story is illegal, see, "Buying of News by Bush's Aides Is Ruled Illegal," by Robert Pear, *New York Times,* October 1, 2005.

Goebbels, "We have made the Reich by propaganda," see, en.thinkexist.com/ quotation/we_have_made_the_reich_by/172707.html.

For an excellent article on secrecy and a closed society, see "President Bush's Penchant for Secrecy Is Moving Us Toward a Closed Society," by Joe W. Pitt, *Washington Spectator* (October 1, 2005).

The reclassification of fifty-five thousand pages in the National Archives: *New York Times,* "U.S. Reclassifies Many Documents in Secret Review," Scott Shane, February 21, 2006.

For a story about the secret "black sites," maintained by the CIA, see *Washington Post,* "CIA Holds Terror Suspects in Secret Prisons," Dana Priest, November 2, 2005.

The quote from Edmund Burke, "The only thing necessary for the triumph of evil is for good men to do nothing," see Biographies, Edmund Burke, blupete.com/Literature/Biographies/Philosophy/Burke.htm.

9. Hate for the Love of Christ

Menninger's "Die we must . . ." and his quote from Freud, Karl Menninger, *Love Against Hate* (N.Y.: Harcourt, Brace & Company, 1942), p. 5.

Pat Robertson's infamous quote: "Just like what Nazi Germany did to the Jews, so liberal America is now doing to the evangelical Christians. . . ." Pat Robertson, interview with Molly Ivins, 1993.

For Robertson's education and mission statement see his official Web site, www.patrobertson.com/Biography/index.asp.

For Jefferson's as well as Madison's writings on the separation of church and state, and the statements of the various justices of the Supreme Court, see, www.theocracywatch.org/separation_church_state2.htm.

Robertson's statements about Hitler, homosexuals, Satanists, and The 700 Club, December 21, 1993, www.geocities.com/CapitolHill/7027/quotes.html, and, www.positiveatheism.org/hist/quotes/revpat.htm.

For an online article on "Homosexuals and the Holocaust" by Ben S. Austin, see, www.mtsu.edu/~baustin/homobg.html.

Talking about apartheid in South Africa, Robertson's statement, "I think 'one man, one vote,'" . . . etc., "The 700 Club," March 18, 1992, www.geocities.com/CapitolHill/7027/quotes.html.

Robertson as to women's rights: "Christ was the head of the household," etc., "The 700 Club," December 8, 1992, see, www.geocities.com/Capitol-Hill/7027/quotes.html.

Robertson's view of Ariel Sharon's stroke, see www.cnn.com/2006/US/01/05/robertson.sharon/49K—April 30, 2006.

Robertson's creative business history, see, www.geocities.com/CapitolHill/7027/business.html.

Robertson's service record, see, en.wikipedia.org/wiki/Pat_Robertson and the cross-examination of Robertson's lawyer, see, www.atrueword.com/index.php/article/articleprint/42/-1/2/.

About LaHaye, his books and ideas, see *Time*, "Meet the Prophet, How an evangelist and conservative activist turned prophecy into a fiction juggernaut," by John Cloud, Rancho Mirage, June 23, 2002, and *The Tim LaHaye Page*, www.tylwythteg.com/enemies/lahaye.html.

Wealth of the Morman Church, see *Time*: "LDS Church 'Most Prosperous' Religion," Associated Press (June 28, 1997), www.lds-mormon.com/wealth.shtml.

Theodore Dreiser's comments on church wealth, etc., www.infidels.org/library/historical/theodore_dreiser/church_and_wealth_in_america.html.

Hitler's pledge to Christians: Adolph Hitler, *The Speeches of Adolph Hitler, 1922–1939*, Vol. 1 (London: Oxford University Press, 1942), pp. 871–72.

Theodore Dreiser's comments on the church, etc., www.infidels.org/library/
historical/theodore_dreiser/church_and_wealth_in_america.html.

10. Kill All the Lawyers

Ann Coulter's hatred of trial lawyers. Interview by Jamie Glazov, *FrontPage
Magazine.com* (January 12, 2004), http://www.frontpagemag.com/arti-
cles/ReadArticle.asp?ID=11689.

Rush Limbaugh, on trial lawyers, www.legalunderground.com/2004/07/
trial_lawyer_in.html.

O'Reilly comment that trial lawyers have a hidden agenda that is antithetical
to the best interests of society, see, http://www.humaneventsonline.com/
article.php?id=2031.

Nancy Grace's comment about greedy lawyers with their hands in the cookie
jar, Grace, *Objection* (N.Y.: Hyperion, 2005), p. 29.

Grace's description of lawyers as snakes, *ibid.,* p. 17.

Pres. George W. Bush's remarks against trial lawyers, president's remarks in
"Ask President Bush Event," Northern Virginia Community College,
Annandale, Virginia, August 9, 2004, www.whitehouse.gov/news/re-
leases/2004/08/20040809-3.html.

Those "parasitic blobs," see, www.justiceseekers.com/index.cfm/aol/1/Menu
ItemID/184/MenuGroup/Home.htm.

De Tocqueville's statement, "It will always be easy for a king to make lawyers
the most useful instruments of his power," see, Russell, *American Legal
History,* www.law.du.edu/russell/lh/alh/docs/deTocq.html.

Caps did not save insurance company significant money, "Malpractice In-
surer Sees Little Savings in Award Caps," by Joseph T. Hallinan and
Rachel Zimmerman, *Wall Street Journal,* November 28, 2004.

The litany of statements by tort reformers that caps will not lower insurance
rates, see, "Public Citizen, Congress Watch," www.citizen.org/congress/
civjus/medmal/articles.cfm?ID=9008.

The quotes from *The Wall Street Journal,* "As Malpractice Caps Spread,
Lawyers Turn Away Some Cases," Rachel Zimmerman and Joseph T.
Hallinan, *Wall Street Journal,* October 8, 2004.

The quote from *The New York Times.* "Behind Those Medical Malpractice
Rates," by Joseph B. Treaster and Joel Brinkley, February 22, 2005.

Some of the states that have held caps on damages unconstitutional—
Wash., N.H, Ore., Kans., Ill., Ariz., Ala.—egisweb.state.wy.us/pub
research/2004/04tm034.pdf.

"Nearly 36 Million People Live in Poverty," by Andrea Hopkins, Reuters,
August 26, 2004, www.commondreams.org/headlines04/0826-24.htm.

The GOA Report, goa.gov/news.items/do3836.pfd.

The Weiss report on HMO profits is reported at, www.atla.org/pressroom/ FACTS/medmal/HealthcareIL.aspx, and, www.house.gov/schakowsky/ MedMal_Bush_MadisonCounty_1_4_05.html.

That in 2004 health and life insurers posted their best profits in a decade, see, "Health insurers rake in records," September 23, 2004, www.Austin .Bizjournals.com.

That three officers in one insurance company insuring doctors in Wyoming received more than the total premiums the company received from doctors in the state: Source, supplemental exhibit for the year 2000 of The Doctors' Life Insurance Company, generated by The Doctors Company.

The figures of iatrogenic deaths each year that exceed deaths from heart disease and cancer, see, "Death by Medicine," Null, Dean, and others, *Health and Living News,* www.healthe=livingnews.com/articles/death_by_medicine_part_1.html.

The figures on the medical profession's discipline of repeat malpractice offenders, Op-Ed, "Bad Doctors Get a Free Ride," Sidney M. Wolf, *New York Times,* March 4, 2003.

The effect of caps on insurance rates for doctors' malpractice premiums, see the study done by Center for Justice & Democracy, "Premium Deceit— the Failure of 'Tort Reform' to Cut Insurance Prices," by J. Robert Hunter and Joanne Doroshow, curewyoming.org/PremiumDeceit.pdf.

Catherine Crier's love of the English system: Catherine Crier, *The Case AGAINST Lawyers* (N.Y.: Broadway Books, 2002), p. 211.

Statistics on the caseloads in the federal court system, see Federal Judicial Caseload Statistics, March 31, 2002, Administrative Office of the U.S. Courts, www.uscourts.gov/statisticsalreports.html.

For the decline of personal injury cases in the state courts, see, National Center for State Courts, "Examining the Work of State Courts," 2003, ncsconline.org/D_Research/csp/2003_Files/2003_Main_Page.html.

The list of lawsuits brought by corporations against one another is quoted from the Association of Trial Lawyers of America's Web site, www.atla .org/homepage/bizvsbiz03.aspx.

For the story on the case by Fox against Al Franken see *New York Times,* August 23, 2002.

About the suit by Caterpillar against Disney, see *Insurance Journal,* "Silly Business Suits Back in Style," September 19, 2005, www.insurancejournal.com/magazines/midwest/2005/09/19/features/60483.htm.

Limbaugh's take on the hot coffee case see, *99,* Shannon's Law: Trial and Error, by James Shannon, March 23, 2005, www.metrobeat.net/gbase/Expedite/Content?oid=oid%3A3306.

About the McDonald's case: excerpted from ATLA fact sheet. © 1995, 1996 by Consumer Attorneys of California and taken by me from, http://www.lectlaw.com/files/cur78.htm.

For a discussion on the U.S. Supreme Court's limiting punitive damages, see, *Goodwin/Procter*, Environmental Law Advisory, April 2003, "Supreme Court Tightens Limits on Punitive Damages," goodwinprocter.com/publications/ELA_PunDamages_4_03.pdf.

Greider's comments about the Democratic Party, see William Greider, *Who Will Tell the People?* (N.Y.: Simon & Schuster, 1992), p. 247.

Grace's comment about hoodwinking criminal defense lawyers, see Nancy Grace, *Objection* (N.Y.: Hyperion, 2005), p. 7.

For Ahab's rage on Moby Dick, see *Books and Writers,* Herman Melville, www.kirjasto.sci.fi/melville.htm.

11. Hate and the New American Slavery

The statistics quoted on the number of solicitations and on personal wealth, credit card debt, net worth, etc., is from *Bankrate.com*'s "Guide to Consolidting Your Debt, www.bankrate.com/brm/news/debt/debt-guide2004/debt-trivial.asp.

Hate at the workplace, see Dozier, *Why We Hate*, Contemporary Books, 2002, pp. 167, 168

Albert Camus, "Without work . . . ," www.brainyquote.com/quotes/authors/a/albert_camus.html.

For a discussion on the sense of being trapped, see Rush W. Dozier Jr., *Why We Hate* (Contemporary Books, 2002), p. 21 et seq.

Statistics on the numbers of workers murdered, assaulted, etc., Dozier Jr., ibid., p. 165.

The study on "desk-rage" is from one cited by Dozier Jr., ibid, p. 167.

Menninger's story about buying the washing machine on time: *Love Against Hate*, supra, p. 283.

De Tocqueville's the incessant endeavoring to procure "petty and paltry things," see Tom Hartmann, *Unequal Protection, The Rise of Corporate Dominance and the Theft of Human Rights*, Rodale, distributed by St. Martin's Press, New York, 2002, p. 223 et seq.

For the revolt of the proles see George Orwell, *1984*, Alred A. Knopf, a Borzoi Book, first published in 1949, pp. 72, 73.

"Two Minutes of Hate" and its effect, see George Orwell, *1984*, pp. 16, 17.

For stats on the number of American jobs sent overseas, etc., see AFL-CIO, News for Working Families, October 20, 2005, www.aflcio.org/issues/jobseconomy/jobs/ns102020004.cfm.

12. The Rise of the Fourth Reich

For the Frank Zappa quote see, en.wikiquote.org/wiki/Frank_Zappa.

The Roosevelt quote was lifted from Lewis Lapham's article in Harper's, "Living in a Fascist State," 10/21/06 *Harper's Magazine* (October 2005).

For a brief history of the Reichstag fire see William L. Shirer, *The Rise and Fall of the Third Reich* (N.Y.: Simon & Schuster Paperback, 1988), and, 9/11review.com/precedent/century/reichstag.html.

For Hitler's statement as to why he invaded Poland, see the Avalon Project, Yale Law School, www.yale.edu/lawweb/avalon/imt/proc/judpolan.htm.

That the Nazis confiscated the property of the Jews and sold it, see Levin and Rabrenovic, *Why We Hate* (N.Y.: Prometheus Books, 2004), p. 151.

For the meaning of *Schutzhaft*—protective custody—see Shirer, *The Rise and Fall of the Third Reich*, supra, p. 271.

"Hitler and the law are one," Shirer, ibid., p. 268.

Halliburton building new cells at Guantánamo, see Reuters, July 27, 2002, commondreams.org/headlines02/0727-02.htm.

For Hitler's quashing of prosecutions for torture, see Shirer, *The Rise and Fall of the Third Reich*, supra, p. 270.

For a discussion on Hitler's promises to the various classes in Germany, Shirer, ibid., p. 261.

Eisenhower's warning of a military-industrial complex, http://coursesa.matrix.msu.edu/~hst306/documents/indust.html.

The seven messages that consistently appear in the fiercest and most thorough campaigns of hate propaganda are an insightful analysis by Jonathan Belman, in an essay entitled, "A Cockroach Cannot Give Birth to a Butterfly and Other Messages of Hate Propaganda," Jonathan Belman, May 2004, http://gseweb.harvard.edu/~t656_web/peace/Articles_Spring_2004/Belman_Jonathan_hate_propaganda.htm.

The quote under the fourth message is from Mr. Belman's work, which he attributes to Kurt Hilmar Eitzen, "Ten Responses to Jewish Lackeys," *German Propaganda Archive* 2004, http://www.calvin.edu/academic/cas/gpa/responses.htm.

The quote from the sixth message is also from Mr. Belman's work, which he attributes to Ernst Hiemer, "The Holy Hate," *German Propaganda Archive* 1998, http://www.calvin.edu/academic/cas/gpa/ds3.htm.

The anti-Semitic quote under the seventh message was also gathered by Belman, above, and is attributed to Ernst Hiemer, "The Holy Hate," German Propaganda Archive 1998, http://www.calvin.edu/academic/cas/gpa/ds3.htm.

Hitler's admonition not to admit you are wrong in the slightest, see *Mein Kampf* 1, chap. 6 (1925).

The statement by Dr. Frank to the judges to consider in each case how the Führer would decide, see Shirer, *The Rise and Fall of the Third Reich*, supra, p. 268.

Murrow's warning about dissent and disloyalty, see antiwar.com/quotes.php.

Martin Luther King's statement about the arrogance of a nation, see, en.wiki quote.org/wiki/Martin_Luther_King,_Jr.

Hitler's Christianity: For his speeches on Christianity and his prayers see, the Christianity of Hitler revealed in his speeches and proclamations, compiled by Jim Walker, nobeliefs.com/speeches.htm.

The quotations from Seymour Hersh's article are from *The New Yorker*, December 5, 2005.

Acceptance speech delivered by Fritz Stern upon receiving the Leo Baeck Medal at the Tenth Annual Dinner of the Leo Baeck Institute, www.lbi.org/fritzstern.html.

The Leo Baeck Institute is a research, exhibition, and lecture center whose library and archives offer the most comprehensive documentation for the study of German Jewish history, see, www.lbi.org/.

"Project for a New American Century" http://www.newamericancentury.org/publicationsreports.htm. See therein "Rebuilding America's Defenses: Strategy, Forces and Resources for a New Century."

Comments on PNAC and RAD http://www.moveon.org/moveonbulletin/bulletin13.html.

Nietzsche's dictum about "a weariness," see www.longevitymeme.org/articles/viewarticle.cfm?article_id=18&page=1-25k-.

The danger of the individual feeling helpless as a prelude to fascism from Eric Fromm, *Excape from Freedom* (Henry Holt and Company, 1941), pp. 207, 208, 216, 239, 240.

13. The End of Hate

John Lennon's concern that our society is being run by insane people for insane objectives, Interview, 22 June 1968, BBC-TV.

About stealth bombers: en.wikipedia.org/wiki/B-2_Spirit, and http://www.cnn.com/US/9903/24/us.kosovo.military/.

For Mohamed ElBaradei's Nobel Lecture see nobelprize.org/peace/laure-ates/2005/.

Jefferson's quote on the judiciary, and the rise of corporations, see, http://etext.virginia.edu/jefferson/quotations/jeff1270.htm.

The birth of corporate personhood, see the Santa Clara case, http://www.radical.org/corporations/SCvSPR1886.html.

Garrison's comment on his excessive speech, see, en.wikipedia.org/wiki/William_Lloyd_Garrison.

FDR's speech: Four Freedoms. www.libertynet.org/~edcivic/fdr.html.

Index